Monuments, Marvels, and Miracles

MONUMENTS, MARVELS, AND MIRACLES

A Traveler's Guide to CATHOLIC AMERICA

MARION AMBERG

Our Sunday Visitor
Huntington, Indiana

Our Sunday Visitor Publishing Division
Our Sunday Visitor, Inc.
200 Noll Plaza
Huntington, IN 46750
1-800-348-2440

ISBN: (Inventory No. T2022)

1. TRAVEL—Special Interest—Religious.
2. TRAVEL—United States—General.
3. RELIGION—Christianity—Catholic.

eISBN: 978-1-68192-339-0
LCCN: 2019953130

Cover design: Amanda Falk
Cover art: Shutterstock
Interior design: Amanda Falk

PRINTED IN THE UNITED STATES OF AMERICA

*To my brother Richard, who lived
with gusto his earthly motto,*

"Life is a grand adventure!"

*He now lives the grandest
adventure of all: eternal life.*

TABLE OF CONTENTS

INTRODUCTION

America's got faith! It's all around us — in grand cathedrals and tiny chapels, in miracle shrines and underwater statues, and even in blessed dirt. Finding these sacred places hasn't been easy — until now! *Monuments, Marvels, and Miracles: A Traveler's Guide to Catholic America* takes you to more than 500 of the country's most intriguing Catholic holy sites, each with a riveting story to tell.

Perhaps it's a story about architecture (the interior of Guardian Angel Cathedral in Las Vegas, Nevada, resembles angel wings). Or a story about Old World traditions (in one Texas church, men sat on one side of the aisle and women on the other). Or perhaps it's a story about Catholic persecution (when Catholicism was outlawed in colonial Maryland, Jesuit priests went incognito), or a revered artifact (the Miraculous Medal Shrine in Philadelphia, Pennsylvania, holds one of the original medals that Saint Catherine Labouré had cast in 1832). Everywhere are found astounding answers to prayer — from Minnesota's Grasshopper Chapel to Coral Miracle Church in Hawaii.

Like America itself, our country's Catholic roots are culturally diverse. Multitudes of nationalities — Irish, Polish, English, Sicilian, Swiss, Portuguese, Lebanese, Vietnamese, Cuban, and many more — settled this land and brought their Catholic traditions with them. Belgians erected tiny wayside chapels in Wisconsin; Germans, grottoes across the land. When early Jesuit missionaries arrived, Indians taught them an indigenous building style: chapels of bark. Surprisingly, America's oldest church isn't American. It's French!

Our road trip — illustrated with dozens of photos to whet your appetite for travel — will be full of adventure. We'll discover healing places. Beautiful places. Hidden places. Places of deep spiritual contemplation. Historic places (the site of America's first known Mass may surprise you). Places where saints walked. But holy doesn't mean stuffy! Many sites are baptized in good humor and sprinkled with fascinating lore. How fast was the Fastest Nun in the West? Why is the Good Thief on his way to sainthood? Who was the Incognito Prince-Priest? (The answers are in the book.)

Put the car in drive and let's go!

HOW TO USE THIS BOOK

This book is divided into seven geographic areas, with each state and the District of Columbia having its own chapter. Typically, the sites for each state are listed north to south, in a mostly clockwise manner. Most states are divided into sections — East and West, or North and South — to help with travel planning. Each state also has a sidebar called Finding Faith (New York and Texas have two) that features a religious attraction or Catholic story unique to that state. Each chapter includes a map, with holy sites assigned a number and Finding Faith sites marked with a blue cross. The index uses these site numbers instead of page numbers for easier reference.

Websites, telephone numbers, physical addresses, and other pertinent information are to help you plan your journey. To verify a site's hours of operation or Mass times, visit the website or call ahead. Some churches may be locked for security reasons, but parish personnel are happy to welcome you if they know your plans. A few sites require reservations. If you can, leave a donation. Many historic churches rely on the good will of visitors to help keep their doors open. And whether indoors or out-doors, these places are holy places and appropriate dress is requested.

And remember, the more than 500 sites high-lighted in the chapters and Finding Faith sidebars are just a fraction of the rich heritage you'll find in your faith travels. Above all, enjoy the journey — and the wonders of America's Catholic faith!

NORTHEAST

CANADA

Burlington

87

Lake Ontario

Syracuse

Albany ★

Buffalo

80

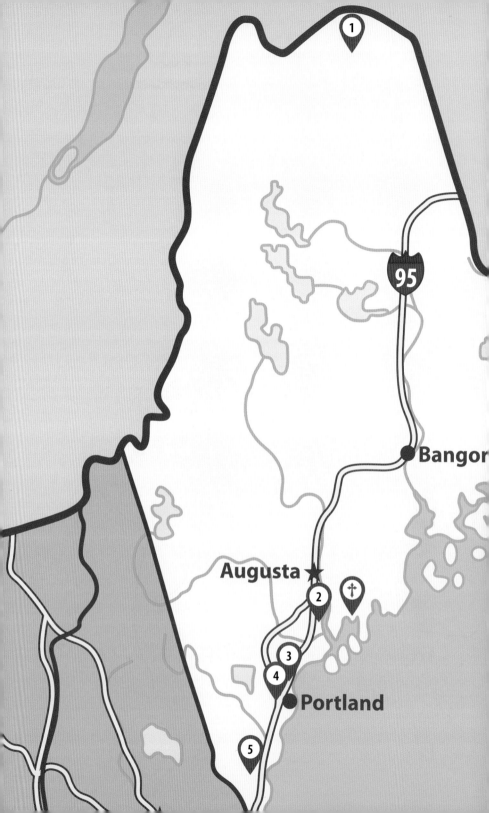

CANADA

MAINE

Atlantic Ocean

NORTHERN MAINE

When Richard Corbin was diagnosed with late-stage Hodgkin's lymphoma in 1969 and given less than a year to live, the twenty-two-year-old cut a deal with the Almighty. In exchange for more years, he pledged to pay it forward. In 1991, he founded **Mizpah** (a Hebrew word meaning "watchtower," which Richard also interpreted as "to help one another"), a 109-acre retreat on the Canadian border at Grand Isle, where people struggling with pain or despair can find comfort and peace. Nature walks include a pond with a floating rosary, the way of the cross, and the way of personal reflection. First Friday Masses are held June–October in the chapel.

Plan your visit: Facebook.com/mizpah.isle. 126 Doucette Road, Grand Isle, ME 04746. (207) 728-3129, (207) 728-7734, or (207) 316-3477.

SOUTHERN MAINE

If folks can come together for a barn raising, why not a church raising? It happened in 1889, at **St. Ambrose Church** in Richmond when townspeople — Catholic and Protestant — gathered to erect the wooden structure. During the church dedication Mass, the congregation held more Protestants than Catholics! The angelic sanctuary mural was a gift of the Russian Orthodox Church.

Plan your visit: allsaintsmaine.com/churches /stambrose. 29 Kimball Street, Richmond, ME 04357. (207) 725-2624.

Who is the First Lady of Maine? Mary! Dedicated in 1869, the neo-Gothic **Cathedral of the Immaculate Conception** in Portland — with attention-getting asymmetrical spires — is a visual walk through salvation history. Stained-glass windows from Munich, Germany, present Mary's role in our redemption (don't miss the window of Mary and Joseph's wedding), and the Venetian mosaic stations of the cross illustrate Christ's sacrifice at Calvary. But it's the portal to heaven that first grabs your eyes: The baptismal font is a "mere" twelve feet tall!

Plan your visit: portlandcatholic.org/cathedral. 307 Congress Street, Portland, ME 04101. (207) 773-7746.

A towering Celtic cross at **Calvary Cemetery** in South Portland marks the grave of Bishop James A. Healy (1830–1900), often regarded as the country's first black bishop and the second bishop of the Diocese of Portland. The eldest of ten children, James Augustine was born near Macon, Georgia, to Irish immigrant cotton planter Michael Healy and Mary Eliza Clark, a former slave of mixed race. Two of Bishop Healy's brothers also became priests, and three of his sisters entered the convent. (Venerable Augustus Tolton is often hailed as the nation's first black Catholic priest. See 149 and 241.)

Plan your visit: portlanddiocese.org /cemeteries-and-funerals/calvary -cemetery-of-south-portland-maine. 1461 Broadway, South Portland, ME 04106. (207) 773-5796.

5 When the Soviet Union invaded Lithuania in 1940 and seized churches and monasteries, Lithuanian Franciscans scattered across the world. In 1947, displaced friars acquired William A. Rogers' 1906 Tudor estate in scenic Kennebunk and founded today's **St. Anthony Franciscan Friary**. Friary grounds include a Lourdes grotto, a Lithuanian Wayside Cross, the Vatican Pavilion Monument of the Militant, Suffering, and Triumphant Church (exhibited at the New York City World's Fair in 1964–1965), and a charming statue of Saint Francis of Assisi playing the violin.

Plan your visit: www.framon.net. 28 Beach Avenue, Kennebunk, ME 04043. (207) 967-2011.

✝ FINDING FAITH
in Maine

Looking for something old? Come to **St. Patrick's Church** in Newcastle. The quaint red-brick church, erected in 1807 in Federal style, is reportedly the country's first church named for Saint Patrick and houses a bell cast in 1818 by Paul Revere. The unique French altar — shaped like a crypt — is one of three known crypt altars in the country. The stained-glass windows came from Sears, Roebuck and Company.

Many early Catholic parishes suffered persecution, including St. Patrick's. One day word leaked out that the Know Nothings, a nativist party that detested Catholic immigrants, planned to burn down the church. Townsfolk removed the church valuables and formed a ring around the church to protect it. Faith won, and St. Patrick's still stands today.

Plan your visit: allsaintsmaine.com/churches /st-patricks. 380 Academy Hill Road, Newcastle, ME 04553. (207) 563-3240.

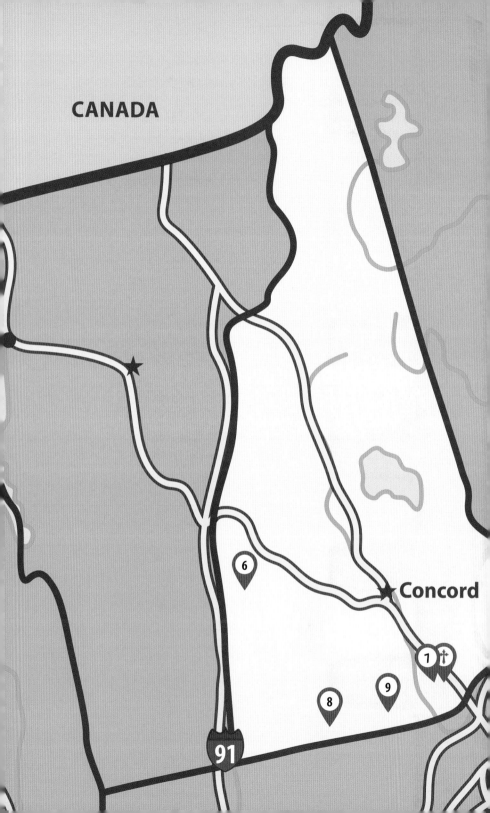

CANADA

Concord

91

NEW HAMPSHIRE

95

Atlantic Ocean

6 ▸ Learn why Our Lady weeps at **La Salette Shrine** near Enfield. The story begins on September 19, 1846, when Our Lady appeared in period dress to two shepherd children near the village of La Salette, France. Around her neck was a cross, with a hammer on one side and pincers on the other. Founded in 1927 by La Salette Missionaries , the rustic retreat — the site of a former Shaker village — includes a chapel, outdoor statuary replicating Our Lady's apparition in France, the Rosary Pond, Calvary with Holy Stairs, and an international exhibit of 450 nativity scenes.

Plan your visit: lasaletteofenfield.org. 410 NH Route 4A, Enfield, NH 03748. (603) 632-7087.

7 ▸ You can "bank" on **Ste. Marie Church** in Manchester, established in 1880. At the turn of the twentieth century, thousands of French Canadians poured into Manchester to work in textile mills. When banks denied the mill workers savings and credit privileges, Ste. Marie pastor Monsignor Pierre Hevey founded the country's first credit union. Established in 1908, St. Mary's Bank is still operat-

8 ▸ ing today. **America's Credit Union Museum** tells Monsignor Hevey's enterprising story.

Plan your visit: Ste. Marie Church: enterthenarrowgate.org. 378 Notre Dame Avenue, Manchester, NH 03102. (603) 622-4615. America's Credit Union Museum: acumuseum.org. 420 Notre Dame Avenue, Manchester, NH 03102. (603) 629-1553.

St. Joseph Cathedral [Finding Faith] ▸

Faith is literally set in stone at **St. Patrick Church** in Jaffrey. For years, folks picked and hauled tons of fieldstone to build the English-looking Gothic stone church; only heaven knows their blood, sweat, and backaches! Heralded as a "unique architectural gem," the Celtic cross-tipped church was dedicated in 1917. An outdoor grotto tells another story of faith: A young boy repeatedly claimed to see a Madonna-like apparition in the brush near the rectory. When the pastor deemed the lad mentally sound, a rock grotto honoring Mary went up.

Plan your visit: stpatricksjaffrey.com. 89 Main Street, Jaffrey, NH 03452. (603) 532-6634.

✜ FINDING FAITH
✝ in New Hampshire

Many people "go to Joseph" in times of need. In a twist of fate, **Saint Joseph Cathedral** of Manchester had a need: furnishings for its period renovation. Designed by renowned American architect Patrick Charles Keely, the 1869 Victorian Gothic cathedral — like many churches in the post-Vatican II period — had been stripped of its marble reredos and altars, even the stations of the cross. Another Keely church, Holy Trinity Church in Boston, saved the Keely cathedral. When the Boston church closed in 2008, Saint Joseph's received its ornate altars, reredos, and six-foot-tall painted bas-relief stations of the cross. The cathedral now glows like never before.

The Austrian stained-glass windows, installed for the cathedral's consecration in 1894, are tales in themselves. It's said that Bishop Denis Bradley, the first bishop of the Diocese of Manchester, was a thorn in artists' sides: He repeatedly altered already-approved designs or moved a scene from one window to another. Called *Meditations of Light*, the glorious windows — from the creation of the world, to Christ with the little children, to the preaching of Saint Patrick — are nothing short of heaven itself.

Plan your visit: stjosephcathedralnh.org. 145 Lowell Street, Manchester, NH 03104. (603) 622-6404.

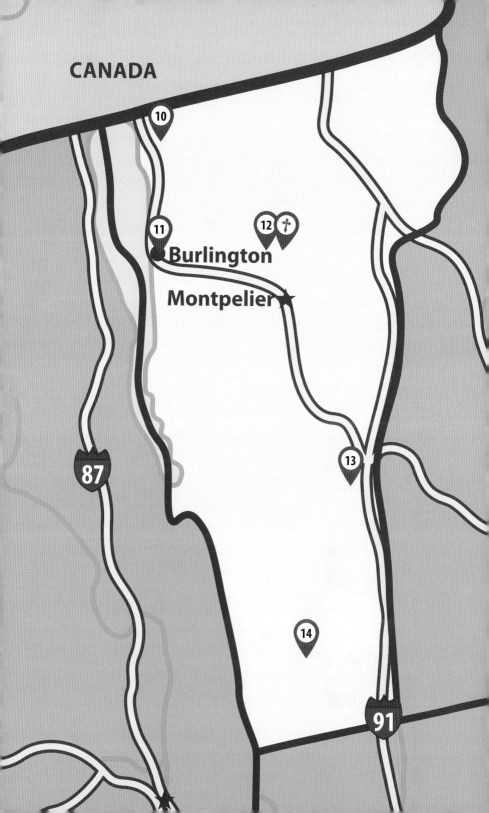

NORTHERN VERMONT

 Walk through history and faith at **Saint Anne's Shrine** on Isle La Motte, overlooking scenic Lake Champlain. Here in 1666 the French built Fort Ste. Anne, Quebec's southern defense, and French Jesuits offered Vermont's first Mass. Devotional areas scattered across the thirteen-acre retreat include a 1909 chapel (a wall of crutches attests to answered prayers), grottoes, the way of the cross, and numerous statues, including Saint Anne teaching her daughter, Mary, and a soaring, gold-leafed Our Lady of Lourdes with a lighted halo of stars.

Plan your visit: saintannesshrine.org. 92 St. Anne's Road, Isle La Motte, VT 05463. (802) 928-3362.

 No passport is needed to visit this palatial French church! Constructed of red sandstone, Burlington's 1887 **Cathedral of St. Joseph** imitates the Chapel of the Palace of Versailles in Paris (the royal chapel built for King Louis XIV). A grand staircase fit for royalty ascends to the arched front doors. It's also the home of New England's oldest French-Canadian national parish, founded in 1850.

Plan your visit: stjosephcathedralvt.org. 29 Allen Street, Burlington, VT 05401. (802) 658-4333.

 Before Werner von Trapp, son of Georg and Maria von Trapp (of *The Sound of Music* fame), left the US to fight in World War II, he vowed to build a chapel of thanksgiving if he returned home safely. On a steep hill behind the **Trapp Family Lodge** near Stowe, Werner and his family erected a tiny stone chapel with a bell tower. It's said that Maria, a Catholic convert, often came here to pray. (See Finding Faith in Vermont.)

Plan your visit: trappfamily.com. 700 Trapp Hill Road, Stowe, VT 05672. (800) 826-7000.

SOUTHERN VERMONT

 Called "sacred and secular treasures," George Tooker's *The Seven Sacraments* are worthy of a renowned museum. Happily for us pilgrims, this collection of paintings adorns **St. Francis of Assisi Church** in Windsor, where the artist converted to Catholicism and was a parishioner. Executed in egg tempera, the seven large murals — unified into a spectacular whole — depict, in Tooker style, similar-looking people radiating an inner light received from partaking of the sacraments. Tooker's strikingly original and symbolic stations of the cross focus on Christ's hands.

Plan your visit: stfranciswindsor.org. 30 Union Street, Windsor, VT 05089. (802) 674-2157.

 High on a hill near Ephesus, Turkey, stands the House of the Virgin Mary, where, according to tradition, the apostle Saint John took the Blessed Mother to live after Christ's ascension and where she was assumed into heaven. On a hill near Jamaica, the Tarinelli family erected, in 2002, **Our Lady of Ephesus House of Prayer**, a replica of Mary's stone house in Turkey. Events include outdoor Lenten stations of the cross, made by snowshoe.

Plan your visit: ourladyofephesushouseofprayer.org. 35 Fawn Ledge Lane, Jamaica, VT 05343. (802) 896-6000.

✤ FINDING FAITH
✝ in Vermont

According to lore, when a priest couldn't convince the bishop to build a church in Stowe, the indomitable Maria von Trapp (see 12) paid him a visit. The bishop said yes! Dedicated in 1949, **Blessed Sacrament Catholic Church** turns heads: Twelve large exterior murals portray Brother Joseph Dutton's work with lepers on the Hawaiian island of Molokai (see Finding Faith in Hawaii). A saint in many minds, Brother Joseph (1843–1931) was born on a farm where the church now stands.

Painted by French artist André Girard in primitive style, the black stick-like figures convey a surprising depth of motion and emotion. In one scene, Saint Damien de Veuster (see 99, 423, and Finding Faith in Hawaii) greets Brother Joseph upon his arrival on Molokai in 1886; in another, a shroud-wrapped leper is lowered into a grave. Inside, Girard's thirty-six painted windows use light to depict Light, the vibrant colors eliciting hope and eternal joy.

Plan your visit: bscvt.com, 728 Mountain Road, Stowe, VT 05672. (802) 253-7536.

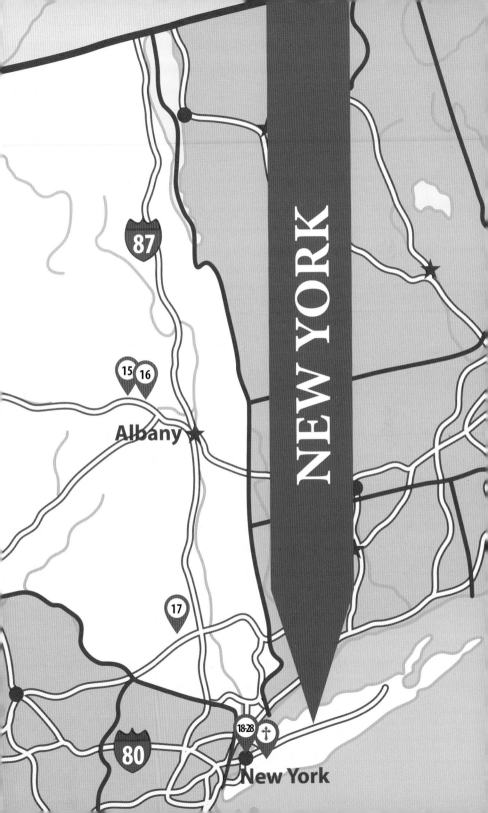

EASTERN NEW YORK

She:kon! Skennon ko:wa! This Mohawk blessing, meaning "Hello! Great Peace be with you!" echoes throughout the **Saint Kateri Tekakwitha National Shrine and Historic Site** at Fonda. Kateri (see 16), a Mohawk maiden and the first canonized Native American, spent much of her life here. Walk where she walked. Praise the Lord of creation (Kateri is patroness of ecology and the environment). Draw water from the spring used for Kateri's baptism on Easter Sunday, April 5, 1676. In a centuries-old barn, the upper level recreates the St. Peter's Chapel of Kateri's day, while the lower level holds a museum of Indian artifacts.

Plan your visit: katerishrine.com. 3636 NY-5, Fonda, NY 12068. (518) 853-3646.

What would you sacrifice for your faith? (Father Isaac Jogues lost his index fingers and thumbs used to hold the Host at Mass.) That question will confront you at **Our Lady of Martyrs Shrine** at Fultonville. Built on the site of a Mohawk Indian village, the shrine marks the 1640s martyrdoms of French Jesuit Saints Jogues, René Goupil, and Jean de Lalande, three of the eight North American Martyrs. Another saint, Kateri Tekakwitha (see 15), was born here in 1656. The grounds include a museum, the Coliseum Church seating 6,500 (reminiscent of Rome's Colosseum where martyrs were slain), statues, shrines, and the ravine where Father Jogues buried the remains of René Goupil.

Plan your visit: ourladyofmartyrsshrine.org. 136 Shrine Road, Fultonville, NY 12072. (518) 853-3939.

Only heaven knows how many souls were saved and lives spared during World War II, thanks to parishioners at the **National Shrine of Our Lady of Mount Carmel** who made millions of scapulars to send to the armed forces. In 1991, the shrine was moved from Manhattan to Middletown. Like a cloud of witnesses, holy Carmelite men and women appear in stained glass, statues, and shrines across the sixty-acre retreat. Of special interest for pilgrims is the Cloister Walk with Carmelite stations of the cross.

Plan your visit: ourladyofmtcarmelshrine.com. 70 Carmelite Drive, Middletown, NY 10940. (845) 343-1879.

NEW YORK CITY

St. Peter's Church in Manhattan is steeped in history. New York's oldest Catholic parish, St. Peter's was established in 1785, four years before George Washington was sworn in as America's first president. Today's Greek Revival temple, erected in 1836, honors Saint Peter in statues and murals, but nothing compels reflection like the gold-leaf inscription in the sanctuary. Added after the September 11, 2001 attacks on the World Trade Center — the church served as a center for rescue and recovery operations — is the Latin translation of Matthew 16:18: "You are Peter, and on this rock I will build my Church, and the gates of Hades shall not prevail against it." The 9/11 Catholic Memorial stands outside the church.

Plan your visit: spcolr.org. 22 Barclay Street, New York, NY 10007. (212) 233-8355.

All the world is a stage except at **St. Malachy's Church**, in Manhattan's Theater District, where actors, musicians, directors, playwrights, and other entertainers come to pray. Spencer Tracy, Gregory Peck, and Rosalind Russell worshiped here; Fred Allen, Don Ameche, and Jimmy Durante served many a Mass. Called the Actors' Chapel, the Gothic Revival church offers a post-theater Saturday night Mass. Don't miss the Artists' Shrine with icons of saintly patrons of the arts, including Saint Vitus (dancers), Blessed Dina Bélanger (concert pianists), and Saint Genesius (comedians).

Plan your visit: actorschapel.org. 239 W. Forty-Ninth Street, New York, NY 10019. (212) 489-1340.

If you feel like dancing while visiting **Our Lady of the Rosary Church** in Manhattan, blame Saint Elizabeth Ann Seton (1774–1821). Constructed in Federal and Georgian styles to complement the 1793 Watson House next door, the church — home of the Saint Elizabeth Ann Seton Shrine — was built on the site where the Seton family lived from 1801 to 1803. It's said that the architects designed the sanctuary to resemble an ornate ballroom because Elizabeth loved to dance! Mother Seton (see 60, 82, and 173), America's first American-born canonized saint, founded the Union's first free Catholic school for girls and the first American congregation of religious sisters, the Sisters of Charity.

Plan your visit: spcolr.org. 7 State Street, New York, NY 10004. (212) 233-8355.

A mosaic is worth 10,000 words at the **St. Frances Cabrini Shrine** in Manhattan. A mosaic filling the entire apse traces the life of Mother Frances Xavier Cabrini (1850–1917), from her childhood in Italy, to her meeting with Pope Leo XIII and his admonition "Not to the East, but to the West," to her work with Italian immigrants in America. The remains of Mother Cabrini are entombed in a glass-enclosed coffin beneath the altar, while a three-story stained-glass image of the saint makes her appear more alive than ever. (See 231 and 325.)

Plan your visit: cabrinishrinenyc.org. 701 Fort Washington Avenue, New York, NY 10040. (212) 923-3536.

22 What's better than one St. Patrick's Cathedral? Two St. Patrick's Cathedrals! And you need only look at the tall outer brick wall of **Old St. Patrick's** in Manhattan — formally known as the Basilica of St. Patrick's Old Cathedral — to know that it's a bastion of American Catholic faith. In the mid-1830s, loopholes were cut into the wall and sharpshooters stationed to defend the church against rioting anti-Catholic nativists. Opened in 1815, the Gothic Revival structure was gutted by fire in 1866 and reopened in 1868. A must-explore: the catacombs under the church.

Plan your visit: oldcathedral.org. 263 Mulberry Street, New York, NY 10012. (212) 226-8075.

23 When Archbishop John Hughes announced plans in 1853 to build a new **St. Patrick's Cathedral** on Manhattan then-farmland, it was ridiculed as Hughes' Folly. Twenty-one years in the building (1858–1879), this magnificent Gothic "folly" boasts 330-foot spires, fifteen altars, nineteen bells (each named for a different saint), and Fifth Avenue bronze doors that weigh over 9,000 pounds each. New St. Patrick's attracts an estimated seven million visitors annually. Buried in the crypt is Venerable Pierre Toussaint (1766–1853), a freed Haitian slave and philanthropist who made his money as a hairdresser for the city's elite women.

Plan your visit: saintpatrickscathedral.org. Fifth Avenue between Fiftieth and Fifty-First Streets, New York, NY 10022. (212) 753-2261.

To experience a medieval chapter in Catholic Church history, visit **The Met Cloisters** — a branch of The Metropolitan Museum of Art in Manhattan — constructed in the 1930s from parts of European medieval monasteries and convents that were falling into ruin. Medieval treasures include stained glass, tapestries, illuminated manuscripts, statuary, vessels and vestments, and even a flabellum, a fan used to shoo flies off priests during Mass. Most revered of all: the Fuentidueña Apse, from a twelfth-century Romanesque church in Spain, with a fresco of Mother and Child. It's thought that the niches in the wall were used to hold the bread and wine for Mass.

Plan your visit: metmuseum.org. 99 Margaret Corbin Drive, Fort Tryon Park, New York, NY 10040. (212) 923-3700.

"I will never forget you. See, upon the palms of my hands I have written your name. Your walls are ever before me" (Is 49:15–16). These poignant words are engraved on a striking bronze statue of Jesus cradling the Twin Towers, in a memorial garden outside **St. Ephrem Church** in Brooklyn. Sculpted by Reto Demetz, the statue honors the nine parishioners who died in the terrorist attacks on September 11, 2001.

Plan your visit: stephremparish-brooklyn.org. 929 Bay Ridge Parkway, Dyker Heights, Brooklyn, NY 11228. (718) 833-1010.

Calvary Cemetery in Queens is literally a "city of the dead": Upward of three million lie here awaiting the resurrection of the body. Consecrated in 1848, the 365-acre cemetery is divided into "Four Calvaries" and named for catacombs in Rome. First Calvary (or Old Calvary) is known as Saint Callixtus; Second, Saint Agnes; Third, Saint Sebastian; and Fourth, Saint Domitilla.

Plan your visit: calvarycemeteryqueens.com. 49-02 Laurel Hill Boulevard, Woodside, NY 11377. (718) 786-8000.

27 **Schoenstatt Chapel** on Staten Island (see 221).

Plan your visit: schoenstattla.com. 337 Cary Avenue, Staten Island, NY 10310. (718) 727-8005.

28 For a bit of Catholic trivia, visit the **National Museum of Immigration** on Ellis Island. When Ellis Island officially opened on January 1, 1892, the first immigrant processed was an Irish Catholic teenager named Annie Moore. Annie and her two younger brothers had sailed from County Cork, Ireland, to meet their parents already living in New York City. A statue of Annie commemorates the historic event and represents the millions of Catholics who passed through Ellis Island in pursuit of religious freedom and the American dream.

Plan your visit: nps.gov/elis/index.htm. (212) 363-3200, libertyellisfoundation.org. (212) 561-4588. Accessible by ferry only.

WESTERN NEW YORK

In trouble? Turn to Our Lady, Help of Christians. In November 1836, Joseph Batt and his family, all from Alsace-Lorraine, boarded the *Mary Ann* and sailed for America. Two weeks into the voyage, the ship encountered a hurricane-like storm and sustained severe damage. Batt invoked Our Lady's protection and vowed to build her a chapel for his family's safe passage. The storm abated and the ship drifted to Ireland, where it was repaired. Safely in America, Batt erected, in 1853, the **Chapel of Our Lady Help of Christians** in Cheektowaga. Throngs of pilgrims began flocking here and the chapel became known as a "second Lourdes."

29

Plan your visit: ourladyhelpofchristians.org. 4125 Union Road, corner of Genesee Street, Cheektowaga, NY 14225. (716) 634-3420.

30 Love the Lord with all your hearts, minds ... and stones. That's the faith story of **Sacred Heart of Jesus Church** in Bowmansville. In the mid-1920s, parishioners collected umpteen tons of stone and turned them into elaborate shrine-grottoes to the Immaculate Conception of Mary (the rough stones and running water give the heart-shaped shrine a timeless feel) and to the Sacred Heart of Jesus (the smooth stones represent the living stones: people), with an altar and a bell tower. Winding stone staircases, each with thirty-three steps signifying Jesus' years on earth, take pilgrims to statues at the top.

Plan your visit: sacredheartshrine.org. 5337 Genesee Street, Bowmansville, NY 14026. (716) 683-2375.

31 Stand with Mary on top of the world at the **Basilica of the National Shrine of Our Lady of Fatima** in Lewiston. Constructed in 1963, the fifty-five-foot-tall, glass-covered, dome-shaped church represents the Northern Hemisphere (complete with a map of the same), with exterior stairs ascending to a thirteen-foot Mary statue on top. Other attractions include a giant heart-shaped illuminated Rosary pool, the Little Chapel of Fatima (a replica of the first chapel built at Fátima, Portugal), and the Avenue of the Saints with more than 130 life-size statues of saints from every race and walk of life.

Plan your visit: fatimashrine.com. 1023 Swann Road, Youngstown, NY 14174. (716) 754-7489.

✟ FINDING FAITH
in New York City …

Can a miracle take one's breath away? It did at the **Basilica of Regina Pacis** in Brooklyn. During World War II, Monsignor Angelo Cioffi and all 12,000 parishioners made a vow to Our Lady to erect a magnificent shrine in her honor for the safe return of their soldiers. During construction of the 1949 Italianate Renaissance structure, the community donated jewelry — wedding rings, lockets, bracelets, jewels, and more — to make crowns for the Regina Pacis painting above the high altar. Days after the painting's coronation, the crowns were stolen.

People flocked to Regina Pacis to pray for the crowns' return. Some days later, a package arrived at the rectory: It was the crowns! Monsignor Cioffi burst into the church and announced the miraculous news. Three people fainted. People still "faint" at the basilica's spectacular artworks, all with legends of their own.

Plan your visit: basilicaofreginapacis.org. 1230 Sixty-Fifth Street, Brooklyn, NY 11219. (718) 236-0909.

... and in Western New York

When Venerable Nelson Baker (1842–1936) began constructing **Our Lady of Victory National Shrine and Basilica** in Lackawanna in 1921, he didn't have a penny. When the magnificent shrine was completed in 1925 (and immediately elevated to basilica in 1926), he didn't owe a nickel! But then, Father Baker lived by miracles, aided by Our Lady of Victory. Once, when faced with high fuel bills, he asked for Our Lady's help and then drilled for gas. The well is still producing today!

While the exterior is constructed mainly of white marble, the basilica's interior is simply angelic — thousands of angels are visible in every possible line of sight, including an angelic host on the eighty-foot-diameter dome painting of Mary's assumption and coronation. Other notable features include the life-size marble stations of the cross (it's said that each station took the sculptor one year to complete) and the indoor Grotto Shrine of Our Lady of Lourdes, hewn out of volcanic rock from Mount Vesuvius in Italy. As in life, Father Baker remains close to Our Lady in death; his remains are interred at the foot of her grotto.

Plan your visit: olvbasilica.org. 767 Ridge Road, Lackawanna, NY 14218. (716) 828-9444.

MASSACHUSETTS

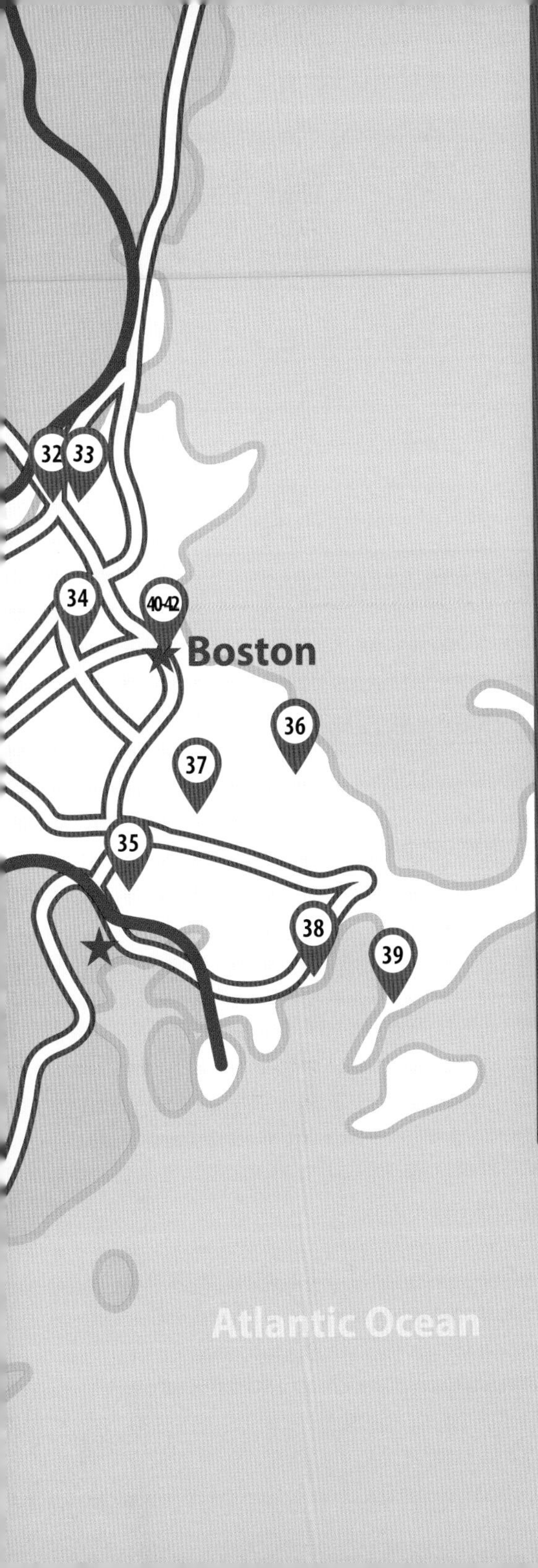

32 33

34

40-42

★ Boston

36

37

35

★

38

39

Atlantic Ocean

EASTERN MASSACHUSETTS

(32) Walk the Via Josephus (Way of Joseph) at **St. Joseph the Worker Shrine** in Lowell. Beautiful stained glass presents his life, from the angelic dream, to the flight into Egypt, to Jesus blessing him at the hour of death. Observe the uniquely colored halos: red, yellow, even blue. Formerly an abandoned church, the shrine's massive wooden trusses make you think that Saint Joseph the Carpenter might have built this himself!

Plan your visit: stjosephshrine.org. 37 Lee Street, Lowell, MA 01853. (978) 458-6346.

(33) You could spend an eternity extracting the religious symbolism presented in stained glass at **Immaculate Conception Church** in Lowell. Dedicated in 1877, the church's brilliant windows include the Seven Sorrows and Seven Joys of Mary, and a rose window depicting thirteen Marian titles spanning the ages — from Our Lady of Hope to Our Lady of Banneux. The window of Our Lady of the Most Blessed Sacrament with a passionflower will test your religious and botanical knowledge. How long does the flower bloom? (Think Holy Week.) What do the five stamens represent? The ten petals? Can you find the nails? Where is the spear?

Plan your visit: iclowell.org. 144 E. Merrimack Street, Lowell, MA 01852. (978) 458-1474.

(34) You'll never forget praying the Rosary at **Our Lady of Fatima Shrine** in Holliston. The granite beads — fastened by marine chain from a ship's anchor — are waist high, and the Our Father beads are even bigger. One of the world's largest rosaries, the 950-foot-long prayer begins atop the Holy Stairs with a larger-than-life crucifixion scene, then encircles the ground below. The Hail Mary beads each bear plaques inscribed with the Hail Mary in a different language, from Arabic to Tamil.

Plan your visit: xaverianmissionaries.org. 101 Summer Street, Holliston, MA 01746. (508) 429-2144.

Do you see what I see? More than 500,000 lights shining so bright at the Christmas Festival of Lights at the **National Shrine of Our Lady of La Salette** in Attleboro. One of New England's largest holiday attractions, the spectacular displays annually draw upward of one million visitors. A pilgrimage destination year-round (many ethnic groups make pilgrimages here), the grounds include the Garden of La Salette Apparition, Holy Stairs, St. Francis's Garden, St. Joseph's Garden, Rosary Walk, and Chapel of Light with its 3,000 candles.

Plan your visit: lasaletteattleboroshrine.org. 947 Park Street, Attleboro, MA. (508) 222-5410.

Portiuncula Chapel in Hanover is more than a "little portion" of Assisi. When Cardinal Richard Cushing built the 1950s hilltop chapel for the Sisters of St. Francis of Assisi of Milwaukee, Wisconsin, and their school for the developmentally disabled (now the Cardinal Cushing Centers), he spared no artistic detail. Every stone, every fresco came from Assisi. The

Hanover facade even depicts the Pardon of Assisi (also known as the Portiuncula Indulgence). Cardinal Cushing (1895–1970) selected the chapel as his final resting place.

Plan your visit: cushingcenters.org. 405 Washington Street, Hanover, MA 02339. (781) 826-6371.

 "The family that prays together stays together," Venerable Patrick Peyton (1909–1992), CSC, famously said. At the **Museum of Family Prayer**, located at Holy Cross Family Ministries in North Easton, pilgrims can retrace Father Peyton's life. Dubbed the Rosary Priest, the Irish native founded Family Rosary apostolate in 1942 and Family Theater Productions in 1947. Artifacts include Father Peyton's rosary, suitcase, film reels, and huge movie projectors — used in South American hinterlands to project movies onto sheets hung from buildings. You'll also find an outdoor Rosary Path with a statue of Father Peyton.

Plan your visit: museumoffamilyprayer.org. 518 Washington Street, North Easton, MA 02356. (800) 299-7729.

 How fortunate that Saint Anthony of Padua is a wonderworker! In the 1990s, **Saint Anthony of Padua Church** in New Bedford needed a miracle — and got one when Father Edmond "Fix-It" Levesque rescued the 1904 Romanesque red sandstone church, with 256-foot-tall steeple, from the brink of destruction. And what a wonder it is: more than 700 angels (some twenty feet tall!), nearly 6,000 lights set in arches, and 117 stained-glass windows. The main attraction? The spectacular *Vision of Saint Anthony*, a thirty-foot-tall frieze with thirty-two statues above the main altar. Surrounded by angels in various colored robes, the Child Jesus — a cross at his back — appears ready to leap into Anthony's waiting arms.

Plan your visit: saintanthonynewbedford.com. 1359 Acushnet Avenue, New Bedford, MA 02746. (508) 993-1691.

Open the gate and step inside the **Mary Garden** at St. Joseph's Chapel in Woods Hole. Created by Frances Crane Lillie in 1932, the devotional garden — believed to be the country's first public Mary garden — features dozens of flowers and herbs that reference

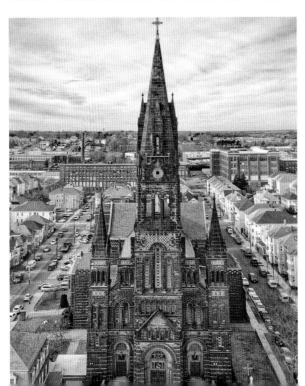

the Virgin Mary. Can you find Our Lady's Mantle? Mary's Star? Our Lady's Slipper? Madonna's Pins? (Hint: Consult the birdhouse-style display box for help.) The two bells in the Angelus Bell Tower are named for Catholic scientists Gregor Mendel and Louis Pasteur.

Plan your visit: falmouthcatholic.org. 33 Millfield Street, Woods Hole, MA 02543. (508) 563-7770.

BOSTON

"Lourdes in the Land of the Pilgrims" was how late nineteenth-century newspapers described today's **Basilica of Our Lady of Perpetual Help**. On August 18, 1883, teenager Grace Hanley, crippled since age four, and her family were praying yet another novena for her healing when Grace suddenly stood up and walked to the altar. She was healed! Since then, multitudes of other seekers have also been healed, as witnessed by two huge receptacles filled with crutches and other aids. Constructed of puddingstone, the 1876 Romanesque church dazzles with its "parade of saints" in statues, murals, and mosaics. Art for thought: A side altar mosaic features Saint Joseph and foster son Jesus, who bear a striking resemblance to each other.

Plan your visit: bostonsbasilica.com. 1545 Tremont Street, Boston, MA 02120. (617) 445-2600.

Named for its relic of the True Cross, the massive neo-Gothic **Cathedral of the Holy Cross** — erected of puddingstone and dedicated in 1875 — is renowned for its enamel-painted glass windows, including a dramatic window of Saint Helena's discovery of the three crosses at Golgotha. When touched by the cross of Christ, a dead woman is shown springing to life and praising the wood of her redemption. A cathedral of many tongues, the parish offers Masses and sacraments in English, Spanish, German, Ge'ez (Ethiopian-Eritrean Rite), and Latin (Extraordinary Form).

Plan your visit: holycrossboston.com. 1400 Washington Street, Boston, MA 02118. (617) 542-5682.

The eye-popping **Madonna Queen of the Universe Shrine**, overlooking Boston Harbor, inspires faith and good works. Located at the national headquarters of the Don Orione Fathers, the thirty-five-foot bronze and copper Madonna statue, standing atop a globe, with a granite backdrop and gold crown-like top, replicates a hilltop statue overlooking Rome. The Roman monument, created by Italian-Jewish sculptor Arrigo Minerbi, honors the Don Orione Fathers who sheltered the sculptor from the Nazis during World War II. Dedicated in 1954, Boston's hilltop Madonna shrine includes a must-visit underground church.

Plan your visit: madonnaqueenshrine.com. 150 Orient Avenue, Boston, MA 02128. (617) 569-8792.

WESTERN MASSACHUSETTS
Every church name tells a story, but at **North American Martyrs Church** in Auburn, even the physical

address, 8 Wyoma Drive, has meaning. Founded in 1952, the church — located on the site of a former Indian village — is named for the eight French Jesuits who were martyred while evangelizing Indians in Canada and upstate New York. The street number 8 commemorates the eight martyrs and the feast of the Immaculate Conception on December 8. *Wyoma*, an Indian word for the outstanding girl of each tribe, honors the outstanding woman of all tribes: Mary, the Mother of God.

Plan your visit: namartyrsauburn.org. 8 Wyoma Drive, Auburn, MA 01501. (508) 798-8779

If Good Saint Anne grants one favor, more favors are sure to follow. That's the testimony of **Saint Anne Church** in Sturbridge (also listed as Fiskdale). In 1879, Monsignor Elzear Brochu, who was in failing health, promised Saint Anne that he would propagate her devotion if he were healed. Four years later, he built the hillside church and prophesied that many healing wonders would be worked here. Healings still happen today! The thirty-five-acre pilgrimage destination is filled with devotional sites, including the fascinating Icon Museum. Amassed and smuggled out of Russia by Assumptionist priests, who served as chaplains to the foreign corps in Moscow from 1934 to 1999, the eighty-plus Russian icons range from Saint Nicholas the Miracle Worker to a six-foot-tall Christ Pantocrator.

Plan your visit: stannestpatrickparish.com. 16 Church Street, Fiskdale, MA 01518. (508) 347-7338.

✤ FINDING FAITH
✝ in Massachusetts

The National Shrine of The Divine Mercy in Stockbridge began with a miracle. In the fall of 1940, Father Joseph Jarzebowski, MIC, a Polish priest trying to flee Nazi Europe and who had been handed Sister Faustina's writings on Divine Mercy, offered Mass before the original Divine Mercy image and entrusted to Divine Mercy his epic journey to America. As it so happened, Divine Mercy intervened more than once. Despite his expired American visa, the Soviets permitted him to travel across Siberia to Japan. While boarding a ship to Japan, officials seized crosses and books, but passed over the priest's belongings. Father Jarzebowski and the Divine Mercy writings arrived in America just seven months before Japan attacked Pearl Harbor.

In 1943, the Marian Fathers acquired Eden Hill — 350 acres in the Berkshire Mountains — and seven years later began construction of the shrine, another miracle. Master wood carver and builder Antonio Guerrieri used no blueprints or architectural plans! The shrine glows with stained glass and mosaics portraying the mercy of God in Scripture as well as the Divine Mercy image itself. Grounds include the Lourdes Candle Grotto, Grove of Saint Francis, Mother of Mercy Shrine, and a life-size way of the cross.

Plan your visit: shrineofdivinemercy.org. 2 Prospect Hill Road, Eden Hill, Stockbridge, MA 01262. (413) 298-3931.

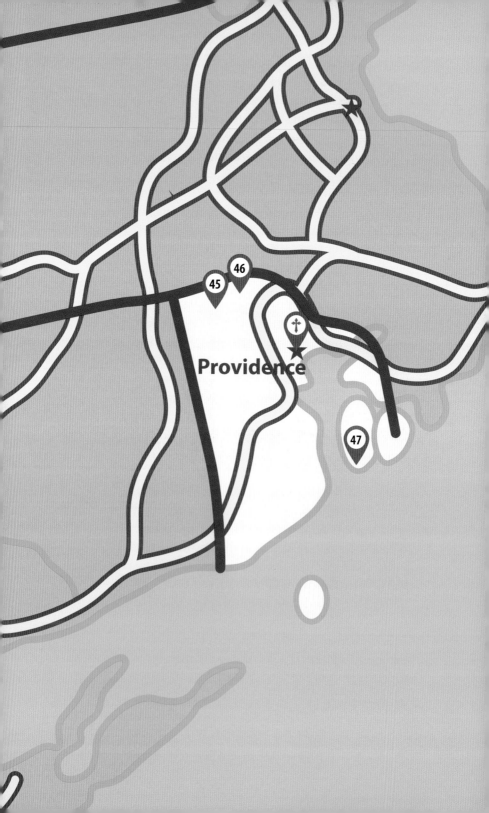

RHODE ISLAND

Atlantic Ocean

45 The world's oldest shrine in honor of the "Little Flower," Saint Thérèse of Lisieux, isn't French. It's American! Started four months after Thérèse was beatified in 1923, **St. Theresa of the Child Jesus Church** (the American spelling of her name at the time) and the outdoor Shrine of the Little Flower in Harrisville are "Little Ways" to Jesus. Devotional sites include the Holy Stairs, which ascend to a replica of Spain's miraculous Limpias Crucifix; sculptor Amedeo Nardini's stone-relief stations of the cross; and the Garden of the Saints. Like roses from heaven, many healings are reported here.

Plan your visit: burrillvillecatholic.org, sainttheresashrine.com. 35 Dion Drive, Harrisville, RI 02830. (401) 568-8280.

46 Like ceiling art? Come to the "Sistine Chapel of America." Built by French Canadians in French Renaissance style in 1913, St. Ann Church in Woonsocket boasts some 175 frescoes. Painted by Florentine artist Guido Nincheri, the frescoes (said to be so beautiful they could convert an atheist) include 475 images of parishioners. Two mischievous boys pose as devils, while a bank teller appears forty times as an angel. When the church closed in 2000, the community rallied to preserve the gem, now called the **St. Ann Arts and Cultural Center**.

Plan your visit: stannartsandculturalcenter.org. 84 Cumberland Street, Woonsocket, RI 02895. (401) 356-0713.

Return to the Kennedy era of Camelot at beautiful **St. Mary's Church** in Newport, where Jacqueline Bouvier and then-Senator John F. Kennedy were married on September 12, 1953. Later, as President and First Lady, the couple attended Sunday Mass here, always sitting in pew number ten. The brownstone Gothic Revival church — with fabulous Tyrolean stained glass — was consecrated in 1849 and is home to Rhode Island's oldest Catholic parish (1828).

Plan your visit: stmarynewport.org. 12 William Street, Newport, RI 02840. (401) 847-0475.

✦ FINDING FAITH
in Rhode Island

The **Cathedral of Saints Peter and Paul** in Providence was built on divine currency: faith. Because Bishop Thomas Hendricken, the first shepherd of the Diocese of Providence, refused to go into debt, the Gothic Revival brownstone was constructed incrementally from 1878–1889 as the pennies rolled in. Stopped short of their planned destiny, the twin 156-foot towers (the spires were never completed) preach a fine sermon: God's work is never finished.

Biblical scenes rarely seen in stained glass are found here. The glorious Old Testament windows include God banishing Cain, Abraham sacrificing Isaac, Jacob stealing Esau's birthright, Jacob's ladder, and Melchizedek blessing Abraham. New Testament windows include Jesus asleep in the boat and Jesus healing the cripple on the Sabbath. On another note, the cathedral organ has a great set of pipes — 6,616, to be exact.

Plan your visit: providencecathedral.org. 30 Fenner Street, Providence, RI 02903. (401) 331-2434.

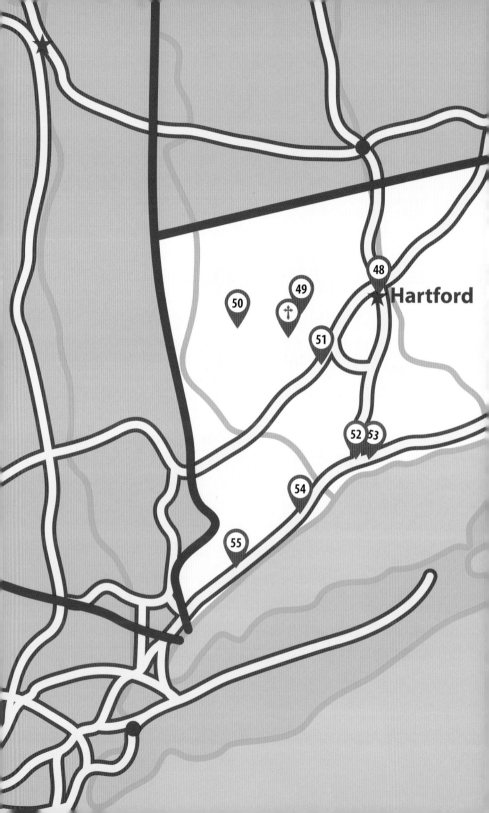

CONNECTICUT

Atlantic Ocean

EASTERN CONNECTICUT

What's behind a door? At the **Cathedral of Saint Joseph** in Hartford — a titanic, limestone-sheathed concrete temple consecrated in 1962 — a dramatic display of divine light and color. Crafted in Paris, the massive art-glass windows, nearly fourteen feet wide and seventy feet tall, preach the Gospel in stupendous larger-than-life scenes. If that don't beat the devil, the *Christ in Glory* sanctuary mural will! Inspired by the Apocalypse, the forty-by-eighty-foot masterpiece is reportedly the largest ceramic tile mural in the world.

Plan your visit: hartfordcathedral.org. 140 Farmington Avenue, Hartford, CT 06105. (860) 249-8431.

WESTERN CONNECTICUT

You can test your iconography skills at **St. Patrick Church** in Collinsville. If Saint Patrick drove the snakes out of Ireland, why are the church door handles here shaped like serpents? The Gothic-style stone church was built in 1933.

Plan your visit: sp4c.org. 50 Church Street, Collinsville, CT 06019. (860) 693-8727.

When two Montfort Missionary Brothers erected the **Lourdes in Litchfield Shrine** at Litchfield, it's said that their "blueprint" was a picture-postcard of Lourdes nailed to a tree. Dedicated in 1958 — the centenary of Our Lady's apparitions to Bernadette — the hillside fieldstone grotto leads to an interactive way of the cross. Wash your hands à la Pontius Pilate at the first station or hammer spikes into a cross at the eleventh station. Children can imitate Christ and carry small crosses up the wooded trail to the summit's larger-than-life Calvary scene.

Plan your visit: shrinect.org. 50 Montfort Road, Litchfield, CT 06759. (860) 567-1041.

When Japan torpedoed the USS *Indianapolis* on July 30, 1945, spewing 900 of its 1,195 crew into the Pacific Ocean, Lieutenant Thomas M. Conway was a spiritual lifesaver. For three days, the thirty-seven-year-old Catholic chaplain swam to his flock — Catholics and Protestants clinging to ship debris — praying with them and absolving their sins. At the **Basilica of the Immaculate Conception** in Waterbury, the Father Conway Memorial honors the last chaplain to die in World War II combat. The statue depicts, in a circle of blue representing the Pacific Ocean, the Waterbury-born priest holding a dying soldier above the waves, rosary and dog tags in hand.

Plan your visit: waterburybasilica.org. 74 W. Main Street, Waterbury, CT 06702. (203) 574-0017.

Blessed Michael J. McGivney (1852–1890) was not only a man of the Gospel but a man ahead of his times. In 1882 at **St. Mary's Church** in New Haven, the young priest founded the Knights of Columbus, a fraternal benefit society that would both invigorate the faith of parish men and financially aid families struck by the death or sudden illness of breadwinners (see 53). Many Knights make pilgrimages to the Gothic Revival stone church to see where the society got its start and to pray at Father McGivney's tomb.

Plan your visit: stmarysnewhaven.org. 5 Hillhouse Avenue, New Haven, CT 06511. (203) 562-6193.

 53 ▸ Walk in Blessed Michael J. McGivney's shoes at New Haven's **Knights of Columbus Museum**. Exhibits and a reliquary room trace the life of Father McGivney, founder of the Knights of Columbus (see 52), and showcase the many humanitarian works of the world's largest Catholic lay organization. The world-class museum is acclaimed for its rotating exhibits of history, art, and faith, and features a 400-year-old cross from atop Saint Peter's Basilica in Rome, a gift of Pope Saint John Paul II.

Plan your visit: kofcmuseum.org. 1 State Street, New Haven, CT 06511. (203) 865-0400.

December 7, 1941 — the day Japan bombed Pearl Harbor — inspired the creation of **St. Margaret Shrine** in Bridgeport. After spending time that day in prayer, Father Emilio Iasiello decided to erect an "oasis of peace," and turned a rocky parcel of land into a meandering pilgrimage of chapels and wayside shrines. Prayer stops include Our Lady of Charity, Saint Sebastian, and Saint Francis of Assisi embracing the Crucified Lord. Saint Margaret Chapel honors Margaret of Antioch, a fourth-century virgin-martyr and vanquisher of demons. According to lore, Margaret was swallowed by a dragon (Satan) but escaped by tickling his throat with a crucifix.

Plan your visit: stmargaretshrine.org. 2523 Park Avenue, Bridgeport, CT 06604. (203) 333-9627.

If the world is our oyster, then **St. Mary's Church** in Norwalk — where oystering is a time-honored tradition — is the great pearl. Standing above a side altar, a statue of Our Lady of Norwalk, dressed in a sea-blue robe with a white veil, holds an oyster in one hand, the Holy Child in the other. Behind them a triptych portrays an oysterman with a rake, the eleven apostles and John the Baptist, and St. Mary's Church. To find the oyster's pearl, look in the Child's tiny hand.

Plan your visit: stmarynorwalk.net. 669 West Avenue, Norwalk, CT 06850. (203) 866-5546.

Lourdes in Litchfield Shrine [50]

✝ FINDING FAITH
in Connecticut

Come to the stable at the **Abbey of Regina Laudis** in Bethlehem: Joseph, Mary, and the Baby Jesus are waiting for you in a 300-year-old, Italian hand-crafted crèche. It's believed that "the Rembrandt of crèches" — a fifteen-by-ten-foot panorama with sixty-eight miniature figures, ranging from the town lamplighter to the Three Kings — was originally a coronation gift to the King of Sardinia in 1720.

The story of the Benedictine abbey, founded in 1947 by two nuns from France, lit up the screen in the 1949 film *Come to the Stable*, starring Catholic actress Loretta Young. Fourteen years later, rising actress Dolores Hart, who appeared in movies with Elvis Presley and played Clare in the 1961 release *Francis of Assisi*, stunned the world when she announced that she was leaving Hollywood and entering the cloistered abbey at Bethlehem.

Plan your visit: abbeyofreginalaudis.org. 273 Flanders Road, Bethlehem, CT 06751. (203) 266-7727.

MID-ATLANTIC

Pittsburgh

★ **Charleston**

[81]

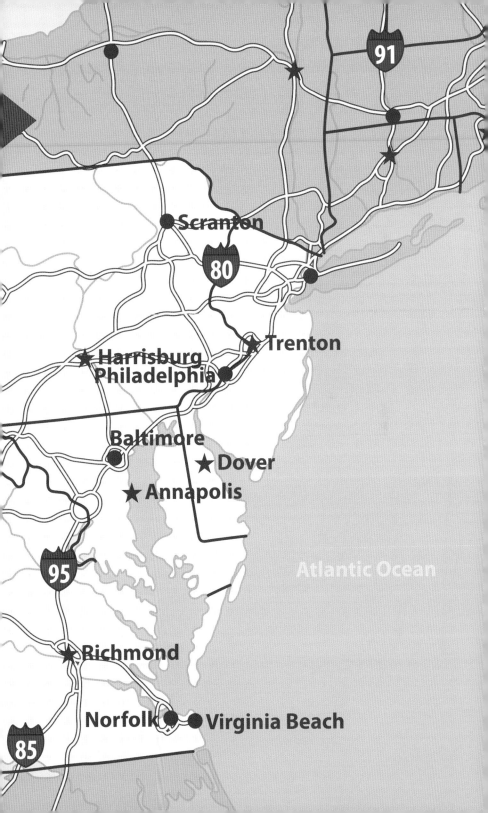

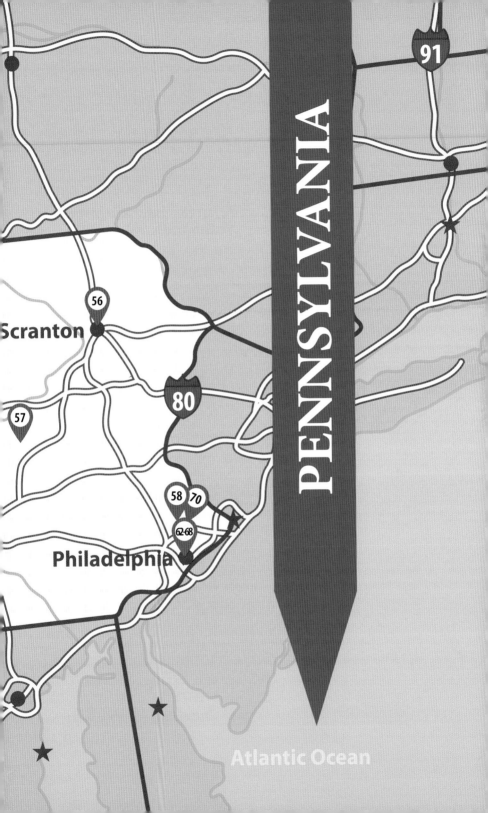

EASTERN PENNSYLVANIA

 Pray at **St. Ann's Monastery and Shrine Basilica** in Scranton and the earth might move under your feet. On July 28, 1913, the monastery's Passionist priests and laity spent the night, amid earthly rumblings, imploring the protection of Saint Ann, patroness of miners. A coal mine subsidence was threatening the monastery, and experts predicted another major slide would doom the building. Suddenly, there came a mighty roar. The "slide" was two huge boulders rolling under the monastery and closing the great fissures! Built in 1927, the present Romanesque Revival church is famous for its novenas to Good Saint Ann.

Plan your visit: stannsmonasterybasilica.org. 1233 St. Ann Street, Scranton, PA 18504. (570) 347-5691.

 Reader's Digest called it "the church that wouldn't burn." Others say the **Assumption of the Blessed Virgin Mary Ukrainian Catholic Church** — a 1911 white clapboard structure with three blue domes overlooking the ghost town of Centralia — is a miracle. In the 1960s, an underground coal seam fire started burning beneath the mining town, bringing down buildings and roads. Would the church collapse too? A subsequent inspection revealed that the church was built not on the coal seam, but on solid rock! An annual pilgrimage is held in August.

Plan your visit: ukrarcheparchy.us/assumption-of-bvm-centralia. North Paxton Street, Centralia, PA 17920. (570) 339-0650.

Miraculous Medal Shrine [62]

Our Lady surely feels right at home at the **National Shrine of Our Lady of Czestochowa** in Doylestown. The Lower Church, a replica of her centuries-old Black Madonna shrine in Jasna Góra, Poland, is located, appropriately enough, on Beacon Hill (Jasna Góra means "bright mountain"). The Upper Church is renowned for its breathtaking Holy Trinity sculpture and humongous stained-glass windows. One bank of windows depicts the history of the United States, the other bank the history of Poland. Founded by the Pauline order (guardians of the Poland shrine) in 1955, the 170-acre retreat includes the original Barn Chapel and a twenty-five-foot statue of Polish Pope Saint John Paul II (see Finding Faith in Maryland, 101, 239, 257, 272, and Finding Faith in Colorado), arms spread wide in greeting.

Plan your visit: czestochowa.us. 654 Ferry Road, Doylestown, PA 18901. (215) 345-0600.

59 A priest in Quaker garb? Strange but true, this happened in the early 1700s near Hanover. Because colonial law restricted the practice of Catholicism, it's said that a Jesuit missionary assumed a Quaker persona as he went about Kingdom business. More fascinating lore awaits you at the **Basilica of the Sacred Heart of Jesus,** erected of stone in 1785. In the mid-1800s, a Tyrolean artist turned the church into a mini-Sistine Chapel, telling the Redemption story through murals. Especially compelling is a painting over the high altar, in which Jesus exchanges his kingly crown for a crown of thorns.

Plan your visit: sacredheartbasilica.com. 30 Basilica Drive, Hanover, PA 17331. (717) 637-2721.

60 When war strikes, angels arise. That's the legacy of **St. Francis Xavier Roman Catholic Church** in Gettysburg. After the Battle of Gettysburg on July 1–3, 1863 — the bloodiest battle of the Civil War — Mother Elizabeth Ann Seton's Sisters of Charity of nearby Emmitsburg, Maryland (see 20, 82, and 173), arrived at the church-turned-makeshift hospital. They nursed the wounded of both armies and prepared souls for eternity. When they ran out of bandages, they ripped parts of their own dresses into strips of cloth. A stained-glass window in the 1852 church commemorates these good women, dubbed the Angels of the Battlefield.

Plan your visit: stfxcc.org. 25 W. High Street, Gettysburg, PA 17325. (717) 334-3919, (717) 334-7711.

The nearly eight-foot-tall bronze statue of Father William Corby, CSC, at **Gettysburg National Military Park** at Gettysburg is an unforgettable scene. On July 2, 1863, the bearded Civil War chaplain climbed atop a boulder (some say the very boulder on which the statue stands) and called New York's Irish Brigade to prayer. As the 530 men knelt on the ground, he raised his right hand in blessing and granted general absolution. A number of the Irish Brigade died that day, in a state of grace. A duplicate statue stands outside Corby Hall at University of Notre Dame in Notre Dame, Indiana (see Finding Faith in Indiana).

Plan your visit: nps.gov/gett/index.htm. 1195 Baltimore Pike, Gettysburg, PA 17325. (717) 334-1124.

PHILADELPHIA

When Father Joseph Skelly, CM, was tasked with raising funds for a minor seminary in 1912, he placed a Miraculous Medal in each appeal letter. The response was miraculous! More miracle stories await at the Vincentians' **Miraculous Medal Shrine**. Out-of-this-world statuary and Venetian mosaics tell the medal's story (don't miss the Lower Shrine), with depictions of Our Lady of the Chair and Our Lady of the Globe. Also displayed is an exact replica of the chair, with a swatch of the original fabric, that Our Lady sat in during her July 18, 1830, visit to Saint Catherine Labouré in Paris. Another must-see: the splendid museum with more than 500 pieces of religious art.

Plan your visit: cammonline.org. 500 E. Chelten Avenue, Philadelphia, PA 19144. (800) 523-3674.

63 Despite being short in stature (his feet didn't reach the stirrups of a horse), Redemptorist Saint John Neumann (1811–1860) is a "miracle giant." Scores of pilgrims testify to healings or special graces received after praying at the **National Shrine of St. John Neumann**, located in the lower level of St. Peter the Apostle Church. Attired in episcopal vestments and miter, the mortal remains of Bishop Neumann — America's first canonized male saint — repose in a glass crypt under the shrine altar, while stained-glass windows in the 1842 upper church and a museum portray his exemplary life. (See 90.)

Plan your visit: stjohnneumann.org. 1019 N. Fifth Street, Philadelphia, PA 19123. (215) 627-3080.

64 The height of a stone's throw determined the height of the very high clerestory windows at the **Cathedral Basilica of Saints Peter and Paul**. Why? To thwart vandalism by the Know Nothings, an anti-Catholic movement of the day. (The lower windows were installed in the 1950s.) Modeled after Rome's Basilica of San Carlo al Corso and opened in 1864, the Roman Corinthian-style brownstone is renowned for its paintings by Constantino Brumidi, the famed artist of the United States Capitol; bronze chandeliers that weigh a half-ton each; and eight side altars. Saint Katharine Drexel (1858–1955), the American missionary, is entombed near the Drexel Family Altar, a gift of the Drexel heiress daughters.

Plan your visit: cathedralphila.org. Eighteenth Street and Benjamin Franklin Parkway, Philadelphia, PA 19103. (215) 561-1313.

Read the Bible in Byzantine icons at the magnificent **Ukrainian Catholic Cathedral of the Immaculate Conception**. The *iconostasis* — a wall of nearly fifty icons that separates the nave from the sanctuary — connects the Old and New Testaments via the prophets, the apostles, and great feasts of the Church year. Constructed in 1966 and modeled after Hagia Sophia in Istanbul, the cathedral's 100-foot-diameter golden dome is covered with one-quarter-inch-square, twenty-two-karat gold-fused Venetian glass tiles, while the interior glows with mosaics, including the *Theotokos* (God-bearer) in the sanctuary. Pilgrims can also venerate a Vatican-authorized, full-size replica of the Shroud of Turin.

Plan your visit: ukrcathedral.com. 830 N. Franklin Street, Philadelphia, PA 19123. (215) 922-2845.

The impossible happens at the **National Shrine of Saint Rita of Cascia**. The Renaissance-style shrine church, constructed in 1907, portrays Saint Rita's "impossible" life in stained glass — from the *Rays of Light* window (according to legend, Rita entered an Augustinian convent through locked doors) to the *Stigmata* window (Rita received a mystical thorn on her forehead). You'll also find testimony to Rita's "impossible" answers to pilgrims' prayers.

Plan your visit: saintritashrine.org. 1166 S. Broad Street, Philadelphia, PA 19146. (215) 546-8333.

67 ▶ Step into **Old St. Mary's Church** and back into Colonial Philadelphia. Built in 1763, the Gothicized brick church was the site of the first public religious commemoration of the Declaration of Independence; members of the Continental Congress officially attended services here four times from 1777 to 1781. Puritan John Adams wrote to his wife, Abigail, "Here is everything that can lay hold of eye, ear, and imagination … I wonder how Luther ever broke the spell." Historic features include an eighteenth-century baptismal font and chandeliers that originally hung in Independence Hall.

Plan your visit: oldstmary.com. 252 S. Fourth Street, Philadelphia, PA 19106. (215) 923-7930.

68 ▶ The bells at **Old St. Joseph's Church** ring out freedom of religion. Established in 1733, the Jesuit church was the first urban Catholic church in the Thirteen Colonies, thanks to Pennsylvania Colony founder William Penn's "holy experiment" of religious tolerance. (Early Catholic churches in Boston and New York City were founded after the American Revolution.) Despite renovations, the present Gothicized church — constructed of red brick in 1838 — retains its striking original altar with double Ionic columns and crucifixion altar painting.

Plan your visit: oldstjoseph.org. 321 Willings Alley, Philadelphia, PA 19106. (215) 923-1733.

WESTERN PENNSYLVANIA

 Christopher Columbus discovered America in 1492. More than 500 years later, you can discover Christopher Columbus at the **Columbus Chapel and Boal Mansion Museum** in Boalsburg. The intriguing story begins in 1908 when Mathilde de Lagarde Boal, a Columbus descendant, inherited the Columbus Castle, c. 1450, at Asturias, Spain. Contents of the castle chapel were shipped to the Boal family estate, where a replica chapel was built. Artifacts include the altar, medieval statues, Renaissance paintings, and centuries-old vestments made from clothing provided by Columbus family women. An annual Mass is celebrated on Columbus Day.

Plan your visit: boalmuseum.com. 163 Boal Estate Drive, Boalsburg, PA 16827. (814) 876-0129.

 As on Pentecost, in 1967 students from Duquesne University were gathered in the Upper Room, a chapel at **The Ark and The Dove** in Gibsonia, when the Holy Spirit descended upon them. Thus began the worldwide Catholic Charismatic Renewal; it's estimated that over 130 million Catholics have since experienced this outpouring of the Holy Spirit. Built in 1924 by Bell Telephone Company as a respite for its female employees, the retreat center includes the three-story mansion dubbed The Ark and a picturesque cottage, The Dove. Pilgrims from around the world come here seeking their own personal Pentecost.

Plan your visit: thearkandthedoveworldwide.org. 10745 Babcock Boulevard, Gibsonia, PA 15044. (724) 444-8055.

Farmer Michael Decker was surely an apple of God's eye. In 1854, while working in his apple orchard at St. Marys, he fell from a tree and severely injured his back. He promised God to build a chapel on that very spot if he recovered. **Decker's Chapel**, twelve by eighteen feet, went up two years later. During World War II, the women of St. Marys gathered daily in the quaint white-frame chapel to pray the Rosary for family in harm's way.

Plan your visit: elkcountyhistoricalsociety.org/deckerschapel.html. Earth Road and State Route 255, St Marys, PA 15857. (814) 776-1032.

PITTSBURGH

It's no blarney: The stone tower of **Old St. Patrick Church** reportedly contains a piece of Ireland's famous Blarney Stone. Inside, the Holy Stairs — ascended on knees only — lead to an altar on the second floor. Possibly the country's only interior Holy Stairs, the penitential steps were modeled after the Scala Sancta in Rome.

Plan your visit: pghshrines.org/st-patrick-1. 1711 Liberty Avenue, Pittsburgh, PA 15222. (412) 471-4767.

Want to get closer to the saints? You can at **Saint Anthony Chapel.** Built in 1880, the chapel houses more than 5,000 relics of saints — from Demetrius' full skeleton in a golden sarcophagus, to a fragment of Mary's veil, to a molar of the chapel's patron, wonderworker Anthony of Padua. Father

Suitbert G. Mollinger, a wealthy Belgian native, amassed the relics and then spent $300,000 of his own money to build the Romanesque-style structure. He later expanded the chapel to accommodate another momentous find: life-size stations of the cross, hand-carved in Germany.

Plan your visit: saintanthonyschapel.org. 1704 Harpster Street, Pittsburgh, PA 15212. (412) 999-4401.

74 You'll never view the horrors of war in the same way after contemplating the revolutionary paintings at **St. Nicholas Croatian Church** (in Millvale). In one mural, a bayoneted Christ on the cross interposes himself between soldiers on a battlefield; in another, Mother Mary, in black mourning gown representing the grieving mothers of war, weeps over her Son. Executed by Croatian immigrant Maxo Vanka in 1937 and 1941, the startling floor-to-ceiling paintings also weave in the social justice issues of the day. A poor Croatian family eats a supper of soup and bread blessed by Jesus; a capitalist, a lavish meal served with a stock market report.

Plan your visit: vankamurals.org. 24 Maryland Avenue, Pittsburgh, PA 15209. (412) 821-3438.

⚜ FINDING FAITH
☦ in Pennsylvania

"From prince to pauper" is the story of Servant of God Demetrius Augustine Gallitzin (1770–1840). Baptized in the Russian Orthodox Church (his godmother was Catherine the Great), the Russian prince converted to Catholicism as a teenager, thereby forfeiting his family's inheritance and royal titles. Taking a pseudonym, "Augustine Smith" sailed for America, where he was ordained a priest in 1795.

Known as the Apostle of the Alleghenies, the incognito prince-priest traveled hill and vale, ministering to souls, and even investigated paranormal disturbances in Kearneysville, West Virginia (see Finding Faith in West Virginia). Arriving in Loretto in 1799, Father Gallitzin built a church in honor of Saint Michael the Archangel. A century later, Pittsburgh steel magnate Charles M. Schwab, who had spent much of his childhood in Loretto, erected the Romanesque-inspired **Basilica of Saint Michael the Archangel**. He also commissioned the outdoor statue of Father Gallitzin and the crypt below it.

Plan your visit: basilicasm-loretto.org. 321 St. Mary Street, Loretto, PA 15940. (814) 472-8551.

NEW JERSEY

Atlantic Ocean

75 Experience the message of Fátima at the **National Blue Army Shrine of Our Lady of Fatima,** a 150-acre retreat near Asbury. Standing on a crown of twelve stars, atop the 130-foot-tall open-air chapel, is a twenty-four-foot bronze statue of the Immaculate Heart of Mary, a rosary in hand. Other Fátima devotional sites include the Capelinha, an exact replica of the original chapel built at the Fátima apparition site in Portugal, and statues of Our Lady and the three shepherd children with sheep. Also on the grounds is a replica of the Holy House of Loreto.

Plan your visit: bluearmy.com. 674 Mountain View Road E., Asbury, NJ 08802. (908) 689-1700, ext. 210.

76 "Greater love has no man than this, that a man lay down his life for his friends." On February 3, 1943, John 15:13 became real in the North Atlantic. Four chaplains aboard the German-torpedoed USAT *Dorchester* — Methodist minister George L. Fox, Rabbi Alexander D. Goode, Dutch Reformed minister Clark V. Poling, and Catholic priest John P. Washington — gave up their life jackets so four sailors might live. Outside Saint Stephen's Church in Kearny, Father Washington's last assignment before going off to war, the **Four Chaplains Monument** honors their selfless heroism. Sculpted by Timothy Schmalz, the nearly sixteen-foot-tall bronze statue portrays the chaplains praying, each according to his faith tradition, as

the ship goes down. The Archdiocesan Sanctuary of the Four Chaplains is found inside the church.

Plan your visit: ststephenkearny.com. 141 Washington Avenue, Kearny, NJ 07032. (201) 998-3314.

In 1895, when a hellish fire devoured the interior of **St. Anthony of Padua Church** in Jersey City, the only item not torched was a large wooden crucifix above the main altar. The Miraculous Crucifix, revered by generations of Polish parishioners, is now enshrined in a side chapel. Restored to its original grandeur, the Victorian Gothic brownstone — known as the mother church of Polonia in New Jersey — features a magnificent, three-story, white marble high altar, the life-size angel candelabra imparting a heaven-on-earth feel. The church is loaded with Franciscan images. How many can you identify?

Plan your visit: saintanthonyjc.com. 457 Monmouth Street, Jersey City, NJ 07302. (201) 653-0343.

Children are a gift of the Lord, and many such gifts begin with a visit to the **National Shrine of St. Gerard Majella** at St. Lucy's Church in Newark, a neo-Renaissance beauty built by Italians and Sicilians in the 1920s. Infertile couples come to implore Saint Gerard's intercession for a miracle baby, while women with problem pregnancies seek relief with "holy hankies" — sacramental handkerchiefs touched to a first-class relic of Saint Gerard. Ceiling murals in the shrine chapel paint the saint's life, from his baptism, to feeding the poor, to his death-bed vision of Mary with the Baby Jesus.

Plan your visit: saintlucy.net. 118 Seventh Avenue, Newark, NJ 07104. (973) 803-4200.

Great medieval churches weren't built overnight, and neither was the **Cathedral Basilica of the Sacred Heart** in Newark. The cornerstone for the French Gothic-inspired cathedral was laid in 1899, and the imposing edifice was dedicated in 1954. The cathedral is also world-unique. Rather than standing flush with the granite structure, the two 232-foot towers are rotated forty-five degrees inward, like gigantic hands guiding you inside. And what a glorious sight you'll find within: twenty-three altars; some 200 Munich stained-glass windows crafted in eleventh-century medieval style, including a thirty-six-foot-diameter rose window portraying the last Judgment; and approximately 200 statues, from large to very small, of bishops, archbishops, and saints from around the world.

Plan your visit: cathedralbasilica.org. 89 Ridge Street, Newark, NJ 07104. (973) 484-4600.

If you believe in "God-incidences," you'll love the **St. Padre Pio Shrine** in Landisville. It's said that one of Padre Pio's favorite foods was squash; the shrine is located on a former squash field. The maiden name of Padre Pio's grandmother was D'Andrea;

Italian-American produce growers Peter and Marie D'Andrea erected the triangular, four-story, open-air shrine.

Plan your visit: stpadrepioshrinenj.org. US Highway 40 and Central Avenue, Landisville, NJ 08326.

✠ FINDING FAITH
in New Jersey

You don't need to travel to Turin, Italy, to venerate the Holy Shroud of Turin, where it's rarely on
public display. Instead, visit the Dominican **Monastery of Our Lady of the Rosary** in Summit,
which holds a 400-year-old certified true copy
of the Shroud of Turin. The fascinating story began in 1624 when Maria Maddalena of Austria,
Grand Duchess of Tuscany and wife of Cosimo
de Medici, commissioned a replica, which was
placed for a time on the original Shroud. When
the replica was removed, a blood stain was found
on the replica that matched a stain on the original. The Grand Duchess gave the replica to the
Dominican nuns of St. Catherine's Monastery in
Rome.

In 1924, St. Catherine's nuns transferred
the replica to the Summit Dominican nuns in
thanksgiving for their help after World War I.
Even more intriguing: In 1987, scientists con-
firmed that the blood stain on the replica was
human blood and of the same blood type as that
found on the original Shroud of Turin. The holy
replica can be venerated in the nuns' neo-Gothic chapel, which features clerestory stained-glass
windows depicting the Mysteries of the Rosary.

Plan your visit: summitdominicans.org. 543
Springfield Avenue, Summit, NJ 07901. (908)
273-1228; steparish.org, South Clayton and
Cedar Streets, (302) 652-3626.

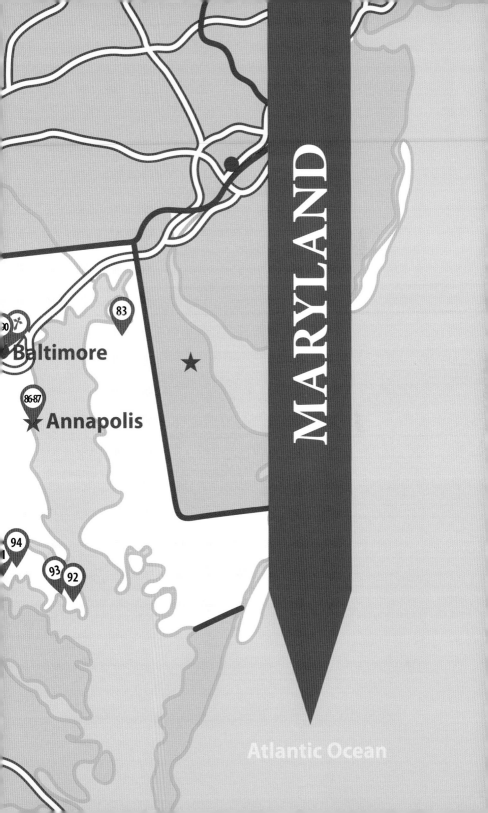

81 Father Jean DuBois, a refugee from France, was traveling through Emmitsburg in 1805 when he saw a heavenly light on a hill. Finding a "blessed spot," he erected a crude cross. From those humble beginnings evolved the **National Shrine Grotto of Our Lady of Lourdes.** Like the Lourdes Grotto in France, the waters of the grotto spring are a popular pilgrimage destination. The mountain retreat also features numerous prayer stations, including the Shrine of St. Sharbel and St. Mary's Glass Chapel. A ninety-five-foot campanile, crowned with a golden statue of Our Lady, is visible for miles around.

Plan your visit: nsgrotto.org. 16330 Grotto Road, Emmitsburg, MD 21727. (301) 447-5318.

82 Mother of five. Widowed. Catholic convert. Founder of the Sisters of Charity of St. Joseph. First American-born canonized saint. Who is she? Saint Elizabeth Ann Seton (1774–1821). Her storied legacy is preserved at the **National Shrine of Saint Elizabeth Ann Seton** at Emmitsburg. A museum showcases artifacts, while the Basilica of Saint Elizabeth Ann Seton inspires prayer before the Altar of Relics, where her remains are interred. Other features include two homes where Mother Seton lived and St. Joseph Cemetery with Mortuary Chapel, built by her son, William, in her memory. (See 20, 60, and 173.)

Plan your visit: setonshrine.org. 339 S. Seton Avenue, Emmitsburg, MD 21727. (301) 447-6606.

Brick Chapel of 1667 [93]

83 When Catholicism was outlawed in the English colonies, Jesuit priests were forced to live a double life. In 1704, they bought a 1,200-acre plantation from a Bohemian outside Warwick and took up lives as "bachelor farmers." They rode on horseback around Pennsylvania, Delaware, and Maryland, clandestinely saying Mass in private home chapels. Constructed of brick c. 1792, **Old Bohemia** — formally called the St. Francis Xavier Shrine — looks much the same today with its wooden high altar, altar rail, and plain glass windows. The old Jesuit tombstones bear no "SJ"; priests were buried incognito, just as they had lived.

Plan your visit: stjosephmiddletown.com. 1690 Bohemia Church Road, Warwick, MD 21912. (302) 378-5800.

84 Tony, Tony, come around … to the **Shrine of St. Anthony** at Ellicott City. Part of St. Joseph Cupertino Friary, erected by Conventual Franciscan friars in 1930 as a miniature version of Sacro Convento in Assisi, the shrine honors Saint Anthony of Padua in art and lore. Inside, a biblical tree motif recalls the saint's many hours praying in a treehouse (try it — there's a treehouse-like platform on grounds), while outdoor art includes a statue depicting the legend of Anthony and the donkey. Grounds also include walking trails and a shrine of Saint Maximilian Kolbe.

Plan your visit: shrineofstanthony.org. 12290 Folly Quarter Road, Ellicott City, MD 21042. (410) 531-2800.

85 When you look at **Old St. Mary's Church** (also called Our Lady's Chapel) in Rockville, you'd never guess that agents of the Underground Railroad operated here. In 1854, they helped fugitive slave Anna Maria Weems, who disguised herself as a male carriage driver, escape to Canada. The "freedom church," with white-painted brick exterior, dates from 1817.

Plan your visit: stmarysrockville.org. 520 Veirs Mill Road, Rockville, MD 20852. (301) 424-5550.

86 Step inside **St. Mary's Church** in Annapolis and you might feel like you're in a planetarium. The star-studded blue ceiling replicates the constellations that lit up the night sky when the Gothic-design church was dedicated in January 1860. Four granddaughters of Charles Carroll of Carrollton, the only Catholic signer of the Declaration of Independence (see 87 and 99), donated the church property to the Redemptorists in 1852.

Plan your visit: stmarysannapolis.org. 109 Duke of Gloucester Street, Annapolis, MD 21401. (410) 990-4100.

87 Soak up Colonial history next door at the **Charles Carroll House and Gardens**. Charles Carroll of Carrollton (1737–1832) (see 86 and 99) was born here, and during anti-Catholic days, crypto-priests said Mass in the Carrolls' private chapel.

Plan your visit: charlescarrollhouse.org. 107 Duke of Gloucester Street, Annapolis, MD 21401.

BALTIMORE

Servant of God Mary Lange (c. 1794–1882) had four strikes against her when she arrived in Baltimore around 1813: She was black, she was a woman, she spoke French, and she wanted to offer herself to the Lord. But nothing could stop Caribbean-born Elizabeth Lange from founding, in 1829, the Oblate Sisters of Providence — the world's first order of black religious sisters. Their charism: to educate and evangelize African-Americans. The remarkable story is told in stained glass at **Our Lady of Mount Providence Chapel**, where Mother Mary Lange is interred.

Plan your visit: oblatesisters.com. 701 Gun Road, Baltimore, MD 21227. (410) 242-8500. Reservations required.

The **Cathedral of Mary Our Queen** — a 1954 modified Gothic structure with Art Deco accents — was financed by a fire! As the story goes, when the Great Baltimore Fire of 1904 was headed toward Thomas J. O'Neill's dry goods store, the wealthy businessman enlisted the prayers of a nearby convent. Just as the fire was about to lick the store's south walls, the winds shifted. In thanksgiving, O'Neill bequeathed funds for a new cathedral. Befitting the Queen of Heaven, the 373-foot-long building resembles a fortress and features more than 385 sculptures, 398 panels of stained glass, and four side altars, including one dedicated to Saint Thomas More (Thomas O'Neill's patron saint).

Plan your visit: cathedralofmary.org. 5200 N. Charles Street, Baltimore, MD 21210. (410) 464-4000.

90 ▶ Pray at the **National Shrine of Saint Alphonsus Liguori** and you might be on your way to canonization. That's what happened to Redemptorists Saint John Neumann (see 63) and Blessed Francis Xavier Seelos (see 164); both served as pastors here. It also happened to Venerable Maria Kaupas, SSC, who founded the Sisters of St. Casimir and taught at the parish school. Built in 1842 in Gothic Revival grandeur, the red-brick church even feels saintly. The elevated pulpit is reached by a winding staircase; the star-shaped vaults are like portals to heaven. A bevy of saints — in statues and stained glass — seem to say, "We made it, so can you!"

Plan your visit: stalphonsusbalt.org. 114 W. Saratoga Street, Baltimore, MD 21201. (410) 685-6090.

ST. MARY'S COUNTY

91 ▶ When the *Ark* and the *Dove* — two English ships carrying Catholic and Protestant colonists — landed at **St. Clement's Island** (now a state park) in the Potomac River on March 25, 1634, a new day dawned in America. Father Andrew White, SJ, offered the first Mass in the English-speaking colonies, and Leonard Calvert read Lord Baltimore's decree granting religious toleration to all. (Catholics were later persecuted, however, as history records.) A museum captures the epic story, and a forty-foot cross marks the historic landing.

Plan your visit: visitstmarysmd.com/see-do/detail/st.-clements-island-state-park. 38370 Point Breeze Road, Coltons Point, MD 20626. (301) 769-2222. Island access by water taxi.

The year 1634 was a "year of firsts" in Maryland. Colonists founded St. Mary's City, the first capital of Maryland, and Jesuits offered America's first English Masses (see 91). In 1667, a tall brick chapel with a soaring vault went up. When the Church of England became the official state church of Maryland in 1702 and Catholics were subsequently denied the right to public worship, Jesuits dismantled the church and floated the bricks downriver to their plantation at St. Inigoes to build a new manor house. All that remains today is **St. Ignatius Church**, erected in 1785, and the old Jesuit cemetery.

Plan your visit: visitstmarysmd.com/site/detail /st.-ignatius-church. 17682 Villa Road, St. Inigoes, MD 20684. (301) 862-4600.

When Maryland's colonial capital was relocated to Annapolis in 1695, Historic St. Mary's City was deserted, until the 1980s when it was resurrected as an 800-acre living history museum. Up went a replica of the **Brick Chapel of 1667** (see 92) over its original foundation. Pilgrims can also explore the *Dove*, a facsimile of the English square-rigged ship (see 91), and buildings recreating the life of Maryland's first settlers.

Plan your visit: hsmcdigshistory.org. 18751 Hogaboom Lane, Lexington Park, MD 20653. (240) 895-4990.

Hailed as the oldest extant Catholic Church in the original Thirteen Colonies, **St. Francis Xavi-**

er Church in Leonardtown is more than a page in history; it's an entire book! Jesuits built the first church in 1662, replaced by the current church in 1731. Some speculate the Protestant-looking design spared the church from being torched during Maryland's anti-Catholic era. Note the brick ends (front and back) that give the frame structure a quasi-octagonal shape. Also on site is a 1789 Jesuit manor house.

Plan your visit: stfrancisxavierchurch.org. 21370 Newtowne Neck Road, Leonardtown, MD 20650. (301) 475-9885.

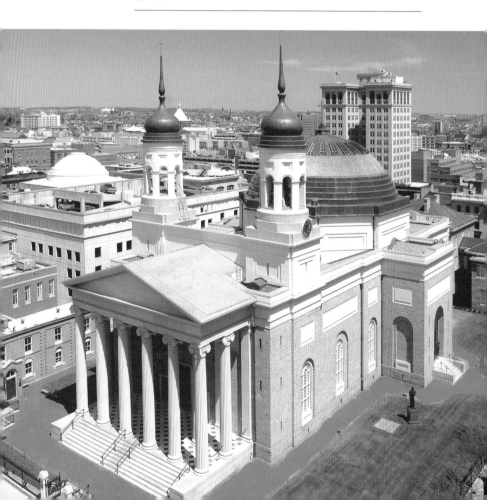

✝ FINDING FAITH
✝ in Maryland

You've heard of the *Baltimore Catechism*. How about the Baltimore Basilica? Formally called the **Basilica of the National Shrine of the Assumption of the Blessed Virgin Mary**, the Baltimore church — also known as America's First Cathedral — is the mother church of Catholic America. It's said that Bishop John Carroll, America's first bishop, wanted a uniquely American cathedral, and chose a Neoclassical look that also represented democracy and freedom of worship. The architect was Benjamin Henry Latrobe, contracted by Thomas Jefferson to build the United States Capitol. The cornerstone was laid in 1806.

The skylights in the Capitol building inspired Latrobe's design for the basilica's grand dome: twenty-four skylights that let in heaven's pure light. Features include dome paintings of the Ascension of Jesus and the Assumption of Mary, two 1821 Rafael Angels flanking the altar, and a Gothic monstrance caught (literally) by a local fisherman. Outside, the fish-shaped Pope Saint John Paul II Prayer Garden (see 58, 101, 239, 257, 272, and Finding Faith in Colorado) includes statuary and a mural depicting flowers associated with Mary. And yes, the *Baltimore Catechism* began here in 1885.

Plan your visit: americasfirstcathedral.org. 409 Cathedral Street, Baltimore, MD 21201. (410) 727-3565, ext. 220.

★ **Dover**

DELAWARE

Atlantic Ocean

95 ▶ **St. Elizabeth Catholic Church** in Wilmington is, well, "Elizabethan." A woman named Elizabeth gave $5,000 to build the nation's first church (1908) named for Saint Elizabeth, cousin of the Blessed Mother; the church's first baptism was a girl christened Elizabeth; and the first pastor composed a hymn and a prayer to the saint. Dedicated in 1947, the current church is filled with images of Elizabeth, who first proclaimed to Mary, "Blessed are you among women, and blessed is the fruit of your womb!" (Lk 1:42).

Plan your visit: steparish.org. South Clayton and Cedar Streets, Wilmington, DE 19805. (302) 652-3626.

96 ▶ Approach **St. Joseph on the Brandywine Church** in Greenville and you're confronted by eternity: More than 5,000 graves surround the historic stone church. The "DuPont church" was erected in 1841 for Irish immigrants working in DuPont powder mills. It's said that Charles du Pont donated the church land, and Alfred I. du Pont provided for the rectory, school, and convent. The church got its distinctive yellow color when Alfred du Pont had it painted the same color as the Du Pont homes.

Plan your visit: stjosephonthebrandywine.org. 10 Old Church Road, Greenville, DE 19807. (302) 658-7017.

✠ FINDING FAITH
in Delaware

Call it a case of "statue envy." In the 1980s, Delaware sculptor Charles C. Parks put on public display, in downtown Wilmington, his thirty-two-foot stainless steel statue of Our Lady of Peace, commissioned by a parish in Santa Clara, California (see 407). In the late 1990s, he exhibited another stainless-steel beauty: a thirty-three-foot Our Lady of the New Millennium, now gracing St. John, Indiana (see 194).

Parishioners at Holy Spirit Catholic Church at New Castle were smitten. They began praying 500,000 rosaries to raise the $500,000 needed for their own Parks statue. Dedicated in 2007, **Our Lady Queen of Peace** stands thirty-two feet tall and weighs more than four tons. But this mega-Madonna isn't solid metal: Her gown is made of welded strips of stainless steel. At times her gown looks silver; at other times, golden.

Plan your visit: holyspiritchurchde.org. 12 Winder Road, New Castle, DE 19720. (302) 658-1069.

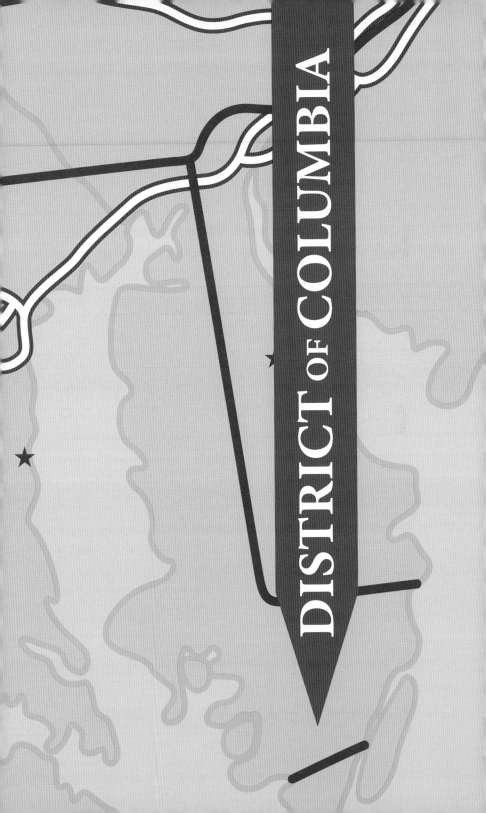

DISTRICT OF COLUMBIA

97 "They comforted the dying, nursed the wounded, carried hope to the imprisoned, gave in his name a drink of water to the thirsty." These words on the **Nuns of the Battlefield Monument** honor more than 600 religious sisters who nursed Union and Confederate soldiers on battlefields and in makeshift hospitals during the American Civil War. Dedicated in 1924, the bronze bas-relief depicts twelve nuns in habits representing their various orders, including a Daughter of Charity in distinctive cornette headgear.

Plan your visit: At intersection of M Street NW and Rhode Island Avenue NW, Washington, D.C., 20036

98 The **Cathedral of St. Matthew the Apostle** is forever noted in American history. The stately redbrick church was the scene of President John F. Kennedy's funeral Mass on November 25, 1963. A plaque marks the spot where his casket rested, and it was here, in front of the church, that three-year-old John F. Kennedy Jr. saluted his father's casket. The Romanesque-Byzantine cathedral, dedicated in 1913, is embellished with brilliant mosaics, including *Saint Matthew and the Angel* and *The Angels of the Crucifixion*. Matthew also gets his due in murals: one of Jesus calling him, the other of his martyrdom.

Plan your visit: stmatthewscathedral.org. 1725 Rhode Island Avenue NW, Washington, D.C. 20036. (202) 347-3215.

Franciscan Monastery of the Holy Land [100]

It's a monumental walk through history at the **National Statuary Hall,** located in the United States Capitol, where statues of prominent Americans from each state are displayed. Honored Catholics include Venerable Eusebio Kino, SJ, missionary and explorer (Arizona; see Finding Faith in Arizona); Saint Damien de Veuster, friend to lepers (Hawaii; see Finding Faith in Vermont, 423, and Finding Faith in Hawaii); Edward Douglass White, Chief Justice of the United States (Louisiana); Charles Carroll, a signer of the Declaration of Independence (Maryland; see 86 and 87); Mother Joseph Pariseau, architect and builder (Washington; see Finding Faith in Washington); and Father Jacques Marquette, SJ, French missionary and explorer (Wisconsin; see 169–171).

Plan your visit: visitthecapitol.gov. First Street and East Capitol Street, Washington, D.C. 20004. (202) 226-8000.

 You won't need a passport to visit this Holy Land! The **Franciscan Monastery of the Holy Land in America** replicates the famous shrines of Christ's life and more. See the Grotto of the Annunciation, where the Archangel Gabriel visited Mary; rejoice at Christ's birth at the Bethlehem Grotto; and pray with Our Lord at the Grotto of Gethsemane. You'll find the "Roman catacombs" under the neo-Byzantine Main Church, erected in 1898, and laid out in the form of a fivefold Jerusalem cross.

Plan your visit: myfranciscan.org. 1400 Quincy Street NE, Washington, D.C. 20017. (202) 526-6800.

Walk in the light at the **Saint John Paul II National Shrine**. Named for the pope's first encyclical, *Redemptor Hominis* ("Redeemer of Man"), Redemptor Hominis Church tells with glittering Byzantine-style mosaics the history of salvation (see John Paul's "guest appearance" in the Magi scene), while floor-to-ceiling mosaics in the Luminous Mysteries Chapel illustrate the Mysteries of Light that he added to the Rosary in 2002. A permanent exhibit presents John Paul's life — from boyhood, to life in Nazi-occupied Poland, to his twenty-six-year pontificate. (See 58, Finding Faith in Maryland, 239, 257, 272, and Finding Faith in Colorado.)

101

Plan your visit: jp2shrine.org. 3900 Harewood Road NE, Washington, D.C. 20017. (202) 635-5400.

✠ FINDING FAITH
✝ in Washington, D.C.

It isn't a parish church, but every American Catholic is a member. It's hailed as the largest Roman Catholic church in North America and as one of the ten largest churches in the world. Covering more than 18,300 square feet, the majestic Trinity Dome mosaic employed more than 14 million pieces of Venetian glass. Not one steel structural beam or column was used in its construction. Where are you? *Ave Maria!* At the **Basilica of the National Shrine of the Immaculate Conception**. Thirty-nine years in the building (1920–1959), the Byzantine-Romanesque megachurch boasts more than eighty chapels and oratories, many dedicated to Marian appellations of America's diverse immigrant church — from Altötting (Bavaria) to Vailankanni (India) to La Vang (Vietnam). Especially poignant is Our Mother of Africa Chapel, with a floor image of the slave ship *Henrietta Marie* and a bronze statue of an African Mary and Child, her strong facial features conveying, "I know your every sorrow."

***

Plan your visit: nationalshrine.com. 400 Michigan Avenue NE, Washington, D.C. 20017. (202) 526-8300.

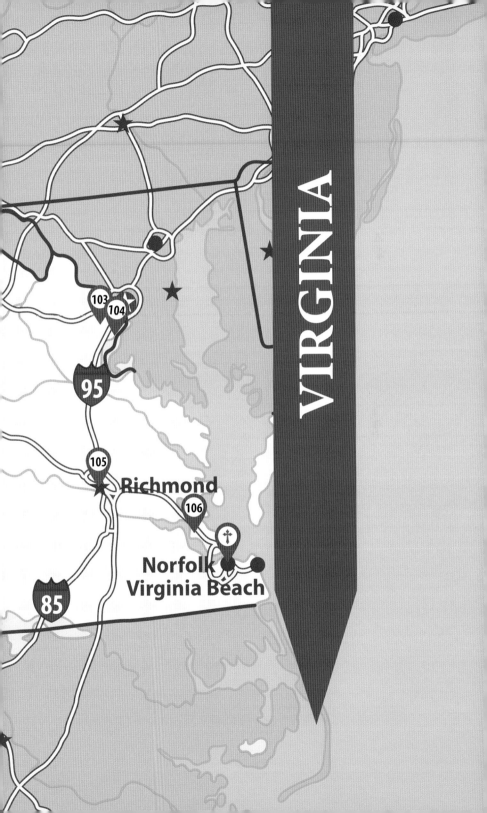

102 John Carrell Jenkins, a Confederate soldier who died during the Civil War in 1861, is forever remembered at **St. John the Baptist Roman Catholic Church** in Front Royal. Jenkins' family built the Shenandoah Valley church with his money and donated the altar, sacred vessels, vestments, sanctuary lamp, bell, and pews. Bishop John J. Keane remarked at the 1884 dedication, "Its cornerstone comes from the battle-field of Manassas ... its red brick was made from the soil of Front Royal, saturated with the blood of the soldiers of the Confederacy."

Plan your visit: sjtb.org. 120 W. Main Street, Front Royal, VA 22630. (540) 635-3780.

103 For three long days after the 1862 Second Battle of Manassas (also called the Second Battle of Bull Run), Clara H. Barton, a government clerk, tended to the wounded and dying in drenching rains as doctors performed surgery in the only dry place around: **St. Mary of Sorrows Catholic Church** at Fairfax Station. Barton's experiences led her to found the American Red Cross; a plaque on church grounds honors her heroic service. Dedicated in 1860, the quaint two-story clapboard structure is literally seated in history. In restitution for war-damaged pews, President U. S. Grant ordered the wooden pews still used today.

Plan your visit: stmaryofsorrows.org. Ox Road and Fairfax Station Road, Fairfax Station, VA 22039. (703) 978-4141.

104 The **Basilica of Saint Mary** in Old Town Alexandria is full of firsts. Founded in 1795, Saint Mary's was the first Catholic parish in the Commonwealth of Virginia (which included West Virginia until it became a state in 1863). The first donor was George Washington, the country's first president, who gave $1,200 in today's currency, and the first church was built by Father Francis Ignatius Neale, SJ, twice president of Georgetown College. The current Gothic Revival church dates from 1826.

Plan your visit: stmaryoldtown.org. 310 S. Royal Street, Alexandria, VA 22314. (703) 836-4100.

105 The **Cathedral of the Sacred Heart** in Richmond might be the world's only cathedral financed by the munificence of just one family. Catholic philanthropists Thomas Fortune Ryan and his wife, Ida Barry Ryan, donated $500,000 (an estimated $14 million in today's currency) to build the 1903 Italian Renaissance Revival gem. Highlights include the cornerstone made of a stone block from the Garden of Gethsemane, elaborate wrought-iron grillwork, and stupendous ceiling artwork. Inscribed above the front doors is John 14:15: "If Ye Love Me Keep My Commandments." The cathedral also houses the Museum of Virginia Catholic History.

Plan your visit: richmondcathedral.org. 823 Cathedral Place, Richmond, Virginia 23220. (804) 359-5651.

The **National Shrine of Our Lady of Walsingham** in Williamsburg has a long history — all the way back to 1061, when Our Lady asked Lady Richeldis to build a replica in England of the Holy House in Nazareth, where the Annunciation occurred. Our Lady promised that "whoever seeks my help there will not go away empty-handed." Gracing the American shrine, dedicated in 1942, is an exquisite wood-carved statue of Our Lady of Walsingham seated on a throne, the Christ Child in her lap. (See 355.)

Plan your visit: facebook.com /NationalShrineofOurLadyofWalsingham. 520 Richmond Road, Williamsburg, VA 23185. (757) 229-3631.

You'd never know by looking at **St. Andrew's Catholic Church** that Roanoke's first Mass was offered in railroad passenger coach car number six. Completed in 1902 in High Victorian Gothic style, St. Andrew's superb stained glass will test your saintly knowledge. Which seven apostles are shown in *The Last Supper*? Which saint was beheaded? (Tradition holds the soldier botched the job and she lay dying for three days.) Why is Saint Joseph wearing lavender and brown robes?

Plan your visit: standrewsva.org. 631 N. Jefferson Street, Roanoke, VA 24016. (540) 344-9814.

✠ FINDING FAITH
† in Virginia

Like the Statue of Liberty, the **Basilica of St. Mary of the Immaculate Conception** in Norfolk carries a big torch: freedom of worship. Founded in 1791 as St. Patrick's Church by refugees fleeing the French Revolution, the church soon became home to European immigrants. A few decades later, the Know Nothings — vehemently anti-Catholic and anti-immigrant — began terrorizing the church. But that didn't deter Father Matthew O'Keefe from offering interracial Masses.

In 1856, the church burned down, ignited by the Know Nothings, people say. Only a wooden crucifix, a symbol of the people's faith, was left unscathed. Two years later, a new Gothic Revival church was dedicated to Mary of the Immaculate Conception — one of the first churches named for Pope Pius IX's 1854 decree that defined the Immaculate Conception of Mary as a dogma of the Catholic Church. St. Mary's is the nation's first black church elevated to a basilica.

Plan your visit: www.basilicaofsaintmary.org. 232 Chapel Street, Norfolk, VA 23504. (757) 622-4487.

Cathedral of the Sacred Heart [105]

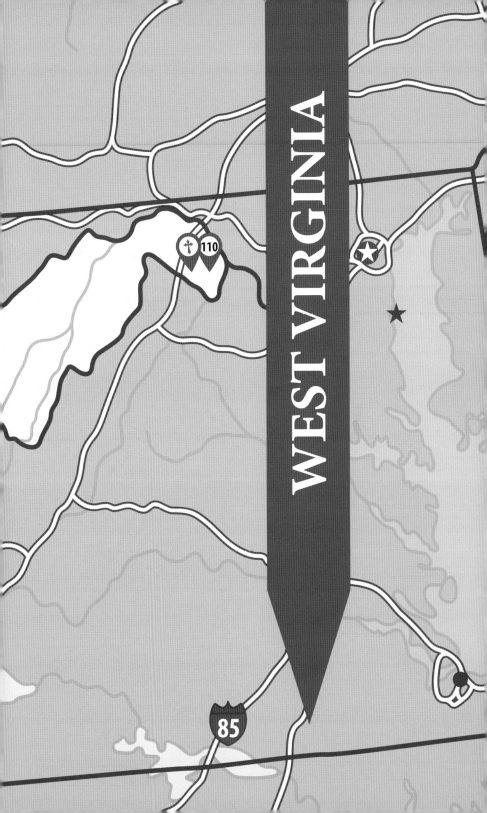

Now hear the word of the Lord at the **Cathedral of St. Joseph** in Wheeling. Imitating Italy's Prato Cathedral, St. Joseph's has two pulpits — one indoors and one outdoors. Together the two pulpits preach a fine sermon: The Word is received internally and lived externally. Dedicated in 1926, the Lombardi Romanesque cathedral is a Byzantine paradise inside — from Felix Lieftuchter's (see Finding Faith in Ohio and Finding Faith in Utah) brilliantly colored apse mural *Enthroned Christ and the Communion of the Saints* to George Sotter's medieval-style stained glass.

Plan your visit: saintjosephcathedral.com. 1300 Eoff Street, Wheeling, WV 26003. (304) 233-4121.

 It's almost heaven at **Our Lady of the Pines Church** at Parsons (southwest of Thomas), on the Seneca Trail. Built in 1957–1958 by Lithuanian immigrant Peter Milkint and wife Elizabeth in memory of their parents, the miniscule stone chapel seats twelve. Milkint, a nurseryman, carved the six tiny wooden pews, the tabernacle, and the stations of the cross.

Plan your visit: visitmountaineercountry.com/business/our-lady-of-the-pines. US Highway 219 at 101 Breedlove Road, Parsons, WV 26287. (800) 458-7373.

 Upon this rock, literally, **St. Peter's Church** at Harpers Ferry was built in 1830, and nothing could prevail against it — not even the Civil War! De-

spite heavy bombardment (Harpers Ferry shifted between Union and Confederate control fourteen times), St. Peter's was the only church in town to escape destruction. It's said that Father Michael Costello, a daring Irish native, saved the steep hillside church by nailing the British Union Jack to the steeple. The church was torn down in 1896, and the present neo-Gothic structure was erected on the original foundation. The Appalachian Trail runs past the church.

Plan your visit: stjameswv.org. 110 Church Street, Harpers Ferry, WV 25425. (304) 725-5558.

111 The town of **Saint Marys** began with a vision. According to lore, Alexander Creel was traveling by steamer on the Ohio River when Our Lady appeared to him. Pointing to the shore, she said, "Behold the site of what will, some day, be a happy and prosperous city." In 1849, Creel had the town platted and named it Saint Marys.

Plan your visit: wvtourism.com/company/city-of -st-marys/

✞ FINDING FAITH
in West Virginia

If the poltergeist story behind **Priest Field Pastoral Center** in Kearneysville wasn't so well documented, nobody would believe it. In the 1790s, Lutheran farmer Adam Livingston and his family began experiencing demonic manifestations. Burning logs leaping from the hearth. Chickens with severed heads. Crescent moon-shaped holes cut into cloth and leather. The nightmare continued for months.

One night during a dream, Livingston saw a "minister in peculiar robes" and heard a voice say, "This is the man who can relieve you." Livingston found the man — Father Dennis Cahill, a Catholic priest. Though he had been vehemently anti- Catholic, Livingston begged the priest for help. Father Cahill exorcised the home, the demonic activities ceased, and the Livingston family converted to Catholicism. Despite his initial skepticism, Father Demetrius Gallitzin (see Finding Faith in Pennsylvania) thoroughly investigated and verified the Livingstons' incredible story. Livingston also donated thirty-eight acres to the Catholic Church, now the site of a retreat center and a haven of peace for all.

Plan your visit: priestfield.org. 4030 Middleway Pike, Kearneysville, WV 25430. (304) 725-1435.

SOUTHEAST

Fort Smith

Memphis

Na

Little Rock

Birmingham

Shreveport

Meridian

Jackson

Baton Rouge

Biloxi

Mobile

New Orleans

Gulf of Mexico

NORTH CAROLINA

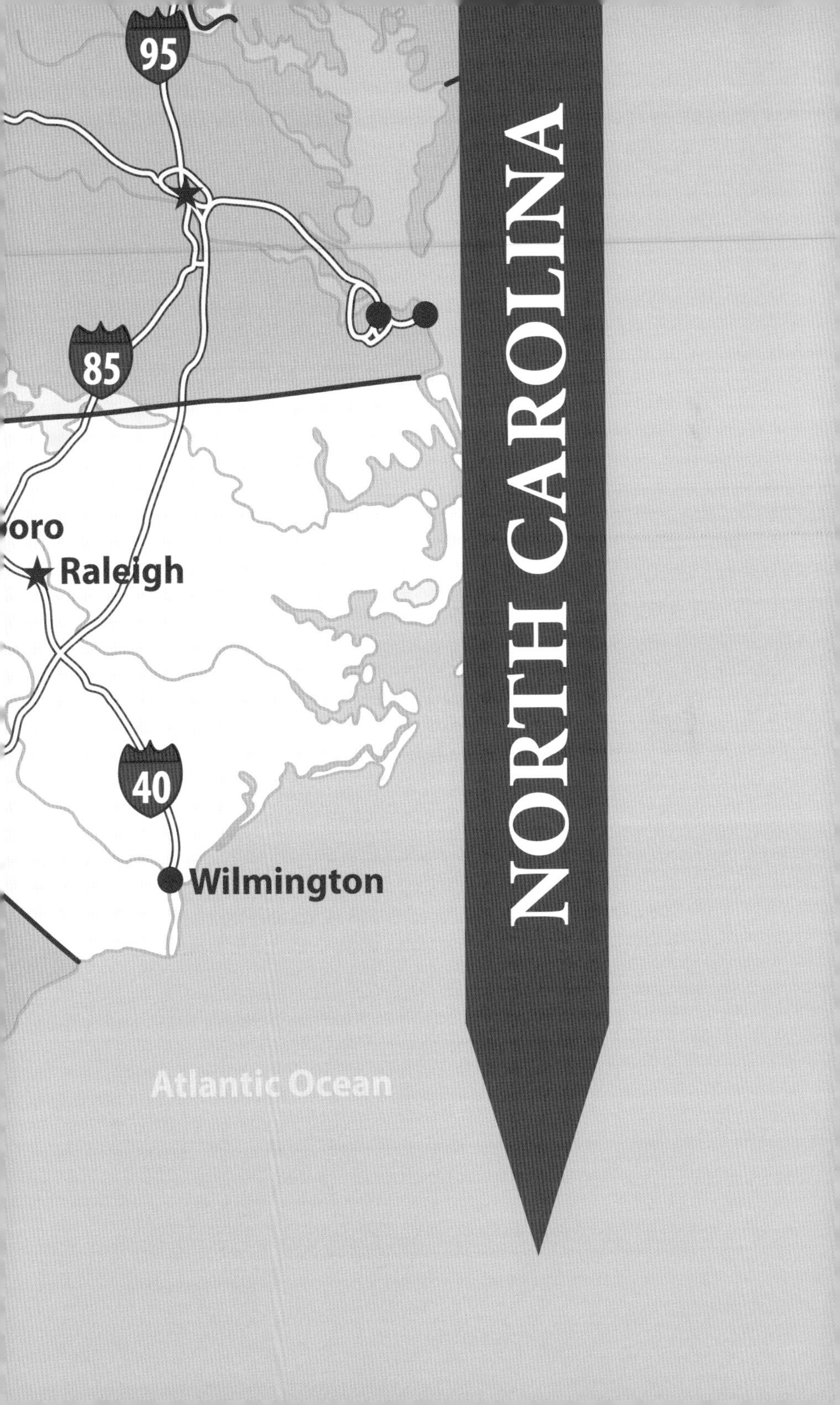

112 This is a tale of three Margarets and a builder-turned-priest. Dubbed the Apostle of the Smokies, William Murphy helped erect a number of churches across the region, but Maggie Valley stole his heart. Here, in the late 1960s, he built **St. Margaret of Scotland Catholic Church** — with massive windows taking in God's wondrous creation — in memory of his mother, Margaret. Then Murphy entered the seminary and was ordained, in 1972, at the age of eighty. A year later, he returned to Saint Margaret's, where he served until his death in 1991 at the age of ninety-nine.

Plan your visit: stmargaretofscotlandmv.org. 37 Murphy Drive, Maggie Valley, NC 28751. (828) 926-0106.

113 When Beverly Barutio was diagnosed with late-stage cancer in 1981, she promised Saint Jude, patron of desperate causes, that she would build him a chapel if she lived. And she did, in a little Blue Ridge Mountain town called Trust (just north of Luck). Constructed of cedar, tiny **St. Jude's Chapel of Hope** seats eight, and features a belfry and stained glass. Outside, a mountain brook tumbles by like a stream of grace.

Plan your visit: romanticasheville.com/st -judes-chapel. State Highways 209 and 63, 14535 NC-209, Hot Springs, NC 28743. (877) 262-3476.

114 Give thanks with a grateful heart and ring the Gratitude Bell at **Belmont Abbey College** in Bel-

St. Jude's
Chapel of Hope

"I will lift up mine
eyes unto the hills
from whence cometh
my help."

Everyone Welcome
stop - rest - reflect

mont. Daily, between noon and three o'clock p.m., visitors are invited to ring the bell in thanksgiving for a blessing in life. Forged in 1915, the bell is inscribed with "Holy Name." Other must-see campus sites include the rustic, glass-walled Saint Joseph Adoration Chapel and the Abbey Basilica of Maryhelp (in honor of Mary, Help of Christians). Benedictine monks founded Belmont Abbey in 1876.

Plan your visit: belmontabbeycollege.edu. 100 Belmont-Mt. Holly Road, Belmont, NC 28012. (704) 461-6700.

115 You'll need your Bible at Charlotte's **St. Peter Catholic Church**, erected in Victorian Gothic style in 1893. Based on chapter 21 of Saint John's Gospel, the great sanctuary triptych — oil on aluminum by artist John Collier — is an allegorical fishing expedition. Why is Jesus holding a fishing line? How many fish did the apostles catch? Why do the backs of two apostles resemble rocks? Why is one apostle wearing blue jeans and a leather jacket? And why does one boat look like a bass boat? (This *is* North Carolina, after all!)

Plan your visit: stpeterscatholic.org. 507 S. Tryon Street, Charlotte, NC 28202. (704) 332-2901.

✞ FINDING FAITH
in North Carolina

When you enter the **Basilica of Saint Law-rence, Deacon and Martyr**, in Asheville, you're teleported back in time to Spain and the era of great-domed churches. Asheville's dome — fifty-eight by eighty-two-feet — is reputedly the largest freestanding elliptical dome in North America. Designed by Rafael Guastavino (of Carnegie Hall and Grand Central Station fame), this turn-of-the-twentieth-century Spanish Renaissance gem used no wooden or steel beams in its construction. Instead, the entire structure is made of tiles and other masonry elements.

Adding to the Old World ambience are two seventeenth-century artworks: a painting of the Visitation by Massimo Stanzione in the Chapel of Our Lady, and a hand-carved walnut tableau of the crucifixion above the high altar. Other features include the polychrome terra cotta reredos with life-size reliefs of the four evangelists and the archangels Michael and Raphael, and the marble boat-shaped altar, a duplicate of that used by Pope Paul VI (a boat is symbolic of the Church). Outside, a Saint Lawrence statue holds a gridiron. It's said that as Lawrence was being grilled to death, he quipped, "Turn me over. I'm done on this side!"

Plan your visit: saintlawrencebasilica.org. 97 Haywood Street, Asheville, NC 28801. (828) 252-6042.

SOUTH CAROLINA

117

118-9

Charleston

Atlantic Ocean

116 How great is the faith at **St. James the Greater Mission** near Walterboro? Built in 1833, the first church served both Irish Catholic planters and their baptized Catholic slaves. The church burned in 1856. When the Irish fled the Lowcountry post-Civil War, their freed Catholic slaves were forgotten. But the blacks didn't forget the Faith: They worshiped together — without priest or church — until 1892, when a priest happened by. Today's red-painted church, erected in 1935, features an 1894 altarpiece of Saint Peter Claver (see Finding Faith in Missouri) ministering to slaves in Cartagena, Colombia. Also on the grounds is an old red schoolhouse and an interracial cemetery dating from 1835.

Plan your visit: 3087 Ritter Road, Walterboro, SC 29488. (843) 549-5230.

 Encounter history at the Trappist monks' **Mepkin Abbey** at Moncks Corner. American patriot Henry Laurens, president of the Continental Congress and later imprisoned by the British in the Tower of London, bought the plantation site in 1762. Fast forward to 1936, when publishing magnate Henry Luce and wife Clare Booth Luce, who converted to Catholicism in 1946, acquired the estate and added the formal gardens. In 1949, they donated 3,000 acres to the Trappists. Self-guided tours include the beautiful gardens; medieval-inspired abbey church; and burial grounds of Henry Laurens, Henry and Clare Luce, and plantation slaves.

Plan your visit: mepkinabbey.org. 1098 Mepkin Abbey Road, Moncks Corner, SC 29461. (843) 761-8509.

"Here's the church and there's the steeple," the finger **118** rhyme goes, but that wasn't always the case at the **Cathedral of St. John the Baptist** in Charleston. For more than a century, folks dreamed of a steeple for their 1890 neo-Gothic brownstone church, but the coffers dictated otherwise. In 2010, the church "grew" eighty-four feet, the new copper-clad steeple nearly doubling its height. Gorgeous stained glass includes fourteen large two-light windows depicting the life of Christ from the Nativity to the Ascension, and a five-light window of Da Vinci's *Last Supper*.

Plan your visit: charlestoncathedral.com. 120 Broad Street, Charleston, SC 29401. (843) 724-8395.

The Faith marches on at **Saint Mary of the An- 119 nunciation Church** in Charleston. Nothing — not a schism, not Charleston's Great Fire of 1838 that burned the church to the ground, not even the Civil War — could extinguish the mother church of the Carolinas and Georgia. Opened in 1839, the Greek Revival structure resembles an art gallery inside: twenty-three paintings (copies of masterpieces rendered by Caesare Porta of Rome) decorate the walls. The portrait of Saint Peter raises a question: Why six toes on his right foot?

Plan your visit: sma.church. 95 Hasell Street, Charleston, SC 29401. (843) 722-7696.

✤ FINDING FAITH
in South Carolina

Where was America's first Mass? Florida? New Mexico? Or was it in South Carolina? According to one account, Spanish explorer Lucas Vázquez de Ayllón, along with 600 soldiers, colonists, African slaves, and priests, landed in 1526 at Winyah Bay, near present-day Georgetown. While short-lived (some say only three months), the colony of San Miguel de Guadalupe reportedly made for a number of "firsts," including the country's first Mass.

In 1899, nearly 375 years after the colony disbanded, Georgetown Catholics erected their first permanent church. Dedicated to **St. Mary Our Lady of Ransom**, the Romanesque, pressed-brick structure is known for its German stained-glass windows featuring lesser-known images, including Our Lady of Ransom, Saint Frances of Rome, and the Apostle John writing the Gospel on the Isle of Patmos.

Plan your visit: stmaryourladyofransom.org. 317 Broad Street, Georgetown, SC 29440. (843) 546-7416.

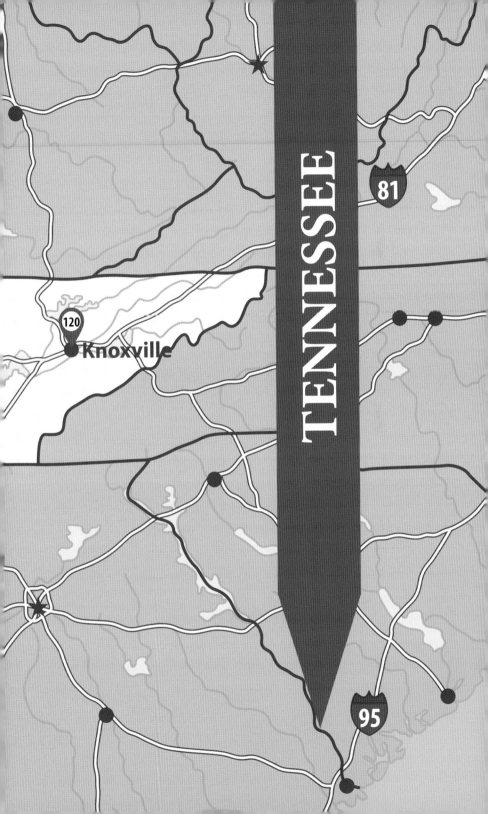

TENNESSEE

Knoxville

120

81

95

120 What can you do with 300,000 bricks, 400 tons of steel, forty miles of wood trim, 20,000 pieces of limestone, and 101 light switches? Build the magnificent **Cathedral of the Most Sacred Heart of Jesus** in Knoxville! Dedicated in 2018, the Roman architecture-style church emulates the greatest European cathedrals — from its 144-foot-tall dome; to its ten-foot-long white marble altar (quarried from the same source as Michelangelo's *Pietà*); to its twenty-five-foot-tall dome painting of Jesus, his pierced Sacred Heart surrounded by a crown of

thorns. Other must-see artworks include Saint Luke holding an icon of Mother Mary and the Infant Jesus (Luke is hailed as the Church's first iconographer), and Saint Francis of Assisi appearing with cathedral builder Bishop Richard F. Stika's pet cockapoo dogs.

Plan your visit: shcathedral.org. 711 S. Northshore Drive, Knoxville, TN 37919. (865) 588-0249.

When yellow fever hit Chattanooga in 1878, thousands of folks lit out for the hills, but Servant of God Patrick Ryan (1845–1878) stayed behind to tend to his flock, dying of the scourge himself. The thirty-three-year-old priest's last request was "Bury me in Chattanooga among my people." He was, three times: first in a churchyard, eight years later in Mount Olivet Cemetery, and in 2019 at the **Basilica of Sts. Peter and Paul**, his parish at the time of death. Father Ryan's remains are entombed beneath the Fourteenth Station of the Cross (Jesus is laid in the tomb). Like his Lord, he gave his life so others might live.

Plan your visit: stspeterandpaulbasilica.com. 214 E. Eighth Street, Chattanooga, TN 37402. (423) 266-1618.

In early 1933, Our Lady of Banneux (also called Our Lady of the Poor) appeared eight times to eleven-year-old Mariette Beco in Banneux, Belgium. Nearly fifty years later, near New Hope, Benedictine monks and local craftsmen erected the **Virgin of the Poor**

Shrine. A replica of the Banneux shrine — even the mountainous setting and springs echo the Belgian site — the stone chapel beckons visitors with its exterior mosaic of Our Lady appearing to young Mariette.

Plan your visit: Burns Island Road, New Hope, TN 37380. GPS 35° 1' 39.4788" N, 85° 39' 13.5540" W. (423) 837-7068

123 When you pray at the tomb of Bishop Richard Pius Miles, OP (1791–1860), at **St. Mary of the Seven Sorrows Catholic Church** in Nashville, you're likely praying before a saint. When the bishop's remains were exhumed in 1972, 112 years after his death, his body was found to be incorrupt. Tennessee's first prelate (when he arrived in 1838, he was the only priest in the state), Bishop Miles erected the Greek Revival temple as his cathedral. According to tradition, the stations of the cross date from 1845 and were painted on tin in Czechoslovakia.

Plan your visit: stmarysdowntown.org. 330 Fifth Avenue N., Nashville, TN 37219. (615) 256-1704.

124 Fledgling entertainer Danny Thomas (1912–1991) wasn't joking when he told Saint Jude Thaddeus, patron of desperate causes, "Show me my way in life, and I will build a shrine in your name." Doors opened, success followed, and the Lebanese-American set about fulfilling his vow. On February

Cathedral of the Immaculate Conception [125]

4, 1962, Thomas unveiled a large statue of Saint Jude and officially opened Memphis's world-renowned St. Jude Children's Research Hospital. Thomas's remarkable story is told at the **Danny Thomas/AL-SAC Pavilion,** located on hospital grounds.

Plan your visit: stjude.org. 262 Danny Thomas Place, Memphis, TN 38105. (800) 230-6617.

(125) God created the animals, and animals exalt the Creator at the **Cathedral of the Immaculate Conception** in Memphis. Symbols on the sanctuary arch include a peacock representing the Resurrection; a butterfly, eternal life; a pelican, atonement in blood; a stag, piety; and a unicorn, the Incarnation. The glorious apse mural replicates Bartolomé Esteban Murillo's 1670s painting *The Assumption of the Virgin* (see 134, 146, and 206). Spanish Colonial Revival in design, the cathedral was dedicated in 1938.

Plan your visit: iccathedral.org. 1695 Central Avenue, Memphis, TN 38104. (901) 725-2700.

✠ FINDING FAITH
✝ in Tennessee

The Dominicans are known as the Order of Preachers, and there's a whole lot of preaching going on at **St. Peter Catholic Church** in Memphis, even when no one's in the pulpit! Tour the 1852 Norman Gothic church with fortress-like towers and you'll find Dominicans everywhere: a plaque dedicated to Dominican priests who died of yellow fever while tending to the sick; oil-on-canvas medallions of Dominican saints; stained-glass Dominican holy men and women (don't miss Saint Hyacinth, who walked dry-shod across a river carrying a monstrance and a large statue of Mary).

The preaching continues in the stained-glass window above the main entrance. A memorial to parishioners who served in World War I, the window depicts a soldier and a sailor, praying on bended knees, as a bevy of Dominican saints keep watch. If the saints look oddly similar, there's good reason. As the story goes, every face bears an uncanny likeness to the Dominican pastor at the time the window was installed.

Plan your visit: stpeterchurch.org. 190 Adams Avenue at Third Street, Memphis, TN 38103. (901) 527-8282.

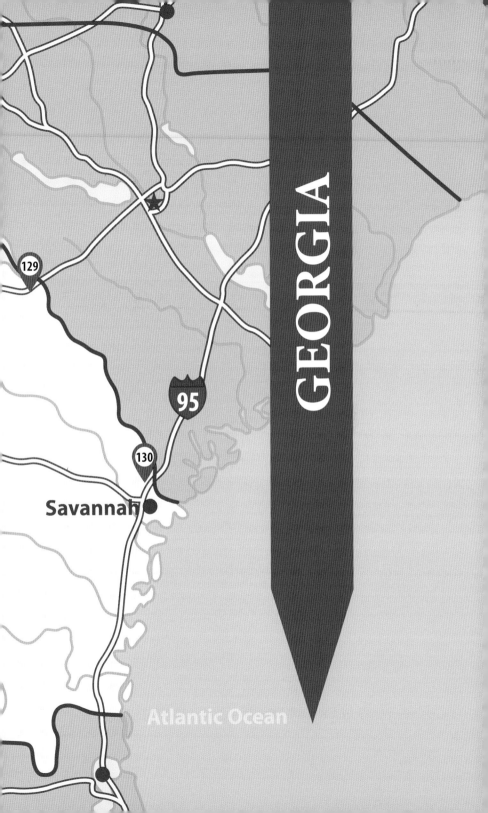

126 The **Cathedral of Christ the King** in Atlanta is a victory of love over hate. The French Gothic-style church, considered one of Atlanta's most beautiful churches, was erected in 1937 on the site of a former Ku Klux Klan mansion — an elegant Southern mansion with white columns that the Klan had hoped to make its "Imperial Palace." Located at what's called Jesus Junction (an intersection with three churches), the cathedral is known for its stained glass and medieval feel.

Plan your visit: cathedralctk.com. 2699 Peachtree Road NE, Atlanta, GA 30305. (404) 233-2145.

127 Can you put old wine in a new wineskin? They did at **Mary Our Queen Catholic Church** in Peachtree Corners. Dedicated in 2019, the white Neoclassical church is filled with century-old religious art and artifacts — stained glass, baptismal font, marble altar, tabernacle, even the pews — from St. Gerard Church in Buffalo, New York, which closed in 2008. If Mary Our Queen Church looks familiar, it is. The design imitates the Buffalo church, a scaled-down replica of the Basilica of St. Paul Outside the Walls in Rome.

Plan your visit: maryourqueen.com. 6260 The Corners Parkway, Peachtree Corners, GA 30092. (770) 416-0002.

128 The Wind of God blows as he wills, and in 1944 twenty-one Trappist monks from Gethsemani Abbey in Kentucky (see 207) founded the **Monastery of the Holy Spirit** near Conyers. Step inside the

Abbey Church, a massive Gothic-inspired concrete structure that took fifteen years to build, and you'll be overcome with otherworldly light. Two tiers of monk-crafted stained-glass windows cast a blue aura over the nave, while the sanctuary is enveloped in a halo of golden light. If God's cathedral, the great outdoors, is calling you, the monastery is a gateway to Arabia Mountain National Heritage Area.

Plan your visit: trappist.net. 2625 Highway 212 SW, Conyers, GA 30094. (770) 483-8705.

A church consecration must go on, even if the altars have to be smuggled in. That's part of the lore of **Most Holy Trinity Catholic Church** (originally called St. Patrick's) in Augusta. During the Civil War in 1863, John P. Mullen, who crafted the three marble altars in Maryland, "slipped" the altars through a Union blockade to their new church home. Georgia's oldest Catholic church, Romanesque Revival in design, is decorated to heaven and back. Observe the stenciled arches featuring symbols of Christ as you approach the altar, and symbols of the apostles as you return.

Plan your visit: themostholytrinity.org. 720 Telfair Street, Augusta, GA 30903. (706) 722-4944.

Only a humble gravestone honors the Angel of Andersonville at the **Catholic Cemetery** in Savannah. During the stiflingly hot summer of 1864, Father Peter Whelan, an Irish native and Confederate chaplain, tended to Union soldiers held at Andersonville Prison — a twenty-six-acre "cattle pen" crammed with 33,000 men. There was no shelter and scant food, and it's said that 10,000 men died of dysentery that summer and fall alone. The "angel" borrowed $16,000 in Confederate script, bought 10,000 pounds of flour, and had it baked into thousands of biscuits. Prisoners called the manna "Whelan's bread."

Plan your visit: diosav.org/offices/cemetery. 1720 Wheaton Street, Savannah, GA 31404. (912) 201-4076.

✠ FINDING FAITH
✝ in Georgia

According to lore, when General William T. Sherman ordered Union troops to burn Atlanta to the ground in 1864, Father Thomas O'Reilly warned, "Burn the Catholic church and every Catholic in the Union army will mutiny." As Providence had it, the majority of Sherman's Atlanta forces were Catholic. The Catholic church, several Protestant churches, and civic buildings were spared.

Father Reilly's wooden church was replaced in 1869 with today's **Catholic Shrine of the Immaculate Conception**. Life-size frescoes of the Twelve Apostles line the ceiling like soldiers themselves. The Gothic Revival shrine is also known as a powerhouse of corporate prayer. During World War II, the congregation prayed the Rosary as part of Mass, fervently imploring the Blessed Mother to safeguard their parishioner-soldiers. Every soldier returned home alive.

Plan your visit: catholicshrineatlanta.org. 48 Martin Luther King Jr. Drive SW, Atlanta, GA 30303. (404) 521-1866.

At nearby Atlanta City Hall, the **Father O'Reilly Monument** honors the priest's gallant intervention.

Plan your visit: 68 Mitchell Street SW, Atlanta, GA 30303

132 Jacksonville

133

134 Orlando

95

Tampa

FLORIDA

Lake
Okeechobee

135
136
Miami

137-8

139

NORTHERN FLORIDA

"Saint Michael the Archangel, defend us in battle!" That's the battle cry of the **Basilica of St. Michael the Archangel** in Pensacola. The parish traces its origin to August 1559, when Spanish explorer Tristán de Luna y Arellano and eleven ships landed at Pensacola Bay and Dominican friars offered Mass. Canonically established in 1781, the first church — a two-story former warehouse — collapsed in 1831. Three subsequent churches were leveled by a hurri-

cane, a fire, and yet another fire. The parish soldiered on and built today's Gothic Revival brick structure in 1883. Note the metal card holders on pew ends (from a bygone custom when parishioners were assigned pews and paid "pew rent"), the wood-carved bowed altar rail, and the rose window of Michael the Archangel, captain of the army of God.

Plan your visit: stmichael.ptdiocese.org. 19 N. Palafox Street, Pensacola, FL 32502. (850) 438-4985.

Our Lady reigns at Jacksonville's **Basilica of the Immaculate Conception**, founded in 1854, the year the Immaculate Conception of Mary was declared a dogma of the Catholic Faith. The original church was sacked and burned during the Civil War. The Great Jacksonville Fire of 1901 took the second church, but miraculously a large Mary statue atop the burned-out structure survived. The present church — a Gothic Revival temple with Munich stained glass and trumpet-blowing angel statues standing on pillars — was dedicated on the feast of the Immaculate Conception (December 8) in 1910.

Plan your visit: icjax.org. 121 E. Duval Street, Jacksonville, FL 32202. (904) 359-0331.

"Baby wanted!": the heartfelt cry of infertile couples who beseech heaven at **Our Lady of La Leche** (Our Lady of the Milk) **National Shrine** at Mission Nombre de Dios (Name of God Mission) in St.

Augustine. Many couples attest that, after praying here, they miraculously conceive and a baby is born nine months later. America's oldest Marian shrine (Spaniards built the original chapel c. 1615), the tiny coquina chapel houses a statue of Mother Mary nursing the Holy Infant. The mission also boasts a 208-foot-tall stainless steel Great Cross commemorating the area's first Mass in 1565.

Plan your visit: missionandshrine.org. 101 San Marco Avenue, St. Augustine, FL 32084. (904) 824-2809.

134 ▶ In 1979, Father F. Joseph Harte, a circuit-riding priest offering Masses in Orlando hotels for Disney World tourists, had a vision: Build a "parish church for the whole world." Consecrated in 1993, Orlando's seventeen-acre **Basilica of the National Shrine of Mary, Queen of the Universe** is simply "Magnificat"! Rosary Garden. Outdoor shrine of Mother Mary with a playful Child Jesus. Art museum (don't miss Bartolomé Esteban Murillo's *The Assumption of the Blessed Virgin*, c. 1640; see 125, 146, and 206). Universe Chapel with mesmerizing stained-glass window of a starry midnight sky. Wherever you turn, your spirit will rejoice in God our Savior.

Plan your visit: maryqueenoftheuniverse.org. 8300 Vineland Avenue, Orlando, FL 32821. (407) 239-6600.

SOUTHERN FLORIDA

 A smuggled statue and an exiled Cuban people — discover an intriguing faith story at Miami's **National Shrine of Our Lady of Charity (*La Ermita de la Caridad*** in Spanish), a 1967 starkly modern edifice facing Cuba some 200 miles away. The statue, a sixteen-inch replica of Our Lady of Charity with the Christ Child, graces a 747-square-foot mural depicting Cuba's Catholic heritage. The statue also tells the miraculous story of its original. In the early 1600s, relates one account, three Cuban farmers got caught in a wicked storm at sea and prayed for their lives. When the storm passed, they found a statue of Mary, bobbing atop a board, with a sign that proclaimed, *"Yo soy la Virgen de la Caridad"* — "I am the Virgin of Charity."

Plan your visit: ermita.org. 3609 S. Miami Avenue, Miami, FL 33133. (305) 854-2404.

 Schoenstatt Chapel in Miami (see 221).

Plan your visit: schoenstattmiamiusa.org. 22800 SW 187th Avenue, Miami, FL 33170. (305) 248-4800.

 Christ is everywhere, even in the depths of the sea. Submerged in twenty-five feet of water at John Pennekamp Coral Reef State Park, near Key Largo, is **Christ of the Abyss** — a nearly nine-foot-tall, two-ton bronze statue of Christ, his arms aloft. Placed here in 1965, the sculpture (also called *Christ of the Deep*) attracts snorkelers and scuba divers who touch Christ's fingertips and then bless themselves.

Plan your visit: pennekamppark.com. 102601 Overseas Highway, Key Largo, FL 33037. (305) 451-6300.

Don't dive or snorkel? Visit an outdoor replica of *Christ of the Abyss* (see 137) and other eye-popping artworks at nearby **St. Justin the Martyr Catholic Church** in Key Largo.

Plan your visit: facebook.com/sjmkeylargo. 105500 Overseas Highway, Key Largo, FL 33037. (305) 451-1316.

When **Our Lady of Lourdes Grotto** at the Basilica of Saint Mary Star of the Sea in Key West was dedicated in 1922, Sister Louis Gabriel, SNJM, a survivor of three major local hurricanes — who also designed and oversaw its construction — prophesied that as long as the outdoor rock grotto stood, "Key West would never experience the full brunt of a hurricane." As parishioners can vouch, there hasn't been a severe storm on the island since! The 1904 basilica is known for its American Victorian architecture and decorative pressed metal panels.

Plan your visit: stmarykeywest.com. 1010 Windsor Lane, Key West, FL 33040. (305) 294-1018.

Ringling Bros. was hailed as "the Greatest Show on Earth." But at **St. Martha Catholic Church** in Sarasota — erected in 1940 in Spanish Mission style — the circus is also revered church history. From 1935 to 1941, Ringling Bros. and Barnum & Bailey Circus (Sarasota was their winter home) staged benefit performances under the big top and donated the receipts to help fund the new church. Mounted on the sanctuary wall are two brightly painted circus wagon wheels. Designated America's Circus Church, Saint Martha's keeps the sacramental records for its traveling performers.

Plan your visit: stmartha.org. 200 N. Orange Avenue, Sarasota, FL 34236. (941) 366-4210.

✛ FINDING FAITH
✛ in Florida

Your heart will be restless until you visit St. Augustine's historic **Cathedral Basilica of St. Augustine**. America's First Parish dates from September 8, 1565, when Spanish admiral and explorer Pedro Menéndez de Avilés came ashore and Father Francisco López de Mendoza Grajales celebrated a Mass of Thanksgiving (often hailed as America's First Thanksgiving) for the fleet's safe arrival from Spain.

Built by the Spanish Crown from 1793 to 1797, the Spanish colonial cathedral is spiritually captivating. The Spanish red ceiling with open timbers pulls eyes heavenward, while murals depict Florida's early Catholic history. Munich stained-glass windows present the life of parish patron Saint Augustine of Hippo, and Smalto glass mosaics illustrate the Last Supper. Looking for the fountain of eternal life? A stone replica of Spanish explorer Juan Ponce de León's baptismal font graces the church entrance.

Plan your visit: thefirstparish.org. 38 Cathedral Place, St. Augustine, FL 32084. (904) 824-2806.

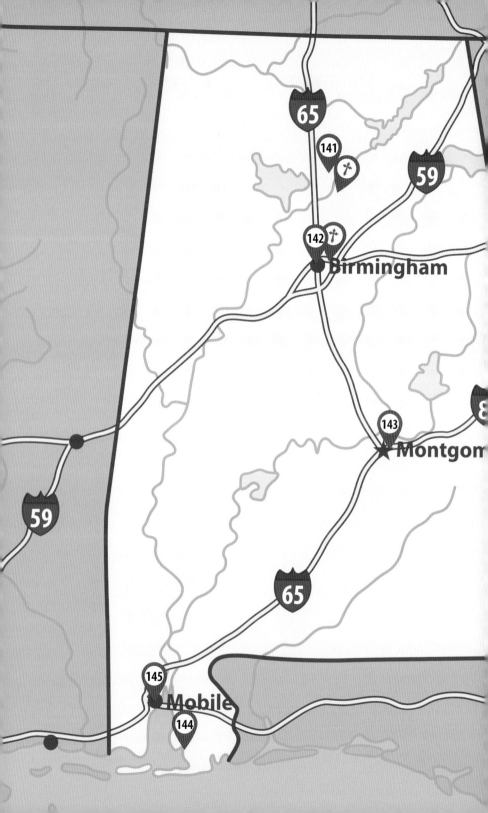

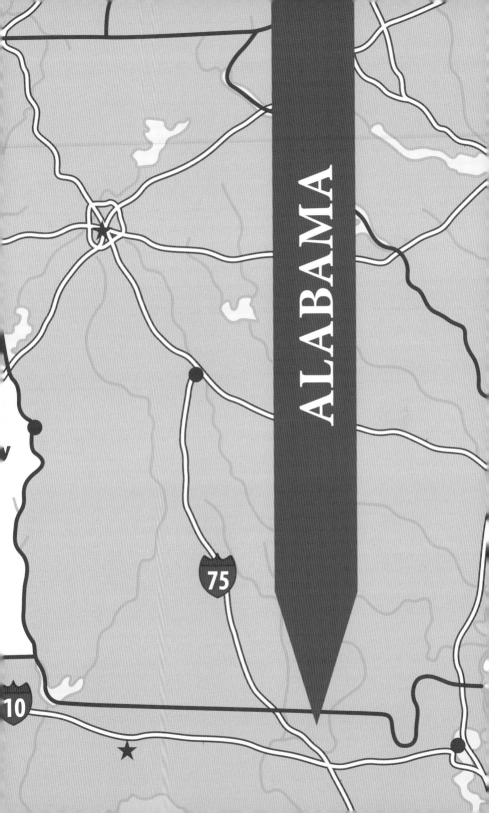

141 Bigger isn't better at **Ave Maria Grotto**, located at St. Bernard Abbey in Cullman. From around 1912 to 1958, Brother Joseph Zoettl, OSB, created a four-acre miniature city filled with 125 tiny versions of famous holy sites and historic monuments: from the Nativity in Bethlehem to Monserrat Abbey in Spain to Mission San Juan Capistrano in California. Anything and everything — costume jewelry, marbles, pebbles and shells, even toilet bowl floats — found new life in Brother Joseph's kingdom. The dome of Saint Peter's Basilica was crafted from an old birdcage.

Plan your visit: avemariagrotto.com. 1600 St. Bernard Drive SE, Cullman, AL 35055. (256) 734-4110.

142 Nothing — not racial threats nor the 1921 murder of Father James Coyle, gunned down by an enraged white minister-Klansman for marrying his Catholic-convert daughter to a Puerto Rican — can stop the **Cathedral of Saint Paul** in Birmingham from preaching God's love for all people. Dedicated in 1893, the red-brick neo-Gothic church features a striking facade with polychromatic banding on the roof and steeples. In a unique stained-glass window of the Holy Family, the Blessed Mother spins wool.

Plan your visit: stpaulsbhm.org. 2120 Third Avenue N., Birmingham, AL 35203. (205) 251-1279.

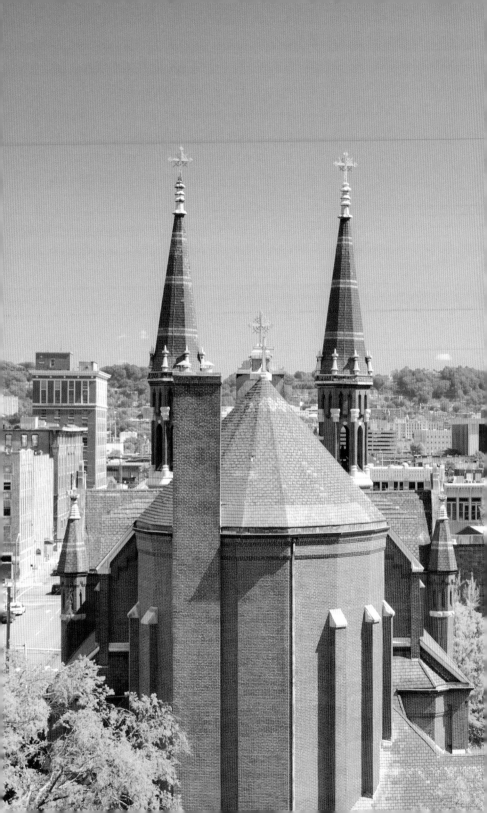

143 Father Harold Purcell had a dream: Improve the lives of black Americans. It came to pass in the mid-1930s, when he founded Montgomery's **City of St. Jude**, a Catholic parish and social services mission. On March 24, 1965, St. Jude's gained national attention when Doctor Martin Luther King Junior and more than 25,000 voting-rights marchers camped on the thirty-six-acre campus and staged the Stars for Freedom Rally. Part of the Selma to Montgomery National Historic Trail, the City of St. Jude includes St. Jude's Church (see the Ten Commandments written on ceiling beams), and an interpretive center commemorating the historic march and St. Jude's role. Also on the grounds is a *Homeless Jesus* statue (see Mt 25:35–40).

Plan your visit: cityofstjude.org. 2048 W. Fairview Avenue, Montgomery, AL 36108. (334) 265-1390, (334) 265-6791.

144 You can go fishing and still get to Sunday Mass at **Sacred Heart Chapel**, located on the edge of Mobile Bay at Fairhope. Just dock at the church pier! The picturesque little white church, with a front porch and stand-alone bell in the front yard, was established in 1876.

Plan your visit: stlawrencefairhope.com. 18673 Scenic Highway 98, Fairhope, AL 36532. (251) 928-5931.

145 The **Cathedral-Basilica of the Immaculate Conception** in Mobile has been tried and tested. Construction began in 1835, only to be interrupted by the Panic of 1837 (the church was consecrated in 1850). During the Civil War, a Union Army ammunition depot exploded, blowing in church windows. Seventy-five years later, a World War II pilot-in-training struck the towers. The Greek Revival masterpiece is best known for its "light show": Munich stained glass presenting events in Mother Mary's life. When sunbeams hit the windows, the church (and Mary) dances in a kaleidoscope of deepest wine reds, bluest Prussian blues, and the most velvety greens this side of heaven.

Plan your visit: mobilecathedral.org. 2 S. Claiborne Street, Mobile, AL 36602. (251) 434-1565.

✠ FINDING FAITH
in Alabama

A child shall lead them, the Good Book says. In the mid-1990s, Mother Angelica, PCPA (1923–2016), founder of the worldwide Eternal Word Television Network (EWTN), was praying at the Sanctuary of the Divine Infant Jesus in Bogotá, Colombia, when the Child Jesus spoke to her. "Build me a temple," the young voice said. Providence then provided five families who funded the **Shrine of the Most Blessed Sacrament** at Our Lady of the Angels Monastery in Hanceville.

Everything — from the Divine Infant statue greeting you on the expansive piazza, to the nearly eight-foot-tall monstrance in the thirteenth-century Italian-style shrine church — exalts the Lord. Note the tabernacle, a scaled-down replica of a Gothic church, and the inlaid jasper crosses on the marble floor that recall the ornamentation in the Jerusalem temple. Other devotional areas on the grounds include the stations of the Most Holy Eucharist (twelve Scriptural events depicting the Eucharist); a Lourdes grotto; a Shroud of Turin replica; and a life-size Nativity scene.

Plan your visit: olamshrine.com. 3224 County Road 548, Hanceville, AL 35077. (256) 352-6267.

Pilgrims can also tour **EWTN** and **Our Lady of the Angels Chapel** in Irondale.

Plan your visit: ewtn.com. 5817 Old Leeds Road, Irondale, AL 35210. (205) 271-2966.

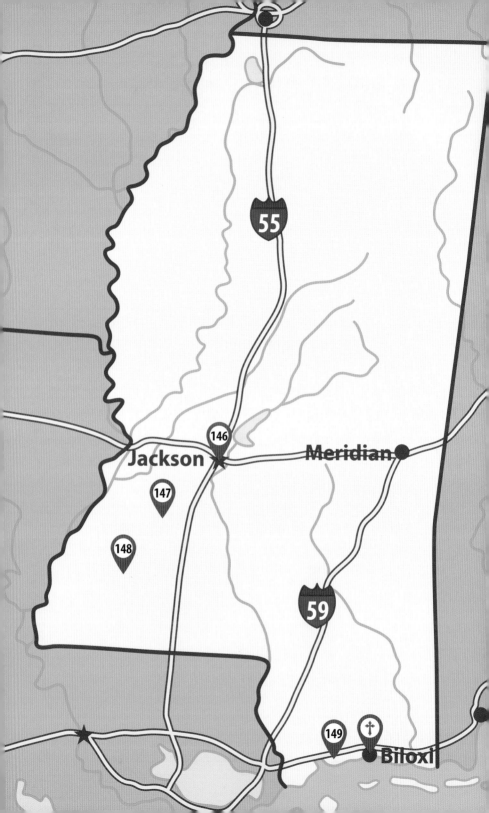

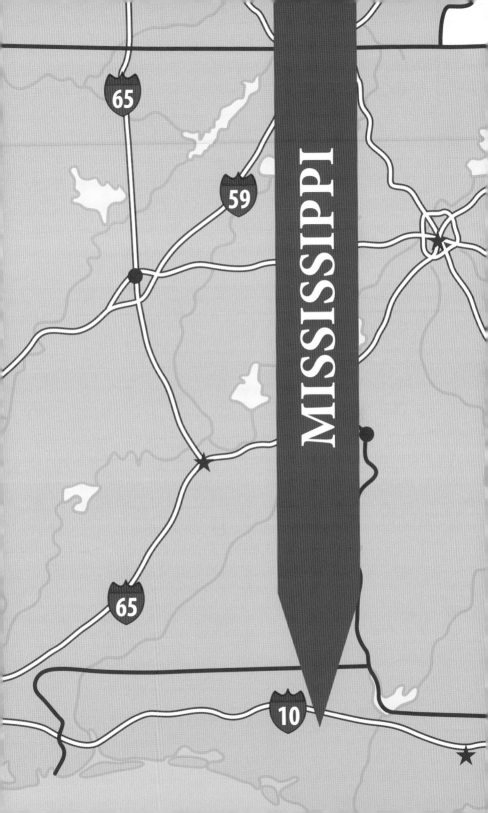

146 The **Cathedral of St. Peter the Apostle Catholic Church** in Jackson is a call to racial unity. On the facade, a Venetian glass mosaic of Christ the Good Shepherd, surrounded by figures representing the world's seven continents, proclaims, "There shall be one flock and one shepherd." The 1897 neo-Gothic structure is also heralded for its stained-glass renditions of three renowned paintings: Raphael's *Transfiguration*, Murillo's *Immaculate Conception* (see 125, 134, and 206), and Sassoferrato's *Madonna of the Thumb* — a wheel window depicting Mary's face and a thumb peeking out from under her blue veil.

Plan your visit: cathedralsaintpeter.org. 123 N. West Street, Jackson, MS 39205. (601) 969-3125.

147 When sunlight hits the cobalt-blue windows at **St. Joseph Catholic Church** in Port Gibson, and fills the nave with an ethereal blue glow and a peace surpassing all understanding, there's only one thing you can do: Cast your cares aside! Interestingly, the light turns purple, the color of the Passion, in a sanctuary niche with a crucifixion painting. The quaint Gothic Revival brick church, with an ornate iron fence, was dedicated in 1863.

Plan your visit: stjosephportgibson.weebly.com. 411 Coffee Street, Port Gibson, MS 39150. (601) 437-5790.

St. Michael Catholic Church [Finding Faith]

Can you hear it? The pealing of prayers at **St. Mary Basilica** in Natchez? As the story goes, when the bell Maria Alexandrina was being cast in Italy in 1848, Princess Torlonia threw a gold ring into the molten mass, then knelt with her husband to pray the Litany of Loreto. The bell, a gift of the prince, arrived at the gorgeous Gothic Revival church in 1850 and has been ringing in the flock ever since.

148

Plan your visit: stmarybasilica.org. 107 S. Union Street, Natchez, MS 39120. (601) 445-5616.

(149) "It is surely a grave injustice to exclude a whole race from the priesthood," penned Father Matthias Christmann, SVD, in 1926. A European immigrant, Father Christmann was the founding rector in 1923 of **St. Augustine Seminary** — the country's first black Catholic seminary — at Bay Saint Louis. On May 23, 1934, the seminary made history: Four black men were ordained to the priesthood. Notable alumni include no fewer than nine bishops. Venerable Augustus Tolton (1854–1897), often cited as America's first black priest, studied for the priesthood in Rome and was ordained there in 1886 (see 241).

Plan your visit: svdsouth.com. 199 Seminary Drive, Bay Saint Louis, MS 39520. (228) 467-6414.

✠ FINDING FAITH
in Mississippi

Don't miss the chance to "net" a beautiful visit to **St. Michael Catholic Church** in Biloxi. Erected of concrete in 1964 and dubbed the Fisherman's Church, the unique cylinder structure with a scalloped roof attracts tourists and pilgrims alike. Inside, elongated stained-glass windows portray the apostles gathering in their catch, depicting both the apostles' role as "fishers of men" and the local seafood industry. The adjacent tiny day chapel echoes the clam shell motif.

The maritime church is also known for its annual Blessing of the Fleet, held in late May or early June at the beginning of Biloxi's shrimping season. A colorful procession of boats files past the blessing boat, where a priest sprinkles each vessel with holy water and prays for God's blessings on the shrimpers, for their safety and a bountiful catch.

Plan your visit: stmichaelchurchbiloxi.com. 177 First Street, Biloxi, MS 39530. (228) 435-5578.

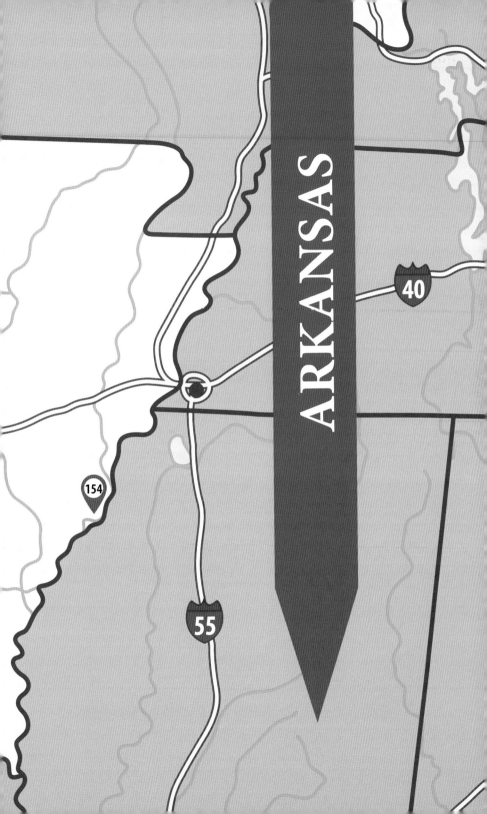

150 Want to make a grand church entrance? Come to **Saint Elizabeth of Hungary Catholic Church** in Eureka Springs. Due to the rugged terrain, the entry to the church — featured in *Ripley's Believe It or Not!* — is through the stand-alone bell tower. The charming turn-of-the-twentieth-century stone church, with a Byzantine-inspired dome, was erected by Richard Kerens in memory of his mother, Elizabeth. Lining the walkway are Carrara marble statuette stations of the cross. It's said that each station took forty days to complete.

Plan your visit: stelizabethar.org. 30 Crescent Drive, Eureka Springs, AR 72632. (479) 253-2222.

151 In April 2008, a hailstorm pounded Fort Smith, but miraculously a new outdoor sign at **St. Boniface Catholic Church** suffered nary a dent. The sign — thirteen by nine feet — shows Boniface chopping down an oak tree worshipped by Germanic pagans. When thunder god Thor didn't strike Boniface dead, many were converted. The Modernistic English Gothic church, completed in 1939, glows with German stained glass that will test your Catholic IQ. What do the seven symbols in Boniface's martyrdom window represent? Why does Doubting Thomas appear in Mary's assumption window?

Plan your visit: stbonifacefortsmith.com. 1820 N. B Street, Fort Smith, AR 72901. (479) 783-6711.

St. Mary's Catholic Church [152]

When World War I prevented artist Fridolin Fuchs (see 266 and 352) from returning home to Germany, he began painting a "Sistine Chapel" at **St. Mary's Catholic Church** in Altus. Set against gold-leaf mosaic backdrops, the murals are arrestingly dramatic. Parishioners posed for various scenes, including the finding of Jesus in the temple and Jesus routing the money changers from the temple (note Fuchs' self-portrait). The Beuronese-style stations of the cross are copies of a once-famous set in a church in Stuttgart, Germany, destroyed in World War II. Who are the boys helping Simon carry the cross in stations five and seven? (See Mk 15:21.) The 1901

Romanesque-inspired hilltop church is also re-nowned for its pressed tin.

Plan your visit: stmarysaltus.org. 5118 St. Mary's Lane, Altus, AR 72821. (479) 468-2585.

153 Ravens reign at the Benedictine monks' **Subiaco Abbey** in Subiaco — in statues, stained glass, and even the abbey's coat of arms. Why the fascination? According to one raven legend (there are several), in the sixth century a wicked priest tried to kill Saint Benedict of Nursia, the father of Western monasticism, with poisoned bread. A raven swooped in and carried the bread away. How many ravens can you find at the 1878 hilltop abbey?

Plan your visit: countrymonks.org. 405 N. Subiaco Avenue, Subiaco, AR 72865. (479) 934-1001.

154 From darkness unto light — the theme of Christianity and of **St. Mary Church** in Helena. Designed by Charles Eames (famous for his Eames chair), the stark, Depression-era brick church is known for its light fixtures that resemble the world: Half of each globe is in darkness, the other half in light. When you enter, you're in darkness, but when you return from holy Communion, you see the light.

Plan your visit: visithelenaar.com/featured -attractions/historic-homes-and-churches. 123 Columbia Street, Helena, AR 72342. (870) 338-6990.

✝ FINDING FAITH
in Arkansas

According to lore, Bishop Edward Fitzgerald halted construction on the taller of the two steeples of Little Rock's 1878 **Cathedral of St. Andrew** until building plans for the nearby Masonic temple were finalized. He wanted his steeple — at 231 feet — to be the highest point in town! From 1890 to 1944, the cathedral's largest bell was part of Little Rock's telegraphic fire alarm system. It sounded, in code, the location of the fire.

A statue of Saint Andrew the Apostle, an X-shaped cross at his back, stands outside the English Gothic Revival granite church, while enormously large stations of the cross await pilgrims inside. German immigrant-sculptor Joseph Sibbel used live models for the stations and included a self-portrait. Can you find it?

Plan your visit: cathedralsaintandrew.org. 617 S. Louisiana Street, Little Rock, AR 72201. (501) 374-2794.

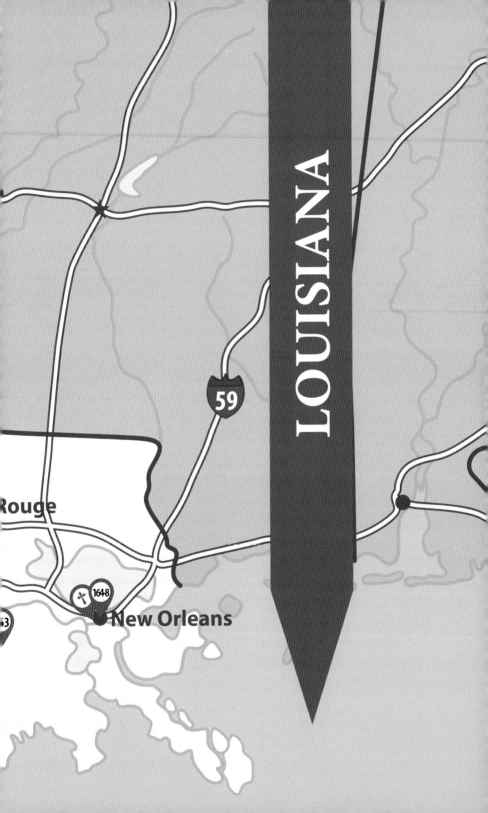

You can't help but embrace the light at **Holy Trinity Catholic Church** in Shreveport: More than 200 light bulbs illuminate the sanctuary dome! The striking 1896 Romanesque Revival church (inside and out) is also known for its stained glass, including a five-panel window dedicated to five priests who lost their lives treating yellow fever victims in 1873. Inscribed at the bottom is John 15:13: "Greater love hath no man than this that a man lay down his life for his friends."

155

Plan your visit: www.holytrinity-shreveport.com. 315 Marshall Street, Shreveport, LA 71101. (318) 221-5990.

Take the road less traveled to **Rock Chapel** at Carmel (near Mansfield). The only sounds here are "prayers of nature": chirping birds, a trickling stream, and the swaying of hardwood trees. Built by German Carmelite friars in 1891, the tiny hilltop stone chapel and marked graves are all that remain of a once flourishing monastery. Restored frescoes and murals include faux wall curtains (so real-looking you'll be tempted to pull them back) and a ceiling paradise with Stars of David.

156

Plan your visit: desotocatholics.org. 1746 Smithport Road, Mansfield, LA 71052. (318) 872-1158. Call ahead for key access.

The **Basilica of the Immaculate Conception**, part of Natchitoches's Historic District, has a long

157

genealogy. The parish dates from around 1717, when Venerable Antonio Margil de Jesús, OFM, offered Mass at Fort St. Jean Baptiste in Natchitoches. The first house of worship went up around 1728, followed by a second in 1734, a third in 1771, a fourth in 1828, a fifth in 1839, and the current church in 1857. This stately "French Lady" is fitted with a French altar, French stations of the cross, a French statue of the Blessed Mother, French chandeliers, and a French wood-carved baptismal font. Note the spiral staircase to the choir loft: It's built into the wall with no central support.

Plan your visit: minorbasilica.org. 145 Church Street, Natchitoches, LA 71457. (318) 352-3422.

 A reproduction of the old fort chapel can be seen at **Fort St. Jean Baptiste State Historic Site**.

Plan your visit: crt.state.la.us/louisiana-state-parks/maps/index. 155 Rue Jefferson, Natchitoches, LA 71457. (888) 677-7853, (318) 357-3101.

 Nothing got past Father Jean Pierre Bellier, not even the Union Army during the Civil War! When Union troops set fire to Alexandria in 1864, some accounts say the priest, who had been an officer in the French Calvary before entering the priesthood, impersonated the voice of General Nathaniel P. Banks and ordered the troops to spare St. Francis Xavier Church. The Army obeyed! Today's gorgeous **St. Francis Xavier Cathedral** was erected in 1895 in Gothic Revival style.

Plan your visit: diocesealex.org/church/st-francis-xavier-cathedral. 626 Fourth Street, Alexandria, LA 71301. (318) 445-1451.

160 You're on "miracle ground" at the **Shrine of St. John Berchmans**, a small chapel at the Academy of the Sacred Heart near Grand Coteau. On December 14, 1866, on this very spot, then-Blessed John Berchmans (1599–1621) appeared to Mary Wilson — a Sacred Heart postulant at death's door — and said, "I come by the order of God. Your sufferings are over." Mary immediately rallied, and the miracle secured the Jesuit's canonization in 1888. Paintings, statuary, and relics tell the heaven-sent story.

Plan your visit: sshcoteau.org. 1821 Academy Road, Grand Coteau, LA 70541. (337) 662-5275. Tours by appointment only.

161 The mother church of the Acadians, **Saint Martin de Tours** in St. Martinville — erected in 1836 (the parish dates from 1765) — is thoroughly French. It boasts an eleven-by-thirteen-foot 1830s French oil painting of Martin of Tours, a French Baroque marble baptismal font said to be a gift from a French king, large French stations of the cross, and an indoor Lourdes grotto. With just a holy card of the French grotto as his reference, freed slave Pierre Martinet constructed the 1870s grotto from bousillage and plaster. The church is also known for its colonial box pews with doors.

Plan your visit: stmartindetours.org. 133 S. Main Street, St. Martinville, LA 70582. (337) 394-6021.

 162 Step inside the wee **Chapel of the Madonna** on the Mississippi River at Bayou Goula, near Plaquemine, and a mighty peace begins to flow. Anthony Gullo, a Sicilian immigrant and sugarcane farmer, erected the chapel in 1903 in thanksgiving for the healing of his son. The nine-foot-square white frame chapel with a steeple is just big enough for an altar, a kneeler, and several people, if everyone holds their breath. The popular feast of the Assumption Mass is held out front.

Plan your visit: Four miles north of Nottoway Plantation on State Highway 405 (River Road), Plaquemine, LA 70764. (225) 545-3635

"Pray and watch what happens" is the heritage of **St. Anne's Church** in Napoleonville. During a yellow fever epidemic, devout folks implored Saint Anne and promised to build her a church if they were spared. The epidemic passed them by, and in 1909 a new church went up. Set among moss-draped oak trees, the neo-Romanesque red-brick structure is a rare gem: five aisles, vaulted metal pan ceiling, and 11,390 linear feet of twenty-three-karat gold leaf. The egg-and-dart frieze is a sermon in itself: The egg signifies life; the dart, death. Together, they represent the journey from life to death to life everlasting.

Plan your visit: bayoulandchurches.com. 417 St. Joseph Street, Napoleonville, LA 70390. (985) 369-6656.

NEW ORLEANS

Blessed Francis Xavier Seelos, CSsR (1819–1867), could read souls. You can "read" his soul at the National Shrine of Blessed Francis Seelos in **St. Mary's Assumption Church**, where the Bavarian native served briefly and where his remains rest in an ornate mini-church-like reliquary. While ministering to yellow fever victims, Father Seelos (see 90) contracted the scourge and died from it. Constructed in German Baroque Revival style, the 1858 brick structure retains its sumptuous ambience — from the richly colored, high altar wooden sculpture of the Coronation of Mary, to the Great Window of stained-glass angels fetching souls from purgatory, to the mahogany confessional where Father Seelos saw into souls and granted absolution.

Plan your visit: stalphonsusno.com. 919 Josephine Street, New Orleans, LA 70130. (504) 525-2495

The historic French Quarter is filled with legends, including two "holy spirits" at the **Cathedral-Basilica of Saint Louis King of France**. It's said that Père (French for "father") Antoine de Sedella appears at Christmas midnight Mass holding a candle, while Père Dagobert chants the Kyrie on rainy days. But then, this iconic 1850s cathedral (the parish was established in 1720) — with its triple steeples and prominent position overlooking Jackson Square — is known to captivate souls. Step inside and catch the spirit of King Saint Louis IX in brilliant stained glass, including his coronation as king, the building of Sainte-Chapelle, and his departure for the Crusades.

Plan your visit: stlouiscathedral.org. 615 Pere Antoine Alley, New Orleans, LA 70116. (504) 525-9585.

On January 7, 1815, General Andrew Jackson and his small motley band of soldiers (with pirates, even) were preparing to fight a very large, well-armed British army in the Battle of New Orleans. Meanwhile, the faithful gathered at the Ursuline Convent chapel in all-night prayer before a statue of Our Lady of Prompt Succor (Quick Help). The mother superior promised Our Lady that, if New Orleans were spared from British control, an annual Mass would be offered in her honor. In 2015, that promise was honored for the 200th time! The large gilded statue of Mary and Child now stands above the altar at the **National Votive Shrine of Our Lady of Prompt Succor**. The shrine also houses the "Sweetheart Statue" (see 167).

Plan your visit: shrineofourladyofpromptsuccor .com. 2701 State Street, New Orleans, LA 70118. (504) 975-9627.

Hailed as the country's finest surviving example of French colonial architecture, the **Old Ursuline Convent Museum** — built from 1748 to 1752 in brick-between-post construction — is a miracle story in itself. On Good Friday in 1788, the Great New Orleans Fire was drawing near the convent when the mother superior ordered everyone to evacuate. Before leaving, one sister placed a small statue of Our Lady of Prompt Succor, dubbed the "Sweetheart Statue" (see 166), in a window facing the fire, and prayed, "Our Lady, unless you hasten to save us, we are lost!" The fire turned on itself and burned out.

Plan your visit: oldursulineconventmuseum.com. 1100 Chartres Street, New Orleans, LA 70116. (504) 529-3040.

168 During one of New Orleans' yellow fever epidemics, Father Peter L. Thevis turned to Saint Roch, invoked against plagues, and pledged to build him a chapel if no one from Father Thevis's parish died from the fever. His flock was spared. A man of his word, the German native erected **St. Roch Chapel** in 1875. Located in St. Roch Cemetery #1, the historic Gothic Revival chapel is filled with anatomical ex-votos and medical artifacts.

Plan your visit: nolacatholiccemeteries.org. 1725 St. Roch Avenue, New Orleans, LA 70117. (504) 482-5065, (504) 304-0576. Call ahead for chapel access and tours.

✤ FINDING FAITH
✝ in Louisiana

Need your prayers expedited? Come to **Our Lady of Guadalupe Church and International Shrine of Saint Jude** in New Orleans. According to lore, around 1921, nuns at the church received a mysterious crate marked "expedite" and found inside a statue of Saint Expedite, a Roman soldier, and a punster at that. In traditional iconography, Saint Expedite — patron saint against procrastination — holds a cross marked *hodie* (Latin for "today") in one hand while one foot stomps a crow (the crow's call sounds like *cras*, Latin for "tomorrow"). The nuns installed the statue inside the church entrance, and it's said the saint has been answering prayers here on the double ever since!

Built in 1826 as a mortuary chapel for yellow fever victims, the church also honors Saint Jude. A shrine awaits petitioners inside the church, while the world's largest Saint Jude statue — seventeen feet tall — stands outside. Also on the grounds is Our Lady of Lourdes Grotto with a catacomb-like candle shrine, where thanksgiving plaques testify to favors received.

Plan your visit: judeshrine.com. 411 N. Rampart Street, New Orleans, LA 70112. (504) 525-1551.

MIDWEST

CANADA

Lake Superior

Lake Michigan

Lake Huron

Lake Ontario

Lake Erie

ul

94

Green Bay

43

Milwaukee

dison ★

dar Rapids

Chicago

ines

eoria

field ★

55

uis

Evansville

gfield

Lansing ★

Grand Rapids

Detroit

Toledo

Cleveland

Fort Wayne

65

70

Indianapolis

Columbus

Cincinnati

Louisville

Frankfort ★

Lexington

81

40

75

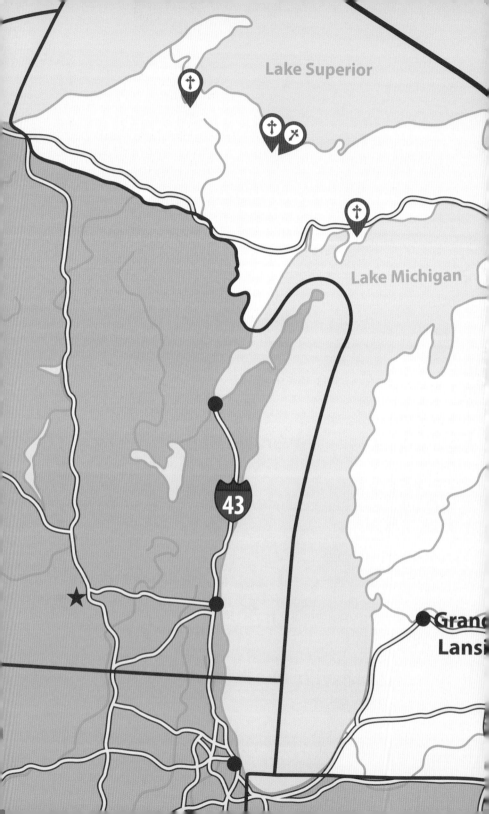

Lake Superior

Lake Michigan

Grand
Lansi

NORTHERN MICHIGAN

 Northern Michigan is Jesuit territory. The great French Jesuit missionary Father Jacques Marquette (1637–1675) (see 99, 170, and 171), who joined French-Canadian explorer Louis Joliet on an epic canoe ride to map the Mississippi River, is buried at **Marquette Mission Park** in St. Ignace, where he established St. Ignace Mission in 1671.

Plan your visit: museumofojibwaculture.net /mission-park.html. 500 N. State Street, St. Ignace, MI 49781. (800) 338-6660.

 The town of St. Ignace is also home to the **Father Marquette National Memorial** in Straits State Park. A monument, interpretive signs, and panoramic views of the Straits of Mackinac take you back to Father Marquette's days. (See 99, 169, and 171.)

Plan your visit: stignace.com/attractions /father-marquette-memorial-2. 720 Church Street, St. Ignace, MI 49781. (906) 643-8620.

 Ever wonder what early missionaries used for a church? Step inside the **Missionary Bark Chapel** at Marquette Park (just below Fort Mackinac) on Mackinac Island. Constructed of birch bark, the replica honors Jesuit priests Claude Dablon and Jacques Marquette, missionaries on the island in 1670–1671. (See 99, 169, and 170.) A towering Father Marquette statue, with rosary and cross, overlooks Haldimand Bay.

Plan your visit: mackinacisland.org/activities /marquette-park. 7200 Huron Street, Mackinac Island, MI 49757. (906) 847-3328.

According to Scripture, God made the world in six days, and it took six days to prepare and attach a seven-ton bronze corpus to a fifty-five-foot-tall redwood cross at the **National Shrine of the Cross in the Woods** at Indian River. Sculpted by Marshall Fredericks, the corpus — twenty-eight feet tall with an arm span of twenty-one feet — was "nailed" to the cross in 1959 with thirteen bolts, each thirty inches long and two inches thick. The cross stands on Calvary Hill, an enormous man-made mountain. Many pilgrims climb the Holy Stairs on their knees.

Plan your visit: crossinthewoods.com. 7078 M-68, Indian River, MI 49749. (231) 238-8973.

The Doll Museum at Indian River is habit forming. Located at the National Shrine of the Cross in the Woods (see 172), the museum houses Sally Rogalski's collection of 525 nun dolls attired in minuscule religious habits. Representing more than 215 religious orders — with habits ranging from black to blue to even pink (note the variety of wimples) — the dolls include a Daughter of Charity in *Flying Nun* headgear, a Carmelite nun with her cream-colored cape, and a Sister of Charity (Saint Elizabeth Ann Seton's order; see 20, 60, and 82) in widow's dress. You'll also find dolled-up bishop, priest, and religious brother mannequins.

Plan your visit: crossinthewoods.com/doll
-museum. 7078 M-68, Indian River, MI 49749.
(231) 238-8973.

 One day, while shoveling a mountain of snow at St.
Mary Catholic Church in Mio, Father Hubert Ra-
kowski promised to build a special shrine to Our
Lady. Honeycombed with grottoes and niches, **Our
Lady of the Woods Shrine** stands forty-three
feet tall and weighs 25,000 tons. The shrine is a
real-life version of the folk tale *Stone Soup*: Many
civic groups, businesses, and church denomina-
tions helped erect the mammoth stone mountain.
Dedicated in 1955, the Marian shrine also honors
the Holy Family, Saint Anne de Beaupré, and Saint
Hubert, patron of hunters.

Plan your visit: olwshrine.org. 100 Deyarmond
Street, Mio, MI 48647. (989) 826-5509.

SOUTHERN MICHIGAN

 It's Christmas Eve year-round at the **Silent Night
Memorial Chapel** in Frankenmuth. Located on
the grounds of Bronner's Christmas Wonderland,
the octagonal chapel is a replica of the Stille Nacht
Kapelle in Oberndorf, Austria, that marks the site
where "Silent Night" was sung for the first time on
Christmas Eve in 1818. The Frankenmuth chapel
includes an altar, an 1818 hand-carved crucifix,
and displays giving the story of Christ's birth in
multiple languages. Outside, plaques translate "Si-

lent Night" into more than 300 tongues, including Apache and Braille.

Plan your visit: bronners.com/history-of -silent-night-chapel. 25 Christmas Lane, Frankenmuth, MI 48734. (989) 652-9931.

When the Ku Klux Klan burned a cross in front of Royal Oak's newly opened Saint Therese of Lisieux Church in 1926, Father Charles Coughlin erected a "cross they could not burn": a ten-story, zig-zag Art Deco tower with a twenty-eight-foot-tall exterior carving of Christ crucified. Other carvings include the Seven Last Words of Christ and the archangels. Known today as the **National Shrine of the Little Flower Basilica**, the shrine includes an

octagonal church (the eight sides signify the Resurrection on the "eighth day"), with seating on two levels. Exterior stonework features carved flowers representing the native flowers of American states.

Plan your visit: shrinechurch.com. 2100 W. Twelve Mile Road, Royal Oak, MI 48073. (248) 541-4122.

DETROIT

When pilgrims seek Saint Anne's intercession at **Ste. Anne de Detroit Church**, they know they have divine favor. Anne is the grandmother of Jesus, and it's hard for grandkids to say no to Grandmother! One of the country's oldest parishes (see Florida and New Mexico for older parishes), Ste. Anne's dates from 1701, when French explorer Antoine de la Mothe Cadillac founded Detroit. Today's grand church, erected in 1886 in Gothic Revival style, is the final resting place of legendary Father Gabriel Richard, PSS (1767–1832). An advocate of education for women, Indians, and the deaf, the French native cofounded the University of Michigan in 1817.

Plan your visit: ste-anne.org. 1000 Sainte Anne Street, Detroit, MI 48216. (313) 496-1701.

When **St. Aloysius Catholic Church** — an Italian-French Romanesque beauty with twenty-six different kinds of marble — was being built in 1930, it had a problem. Where to put the people? The building was hemmed in and had a very narrow footprint: seventy-two by 100 feet. Architects created the "divine theater." Everyone, whether seated on the main level, balcony, or lower level (gazing upward), can see the altar. Dubbed Everybody's Church, St. Aloysius is also known for its Byzantine-style mosaics. The sanctuary centerpiece portrays Christ the Good Shepherd with rows of sheep at his feet.

Plan your visit: stalsdetroit.com. 1234 Washington Boulevard, Detroit, MI 48226. (313) 237-5810.

Old St. Mary's Church in Greektown District "rocks." In the early twentieth century, Father Joseph Wuest constructed three grottoes inside the cavernous church: the Grotto of Gethsemane (Christ's agony in the Garden of Olives), the Baptismal Grotto (John the Baptist baptizing Jesus in the River Jordan, complete with running water), and the Lourdes Grotto (a replica of the famous French shrine). The striking 1884 red-brick structure combines facets of Pisan Romanesque and Venetian Renaissance architecture and features a ninety-foot-high, richly frescoed ceiling.

Plan your visit: oldstmarysdetroit.com. 646 Monroe Avenue, Detroit, MI 48226. (313) 961-8711.

When a ruinous depression swept the nation in the 1890s, **Sweetest Heart of Mary Church** — erected by Polish immigrants for $125,000, a princely sum in that day — was heavily in debt and sold at auction for $30,000. Sweet on Mary, families mortgaged their homes and bought back the Gothic Revival gem. And no wonder! The church is a celestial work of art: spectacular stained-glass windows crowned with Stars of David, rows of lights on the apse ceiling that resemble rays from heaven, and statues and murals galore. Everywhere you look, it's a paradise on earth.

Plan your visit: motherofdivinemercy.org. 4440 Russell Street, Detroit, MI 48207. (313) 831-6659.

A doorkeeper in life, Blessed Solanus Casey (1870–1957) is still opening doors — to heaven. Kneeling before his tomb at the **Solanus Casey Center**, part of St. Bonaventure Monastery, pilgrims invoke the Capuchin Franciscan's intercession and, in Solanus-style, "Thank God ahead of time" for answered prayer. Also see the Creation Garden (sculptures depicting Saint Francis's Canticle of the Creatures), Blessed Solanus Museum, Beatitude Statues (bronze figures of eight twentieth-century people who exemplify the Beatitudes), and St. Bonaventure Chapel, where Solanus played Christmas hymns on his violin to the Baby Jesus. (See 394.)

Plan your visit: solanuscenter.org. 1780 Mount Elliott Street, Detroit, MI 48207. (313) 579-2100.

✠ FINDING FAITH
in Michigan

Strap on a pair of really big snowshoes if you want to retrace the footsteps of Venerable Frederic Baraga (1797–1868). Dubbed the Snowshoe Priest, the Slovenian native trudged hundreds of miles over frozen lakes and through forests to tend to his scattered flock. In summer, he traveled by canoe or boat. (See 242.) You can catch his spirit at these Upper Peninsula sites:

When Father Baraga first visited the Chippewa Indians at Indian Lake in 1832, they were building a log chapel in anticipation of his arrival. Rebuilt in the 1980s, the **Indian Lake Mission Chapel** near Manistique is noted for both its stations of the cross painted on leather and Indian cemetery with traditional burial houses.

Plan your visit: visitmanistique.com/baraga .shtml. Off M-94 on the east side of Indian Lake, near the golf course, Manistique, MI 49854. (800) 342-4282.

Consecrated the first bishop of today's Diocese of Marquette in 1853, Bishop Baraga moved his see from Sault Ste. Marie to Marquette in 1866. The **Baraga House** — his humble "episcopal palace" — preserves his legacy and the room where he died.

Plan your visit: bishopbaraga.org. 615 S. Fourth Street, Marquette, MI 49855. (906) 227-9117.

Present-day **St. Peter Cathedral**, dedicated in 1939, contains Bishop Baraga's crypt, where devotees seek his intercession.

Plan your visit: stpetercathedral.org. 311 W. Baraga Avenue, Marquette, MI 49855. (906) 226-6548.

Nothing captures the Baraga legend like the **Shrine of the Snowshoe Priest at L'Anse**. Overlooking the bay and standing six stories tall, a thirty five-foot statue of the good bishop holds a pair of twenty-six-foot snowshoes in one hand and a seven-foot cross in the other. The five teepees represent the Indian missions that he founded.

Plan your visit: exploringthenorth.com/bishopb /shrine.html. 17570 US Highway 41, L'Anse, MI 49801. (906) 524-7021.

EASTERN OHIO

Wherever Our Lady of Mariapoch goes, pilgrims follow. The story begins in 1696 in Pócs, Hungary, when an icon of the Most Holy *Theotokos* (Mother of God) began to weep and many miraculous healings were reported. When Emperor Leopold I transferred the icon to St. Stephen's Cathedral in Vienna, the bishop ordered a replica icon for the Pócs church. In 1715, the replica began to weep. It wept again in 1905. Hungarians brought the devotion to Ohio and in 1956 dedicated the **Shrine of Our Lady of Mariapoch** near Burton. The Byzantine retreat includes Our Lady's chapel, replicas of the weeping icon, and numerous outdoor prayer stations.

Plan your visit: shrineofmariapoch.com. 17486 Mumford Road, Burton, OH 44021. (216) 469-1425.

Joy to the world, the Lord is come … to the **Nativity of the Lord Jesus Catholic Church** in Akron, the 1991 barn-like design recalling Christ's birth in a stable. Stained glass echoes the Christmas story, while the Bethlehem Cave recreates the Church of the Nativity in Bethlehem — from its low doors to the star on the floor marking Jesus' birthplace. For more joy, visit the Nativity Museum, a collection of more than 500 Nativity sets, crafted from every medium imaginable, even marbles.

Plan your visit: nativityofthelord.org. 2425 Myersville Road, Akron, OH 44312. (330) 699-5086.

In 1960, Maronite priest Father Peter Eid saw a sign: eighty acres for sale. A perfect site for a shrine, he thought, before contacting the owner. "I will never sell to a Catholic," she replied. Father Eid and priest-friends began a novena. Several days later, she called him and said, "Priest, come and take the land. Your Lady is bothering me in my sleep!" Located in North Jackson, the **Basilica and National Shrine of Our Lady of Lebanon**, with a fifty-foot-tall stone tower, is a one-third-scale replica of a Maronite shrine in Harissa, Lebanon. Sixty-four steps (one step for every Rosary prayer) spiral to a granite statue of Our Lady at the top. The annual Assumption pilgrimage, a triduum, is held in mid-August.

Plan your visit: ourladyoflebanonshrine.com. 2759 N. Lipkey Road, Jackson, OH 44451. (330) 538-3351.

Want to visit Italy, France, and the Holy Land in one trip? You can at **Franciscan University** in Steubenville. The Portiuncula Chapel recreates Saint Francis's Portiuncula at Assisi, Italy; the Marian Grotto recalls the grotto at Lourdes, France; and the outdoor Christmas Crèche, with near life-size figures, pays homage to Christ's birth at Bethlehem. Behind the Portiuncula Chapel, a staircase takes you down to bronze stations of the cross, designed by artist Carmelo Puzzolo and cast in the same molds as the stations on Mount Krizevac in Medjugorje.

Plan your visit: franciscan.edu. 1235 University Boulevard, Steubenville, OH 43952. (740) 283-3771.

186 When Mother Mary wants stained-glass windows, nothing can stop their shipment — not even the British blockade of Europe during World War I! That's one of the fascinating stories at the **Basilica of Saint Mary of the Assumption** in Marietta. The 1904 Spanish Renaissance beauty is also touted for its German artworks (the Assumption of Mary is heaven itself) and the *Via Lucis* (the Way of Light), an Eastertide devotion that focuses on Jesus' life after the crucifixion. The fourteen stations include the Resurrection, Jesus revealing himself in the Breaking of the Bread, and Jesus sending forth the Holy Spirit.

Plan your visit: stmarysmarietta.org. 506 Fourth Street, Marietta, OH 45750. (740) 373-3643.

WESTERN OHIO

 187 Every day is All Saints Day at **Maria Stein Shrine of the Holy Relics** in Maria Stein. The former convent houses more than 1,200 relics of saints — from the Three Kings to a piece of Veronica's veil to twentieth-century martyr Blessed Miguel Pro. The shrine was founded in 1875 when relics (many rescued from Italy's pawnshops and street markets) accumulated by two priests, Father Francis de Sales Brunner, CPPS (see 189) and Father J. M. Gartner, were combined into one collection. A painting of Maria Stein (German for "Mary of the Rock") replicates a miraculous image at Mariastein, Switzerland.

Plan your visit: mariasteinshrine.org. 2291 St. Johns Road, Maria Stein, OH 45860. (419) 925-4532.

St. Peter in Chains Cathedral [190]

188 On May 24, 1875, when a statue of Our Lady of Consolation was being carried in a seven-mile procession from St. Nicholas Church in Frenchtown to a new church in Carey, the pouring rain parted like the Red Sea. Rain fell on all sides, but not one drop fell on Our Lady or anyone in the procession. Pilgrims began flocking here, and today's Romanesque **Basilica and National Shrine of Our Lady of Consolation** opened in 1924. The Shrine Park includes stations of the cross and an outdoor altar, located under a seventy-five-foot arch with a golden Mary statue on top. An annual procession is held in mid-August.

Plan your visit: olcshrine.com. 315 Clay Street, Carey, OH 43316. (419) 396-7107.

189 There's a saint for every pilgrim at the **Sorrowful Mother Shrine** in Bellevue. Founded in 1850 by Father Francis de Sales Brunner, CPPS (see 187), the 120-acre wooded retreat includes the Sorrowful Mother Shrine Chapel with large ceiling paintings of Our Lady's Seven Sorrows, an outdoor Pietà Chapel, and dozens of grottoes and shrines honoring Mary and a multitude of other saints. Of special note are the Lourdes Grotto and illuminated stations of the cross.

Plan your visit: sorrowfulmothershrine.org. 4106 State Route 269, Bellevue, OH 44811. (419) 483-3435.

CINCINNATI

Saint Peter in Chains Cathedral is like no other American cathedral: It honors the imprisoned Saint Peter (he's miraculously set free in a stunning mosaic). Constructed of limestone, the 1841 Greek Revival structure, with a striking 220-foot single spire, is humorously dubbed the Bishop Factory: More than twenty bishops have been consecrated here. Must-see artworks include the thirty-five-foot-tall Venetian glass mosaic of Christ giving Peter the keys to the kingdom, Greek-themed murals depicting the stations of the cross, and a processional crucifix with a corpus by Benvenuto Cellini (1500–1571).

Plan your visit: stpeterinchainscathedral.org. 325 W. Eighth Street, Cincinnati, OH 45202. (513) 421-5354.

St. Rose of Lima Church is one of a kind. Painted on a rear brick wall facing the Ohio River, a flood gauge records the water levels of fifteen major floods. In 1937, the river crested at eighty feet (floodwaters invade the church basement at fifty-seven feet)! Flooding hasn't been St. Rose's only calamity. In 1894, an altar boy lighting candles for a wedding accidentally set the 1867 Romanesque church on fire. The couple got married at a nearby church and then returned to watch the blaze.

Plan your visit: strosecincinnati.org. 2501 Riverside Drive, Cincinnati, OH 45202. (513) 871-1162.

(192) They don't make churches anymore like **Old St. Mary's Church** in the Over-the-Rhine Historic District. The city's oldest extant church, St. Mary's — a heavenly mix of Greek Revival exterior with Baroque and Romanesque interior — was constructed in 1841 of handmade bricks baked by women in their home ovens. You're not having an apparition if you visit more than once and see a different large painting of Mary over the high altar! Paintings of the Immaculate Conception, the Annunciation, and the Coronation of Mary are hung in rotation, and you never know which Mary will appear.

Plan your visit: oldstmarys.org. 123 E. Thirteenth Street, Cincinnati, OH 45202. (513) 721-2988.

(193) "Pray the steps" at **Holy Cross-Immaculata Church.** Every Good Friday (and at other times of the year too), thousands of pilgrims climb approximately 100 steps to the hilltop church, saying a Hail Mary or other prayer on each step. Some make the journey on their knees. It's said that during a devilish storm at sea, Archbishop John Baptist Purcell vowed to erect a church atop the city's highest peak if he lived. The Gothic Revival limestone church was erected in 1859. Step inside and study Johann Schmitt's Annunciation painting; some see a mysterious face near the top. (See 204.)

Plan your visit: 2011.hciparish.org. 30 Guido Street, Cincinnati, OH 45202. (513) 721-6544.

✝ FINDING FAITH
in Ohio

Holy Toledo! What a cathedral! Purple, green, red, and chartreuse Spanish roof tiles, a six-foot-tall bronze tabernacle, a mural with a redheaded archangel Gabriel — there's no church like **Our Lady, Queen of the Most Holy Rosary Cathedral** in Toledo. In fact, Rosary Cathedral, as it's called locally, is the world's only Plateresque-style cathedral. Designed after the Primate Cathedral of Saint Mary in Toledo, Spain, Rosary Cathedral's cornerstone was laid in 1926 — exactly 700 years after construction commenced on its medieval sister.

Your eyes will hardly be able to take in the artistic wonders. Fifty exterior bas-relief panels illustrate the history of the Catholic Church, while inside, artist Felix Lieftuchter's epic mural (see 108 and Finding Faith in Utah) begins above the Rose Window with his *Creatio Mundi* (the opening chapter in Genesis), navigates through biblical history along the Spanish vaulted ceiling, and culminates with the glorious apse mural of the Crowning of Mary, Queen of Heaven. Other murals commemorate the Battles of Lepanto in 1571 and Temesvar in 1716 — victories attributed to the power of the Rosary. You can pray the Rosary by following the mysteries (along with their Old Testament counterparts) painted along the dome-like ceilings in the side aisles.

Plan your visit: rosarycathedral.org. 2535 Collingwood Boulevard, Toledo, OH 43610. (419) 244-9575.

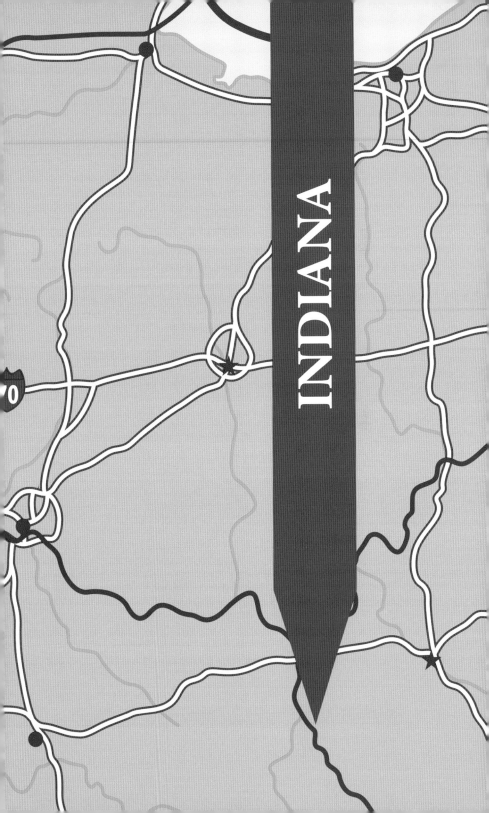

NORTHERN INDIANA

Walk with Christ at the **Shrine of Christ's Passion** in St. John. Lining a hilly trail reminiscent of Jerusalem, forty life-size bronze sculptures recreate Jesus' last days on earth, including the Last Supper, the apostles in the Garden of Gethsemane, Christ's burial, and the breathtaking Ascension. Sculpted by Mickey Wells, the statues are accompanied by audio reflections. Other must-see sculptures include Moses at Mount Sinai with the Ten Commandments and *Our Lady of the New Millennium*, a thirty-three-foot stainless steel wonder sculpted by Charles C. Parks (see Finding Faith in Delaware and 407). St. John the Evangelist Church (see 195) stands sentinel on a hill above.

Plan your visit: shrineofchristspassion.org. 10630 Wicker Avenue, St. John, IN 46373. (855) 277-7474.

Like its namesake, **St. John the Evangelist Church**, in St. John, went out into the world. When the original log church, built in the 1830s, was replaced by larger churches, the log structure was subsequently moved to the fairgrounds, to a school, back to the fairgrounds, and finally to its original home on St. John's property. Its traveling days over, the little log church is now a perpetual adoration chapel. If not the country's oldest adoration chapel, it's certainly one of the most unique and well traveled.

Plan your visit: stjohnparish.org. Corner of Ninety-Third Street and US Highway 41, St John, IN 46373. (219) 365-5678.

SOUTHERN INDIANA

 During World War II, Catholic Italian prisoners-of-war incarcerated at **Camp Atterbury** near Edinburgh had a dream: Build a chapel where they could pray. Permission was granted, and in 1943 they began constructing the eleven-by-sixteen-foot Chapel in the Meadow from scrap materials found around the camp. In Italian style, the prisoners, many of them artisans, painted frescoes of Our Lady, Jesus, and cherubs on the walls and ceiling, and built an altar to their Lord.

Plan your visit: atterburymuscatatuck.in.ng.mil. 3008 Old Hospital Road, Edinburgh, IN 46124. (812) 526-1499.

 Per square inch, tiny **Oldenburg** may be the most Catholic town in America. Dubbed the Village of Spires, the charming German town, platted in 1837, is dwarfed by steeples. A walking tour includes the Sisters of St. Francis's convent chapel (1889) with its distinctive Baroque tower, the convent mortuary chapel (1900), the Old Stone Church (1846) with a Zwiebelturm (onion dome), and Holy Family Church (1862), known for its annual Corpus Christi processions that began in 1846. Around 1890, the church got a new spire — the town "aspired" to have the tallest steeple around!

Plan your visit: franklincountyin.com/resources /brochures. (866) 647-6555; holyfamilychurcholdenburgin.com. 3027 Pearl Street, Oldenburg, IN 47036. (812) 934-3013.

The statue of Our Lady of Consolation at **St. Augustine Catholic Church** in rural Leopold tells a curious tale. During the Civil War, three Union soldiers from Leopold were incarcerated at Andersonville Prison (see 130) and vowed to erect a shrine to Our Lady if they survived. After the war, one soldier traveled to Belgium and commissioned a duplicate statue of Our Lady of Consolation. Or did he steal the statue, as some purport, sparking an international incident? According to some accounts, when King Leopold II of Belgium learned the statue was in a village called Leopold, he was so flattered that he allowed it to stay there. The beautiful statue shows Mary holding the Christ Child, a silver heart suspended from her right hand.

Plan your visit: 18020 Lafayette Street, Leopold, IN 47551. (812) 843-5143.

Laboring in Kentucky's coal mines during World War II, German prisoner-of-war and artist Herbert Jogerst pledged to do "something for God" if he ever regained his freedom. In 1956, a doctor commissioned him to sculpt **Christ of the Ohio**, a towering statue with outstretched arms overlooking the Ohio River near Troy. The monument, visible up and down the river and on the highway below, is illuminated at night. Jogerst's "something" multiplied: He created artworks for Saint Meinrad Archabbey (see 200) and for churches and monasteries across numerous states.

Plan your visit: troyindiana.com/christ-of-the-ohio. 800 Market Street, Troy, IN 47588. (812) 547-7501.

200 A mighty fortress is our God, and the Benedictine monks' **Archabbey Church of Our Lady of Einsiedeln** at St. Meinrad is his bulwark. The turn-of-the-twentieth-century hilltop church, with castle-like turrets and impenetrable sandstone construction, looks like a page out of medieval history. Noted artworks include murals of Saints Meinrad and Benedict (note artist Dom Gregory de Wit's self-portrait), a marble floor Star of David (created from six colors of marble with overlapping triangles), and three marble statues sculpted by Herbert Jogerst (see 199) over the entrance. Founded by Swiss monks in 1854, the Archabbey is one of eleven archabbeys in the world.

Plan your visit: saintmeinrad.org. 200 Hill Drive, St. Meinrad, IN 47577. (800) 581-6905.

201 Need a miracle? Visit **Monte Cassino Shrine** near Saint Meinrad Archabbey, at St. Meinrad. When an 1871 smallpox epidemic claimed the lives of several villagers and infected four more at the abbey, students made a pilgrimage to the shrine and began a novena to Our Lady of Monte Cassino. Not one new case of smallpox broke out. Based on a picture of an early shrine at Einsiedeln, Switzerland, the hilltop chapel is adorned with Marian murals and a hand-carved Swiss statue of Our Lady.

Plan your visit: saintmeinrad.org. 13312 Monte Cassino Shrine Road, St. Meinrad, IN 47577. (800) 581-6905.

202 When Saint Theodore Guerin (1798–1856) and another Sister of Providence were returning from France in 1843, a terrible storm threatened the ship. Mother Theodore invoked Saint Anne's protection and the roaring ocean calmed. Back home at their convent in **Saint Mary-of-the-Woods,** Mother Theodore, foundress of the religious community, built a tiny log chapel of thanksgiving, replaced by Saint Anne's Shell Chapel in 1875. The nautical-themed chapel tells in exquisite shell mosaics the adventurous life of Mother Theodore. Another must-see site is the Shrine of Saint Mother Theodore Guerin, Mother's final resting place.

Plan your visit: spsmw.org. 1 Sisters of Providence Road, Saint Mary-of-the-Woods, IN 47876. (800) 860-1840.

✚ FINDING FAITH
in Indiana

Want to score a spiritual touchdown? Come to **Notre Dame University** at Notre Dame. Decorating the south exterior wall of Hesburgh Library is the famous Jesus mural *The Word of Life*. During football season, the 132-foot-tall Jesus — his upraised arms visible over the north end zone of Notre Dame Stadium — becomes known as Touchdown Jesus! Win or lose, there's more to see at Notre Dame, founded by French native and Holy Cross priest Father Edwin Sorin in 1842.

The Basilica of the Sacred Heart (finished in 1888) will steal yours. Gothic inspired, the church claims the world's largest collection of nineteenth-century French stained glass — more than 116 spectacular windows crafted by Carmelite nuns in Le Mans, France. A popular marriage proposal site, the Grotto of Our Lady of Lourdes is one-seventh the size of its famous French mother. But it's the Main Building (1879) that catapults eyes heavenward. Standing atop the gold-leafed dome is a nineteen-foot, two-ton statue of Our Lady, Notre Dame.

Plan your visit: nd.edu. 100 Eck Center Drive, Notre Dame, IN 46556. (574) 631-5726.

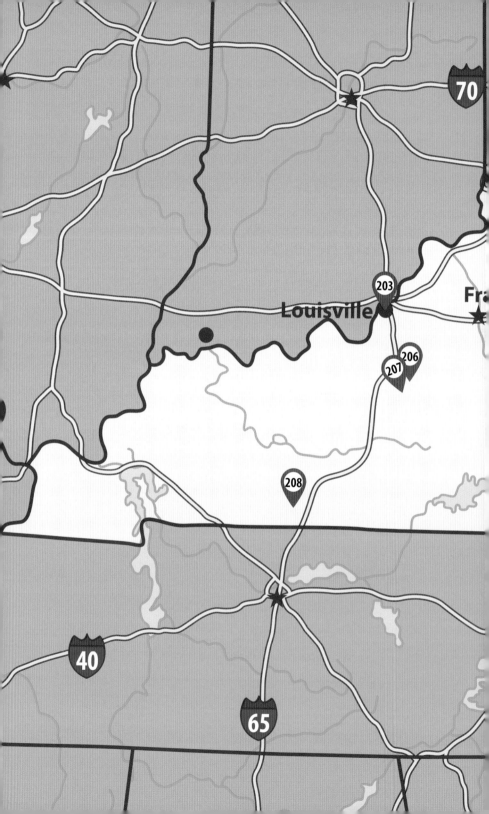

203 "Dem old bones" at **St. Martin of Tours Catholic Church** in Louisville are going to rise again! On New Year's Eve, 1901, the parish received a most unusual delivery: the third-century skeletons of Saints Bonosa, a virgin, and Magnus, a Roman centurion. Tradition holds that when Bonosa was being put to death at the Roman Colosseum in A.D. 207 for her Christian beliefs, Magnus jumped into the ring to save her and was killed himself. Today, they rest in glory — wearing martyrs' crowns and velvet gowns — in glass reliquaries below the two side altars.

Plan your visit: stmartinoftourschurch.org. 639 S. Shelby Street, Louisville, KY 40202. (502) 582-2827.

204 Heaven is our destination, but in Covington it's surely **Mother of God Church**. Erected in 1870, the breathtaking Italian Renaissance church radiates heaven's glory in German. (The German name is *Mutter Gottes Kirche*.) German-born parishioner Johann Schmitt (see 193) painted five large murals depicting the Joyful Mysteries of the Rosary (note the Nativity scene over the altar), while Munich stained glass presents Mary's life. The Litany of Loreto is written in German above window tops; the floor is laid with German Mettlach tiles. If that doesn't get your attention, the 200-foot-tall German clock towers will.

Plan your visit: mother-of-god.org. 119 W. Sixth Street, Covington, KY 41011. (859) 291-2288.

Crestview Hills isn't short on lore. As the story goes, Benedictine monks at **Monte Casino Monastery** near Covington built the six-by-nine-foot stone chapel in 1878 as a retreat from working in monastery vineyards. In 1920, when Prohibition banned the sale of wine across state lines, the monks — now without a source of income — left. Raiders stripped the door, stained glass, foot scrapers, and even the little stone steeple with hand-chiseled cross. Amazingly, in 1965, when word circulated about the chapel's restoration and move to Thomas More University, the steeple and cross were returned.

205

Plan your visit: thomasmore.edu/about/history /monte-casino. 333 Thomas More Parkway, Crestview Hills, KY 41017. (859) 341-5800.

When Bishop Benedict Joseph Flaget (see Finding Faith in Kentucky) erected his Greek Revival "Cathedral in the Wilderness" — today's **Basilica of St. Joseph Proto-Cathedral** — in Bardstown in 1816, it was literally hand-built. Settlers made the bricks, nearly one million of them, on site and turned tree trunks into stately columns. The artwork is worthy of a museum. Gifts of Pope Leo XII, King Louis Philippe of France, and King Francis I of the Two Sicilies, the masterpieces include works by Bartolomé Esteban Murillo (see 125, 134, and 146), Mattia Preti, and Anthony Van Dyck. Outside, the Ten Commandments are written over the arched windows.

Plan your visit: stjosephbasilica.org. 310 W. Stephen Foster Avenue, Bardstown, KY 40004. (502) 348-3126.

 "Return to me," says the Lord. As the story goes, in 1805 Trappist monks from Switzerland settled in Kentucky but left in 1809. Four decades later, in 1847, Trappist monks from France arrived, looking for land, and were directed to the original Trappist site. It was here at the **Abbey of Gethsemani**, in Trappist, that Trappist monk Thomas Merton (1915–1968) penned his best-selling autobiography, *The Seven Storey Mountain*. After visiting his grave — he's known here as Father Louis Merton — many pilgrims hike the knobs. Get a map before setting out; even monks have gotten lost in nature's spectacular maze!

Plan your visit: monks.org. 3642 Monks Road, Trappist, KY 40051. (502) 549-3117.

You can always recognize the Fathers of Mercy: They wear the congregation's badge, the Return of the Prodigal Son, on their black cassocks with black cinctures. True to the congregation's charism, the 2008 Romanesque-style **Chapel of Divine Mercy** at Auburn extends mercy. Above the nave arches is written the Divine Mercy Chaplet, while murals of the Divine Mercy, the Good Shepherd, The Last Supper, and others offer forgiveness and hope. Study the animated faces, all stories in themselves.

Plan your visit: fathersofmercy.com. 806 Shaker Museum Road, Auburn, KY 42206. (270) 542-4146.

✠ FINDING FAITH
in Kentucky

Constructed like a cocoon over and around St. Louis Church in 1849 (the church was later deconstructed and carried, piece by piece, out the front doors), the **Cathedral of the Assumption** in Louisville is both an artistic paradise and a history lesson in frontier Catholicism. During the Bloody Monday election riots of August 6, 1855 — incited by a newspaper editorial speculating immigrant vote tampering and a papist takeover — nativist Know Nothings attacked German and Irish Catholic settlers, and torched their homes and businesses. At least twenty-two persons died. Armed rioters also searched the cathedral and other local Catholic churches for weapons, but none were found.

Step inside the Victorian Gothic Revival church and you'll be whisked into Marian splendor. More than 8,000 six-pointed Stars of David (an early symbol of the Blessed Mother) of twenty-four-karat gold leaf sparkle from the deep blue ceiling, while the 1883 Coronation window, one of the country's largest and oldest hand-painted glass windows, honors Mary, Queen of Heaven. The four sanctuary paintings were a gift of Pope Gregory XVI to Bishop Benedict Joseph Flaget (see 206), the first shepherd of today's Archdiocese of Louisville.

Plan your visit: cathedraloftheassumption .org. 433 S. Fifth Street, Louisville, KY 40202. (502) 582-2971.

Lake Superior

Madison

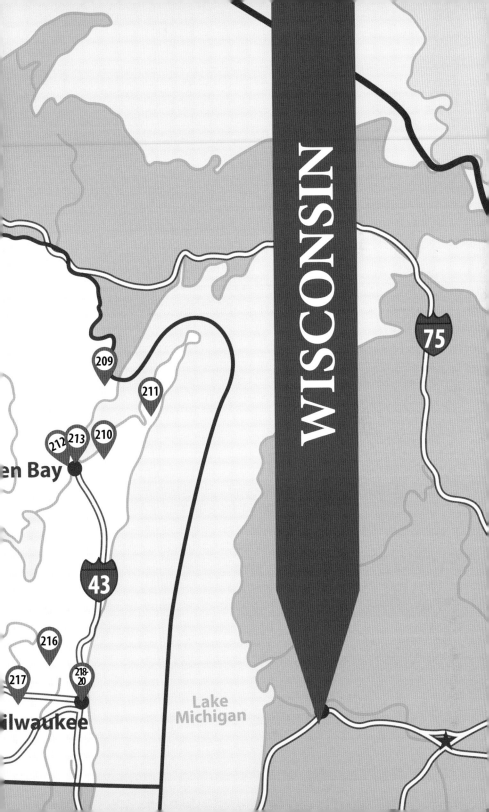

NORTHERN WISCONSIN

 On October 8, 1871, the Great Chicago Fire raced across the Windy City. That same night an even mightier blaze, the Great Peshtigo Fire — the deadliest fire in American history — roared across northeast Wisconsin. Some 1,500 to 2,500 persons perished. Racing ahead of the inferno, Father Peter Pernin ran to St. Mary's Church in Peshtigo and rescued the wooden tabernacle with the Blessed Sacrament. He loaded the tabernacle in a wagon and then pushed the wagon into the Peshtigo River. The next day the tabernacle was found floating on a log, unharmed. The **Miraculous Tabernacle** is displayed at the Peshtigo Fire Museum during the summer and at St. Mary's Church the other months. (See 210.)

Plan your visit: stmaryjosephedwardparish.org. 171 S. Wood Avenue, Peshtigo, WI 54157. (715) 582-3876; peshtigofiremuseum.com. 400 Oconto Avenue, Peshtigo, WI 54157. (715) 582-3244.

 You're on holy ground at the **National Shrine of Our Lady of Good Help** in Champion. In 1859, Our Lady appeared three times to Adele Brise, a twenty-eight-year-old Belgian immigrant. "Gather the children in this wild country and teach them what they should know for salvation," Our Lady told her. Thus began Adele's ministry to the children. Meanwhile, a wooden chapel (and successive buildings, including today's Tudor Gothic chapel) went up. When the Great Peshtigo Fire of October 8, 1871 engulfed the area (see 209), Adele and farm folk processed around the chapel with a statue of Our Lady and prayed. Heaven sent a downpour; the chapel and the people were saved. The shrine is the only Church-approved Marian apparition site in the United States.

Plan your visit: championshrine.org. 4047 Chapel Drive, Champion, WI 54229. (920) 315-0398.

Like a string of rosary beads, dozens of tiny **Belgian Roadside Chapels** dot the countryside in the southern Door Peninsula. Built by Belgian settlers in the Old World tradition, the family wayside chapels — some nine by seven feet — were just big enough for an altar, a few statues, and a kneeler. The houses of prayer were often dedicated to a saint for a favor received ("If you help me, I'll build you a chapel") and were always open to passersby. Though privately owned, many chapels remain open to the public today.

Plan your visit: belgianheritagecenter.org. (920) 825-1328; doorcounty.com. (800) 527-3529.

When Father Claude Allouez, a French Jesuit missionary and explorer, was evangelizing the Indians in northeastern Wisconsin c. 1670, his dwelling and church was a bark chapel that resembled an Iroquois longhouse. A replica of a **Bark Chapel** — a sapling framework with bark covering — can be explored at Heritage Hill State Historical Park in Green Bay. (See 171.)

Plan your visit: heritagehillgb.org. 2640 S. Webster Avenue, Green Bay, WI 54301. (800) 721-5150.

213 ▶ Some might call **St. Willebrord Church** in Green Bay "the church of the Hail Mary pass." Legendary Green Bay Packers football coach Vince Lombardi attended Mass here and undoubtedly begged heaven for a pigskin favor or two. Erected in 1891 by Dutch settlers in High Victorian Gothic style, St. Willebrord Church (spelled with an "e" rather than an "i" because stonemasons carved the name wrong) is one of the stops on the Packers Heritage Trail. A plaque outside the red-brick church tells the story.

Plan your visit: stwillys.org. 209 S. Adams Street, Green Bay, WI 54301. (920) 435-2016; packersheritagetrail.com.

214 ▶ When Father Philip Wagner made a promise, he kept it. While studying for the priesthood in Europe in 1912, he fell gravely ill. He visited the Grotto of Our Lady of Lourdes in France and vowed to build her a shrine if he regained his health and was ordained. Father Wagner, with cobuilder Edmund Rybicki, not only erected a Lourdes shrine but dozens more! Constructed of rock, shells, marbles, tiles, and whatnot, **Rudolph Grotto Gardens** in Rudolph is known for its above-ground Wonder Cave, a Roman-like catacomb with twenty-six shrines alone.

Plan your visit: rudolphgrotto.org. 6957 Grotto Avenue, Rudolph, WI 54475. (715) 435-3120.

SOUTHERN WISCONSIN

Befriend Saint Philomena and she will pay you back! That's the story of Old Jake, a seventy-six-year-old cripple who helped erect the **National Shrine of Saint Philomena**, adjacent to St. Mary Help of Christians Church in Briggsville. On the fourth day of construction, Old Jake was healed and never used a cane again. Erected in 1950, the outdoor shrine resembles the Roman dungeon where the thirteen-year-old Greek virgin-princess was tortured and beheaded c. A.D. 304 for refusing to marry the emperor Diocletian. The shrine boasts a larger-than-life Carrara marble statue of the wonder-working saint and stained glass that illumines her heroic life.

Plan your visit: saintphilomenashrine.org. N565 County Road A, Briggsville, WI 53920. (608) 981-2282.

According to lore, in the 1860s atop a steep hill near Hubertus, a hermit cried out to the Lord and was healed of a partial paralysis. Judging by the discarded medical aids, healings are still happening on this sacred mountain, known today as the **Basilica and National Shrine of Mary Help of Christians at Holy Hill**. After praying in the 1926 neo-Romanesque church, some pilgrims climb 178 winding steps to an observation deck in one of the twin towers. If that doesn't take your breath away, the view will.

Plan your visit: holyhill.com. 1525 Carmel Road, Hubertus, WI 53033. (262) 628-1838.

Schoenstatt Chapel and Retreat Center at Waukesha (see 221). **217**

Plan your visit: schoenstattwisconsin.org /retreat-center. W284 N698 Cherry Lane, Waukesha, WI 53188. (262) 522-4300.

America's oldest church isn't American. It's French! **218** Erected c. 1420, Milwaukee's **St. Joan of Arc Chapel** — originally called Chapelle de St. Martin de Seyssuel — once graced the Rhône River hamlet of Chasse. In 1926, Gertrude Hill Gavin, daughter of railroad baron James J. Hill, acquired the little Gothic chapel and had it shipped, stone by stone, to her French chateau on Long Island, New York. When a 1962 fire gutted the chateau but miraculously spared the attached chapel, the new owners donated the gem to Marquette University. Don't miss the Joan of Arc Stone. According to lore, Saint Joan of Arc (1412–1431) prayed on this very stone and then kissed it before going off to war.

Plan your visit: marquette.edu/st-joan-of-arc -chapel. 1250 W. Wisconsin Avenue, Milwaukee, WI 53233. (800) 222-6544.

Schoenstatt Chapel in Milwaukee (see 221). **219**

Plan your visit: schoenstattwisconsin.org. 5424 W. Bluemound Road, Milwaukee, WI 53208. (414) 453-5344.

220 When Father Wilhelm Grutza built a church, he built a world destination. Designed after Saint Peter's Basilica in Rome, Milwaukee's Polish **Basilica of St. Josaphat** will wow you: marbleized columns, dozens of murals, Austrian stained glass, and a dome larger than the Taj Mahal's. Father Grutza also built green. When the United States Post Office and Custom House in Chicago was slated for demolition, he bought the building, had it dismantled, and shipped — carved stone, light fixtures, granite columns, even doorknobs — by rail to Milwaukee. Completed in 1901, the basilica is often called an

"ignored wonder of the world."

Plan your visit: thebasilica.org. 2333 S. Sixth Street, Milwaukee, WI 53215. (414) 645-5623.

Wherever Schoenstatt — a Marian movement of religious and moral renewal — puts down roots, up goes a replica of the Original Shrine (as it's called) in Schoenstatt, Germany. The movement began in 1914 when Father Joseph Kentenich asked Our Lady to dwell in the centuries-old chapel and work miracles of grace. Around 250 **Schoenstatt Chapels** exist worldwide, with ten in the United States. The first American chapel was erected in 1952 in Madison. The chapels with steeply pitched roofs seat thirty and are filled with identical images, including a picture of Our Lady under the title Mother Thrice Admirable. Schoenstatt chapels are also found in Florida, Minnesota, Nebraska, New York, and Texas, and in Waukesha and Milwaukee, Wisconsin. (See 27, 136, 217, 219, 248, 296, 353, 358, and 368.)

Plan your visit: schoenstatt.de; schoenstattwisconsin .org/madison. 5901 Cottage Grove Road, Madison, WI 53718. (608) 222-7208.

For Truth and Wisdom, stop in **Shullsburg**. During the mid-1800s, Italian-born Father Samuel Mazzuchelli, OP (see Finding Faith in Wisconsin), not only erected Saint Matthew's Church in the old lead-mining town, he also named the streets for godly virtues. For nearly two centuries, folks here have been walking down Faith, Peace, Pious, Justice, Goodness, and Friendship, not to mention Virtue, Happy, Charity, and Mercy. Ironically, or maybe not, Saint Matthew's Church sits on Judgement Street (yes, "Judgement").

Plan your visit: experienceshullsburg.com, shullsburgwisconsin.org. (608) 965-4424.

223 What do you do with assorted gems, heirloom pottery, starfish, petrified wood, fool's gold, perfume bottle stoppers, and 180 tons of stone? If you're Father Mathias Wernerus, you build a roadside attraction. From 1925 to 1930, the German native erected **Dickeyville Grotto** — a series of folk-art shrines — outside Holy Ghost Church in Dickeyville. Dedicated to God and country, artworks include the Grotto of the Blessed Virgin (stalactites make it feel like a real cave), Sacred Heart Shrine, Holy Eucharist Shrine, and Patriotism Shrine honoring presidents Washington and Lincoln.

Plan your visit: dickeyvillegrotto.com. 305 W. Main Street, Dickeyville, WI 53808. (608) 568-3119.

224 There's power in prayer at La Crosse's **Motherhouse of the Franciscan Sisters of Perpetual Adoration**. Beginning on August 1, 1878, at least

two adorers have kept vigil in the stunningly beautiful Adoration Chapel with a gleaming white altar. That's nearly 150 years of nonstop prayer! When a fire devoured the west wing of the convent in 1923, the good sisters kept on praying. Miraculously, the blaze stopped within yards of the chapel and a protective statue of Saint Michael the Archangel.

Plan your visit: fspa.org. 912 Market Street, La Crosse, WI 54601. (608) 782-5610.

225 In December 1531, Our Lady of Guadalupe appeared to Indian peasant Juan Diego in what is now Mexico City. "Go tell the bishop to build a church here," she told him. He did, and a church went up. In the 1990s, then-Bishop Raymond Burke also heeded Mary's request and erected the **Shrine of Our Lady of Guadalupe** near La Crosse. Set high on a wooded bluff, the 100-acre site includes a meditation path, outdoor devotional areas, beautiful gardens, and a seventeenth-century Italian-style shrine church. Don't miss the turquoise-colored dome inside: The stars replicate the night sky when Our Lady visited Juan Diego.

Plan your visit: guadalupeshrine.org. 5250 Justin Road, La Crosse, WI 54601. (877) 799-4059.

✚ FINDING FAITH
in Wisconsin

You can't "faith-see" in southern Wisconsin without tracing the footsteps of Venerable Samuel Mazzuchelli, OP (1806–1864) (see 222). The Italian native designed and built over twenty churches in the tristate area of Wisconsin, Illinois, and Iowa; started numerous schools and parish communities; and founded a teaching congregation of Dominican Sisters at Sinsinawa. He was so beloved by the Irish that they "Irishified" his surname to "Matthew Kelly."

In February 1864, after making a sick call in frigid weather, Father Mazzuchelli contracted pneumonia and died. When his body was being prepared for burial, a penance chain (an iron chain) was found around his waist, parts of it embedded in his skin. His grave and rectory-turned-museum at **Saint Patrick's Church** in Benton are pilgrimage sites.

Plan your visit: 237 E. Main Street, Benton, WI 53803. (608) 759-2131.

Father Mazzuchelli's penance chain and other priestly relics can be viewed at the **Sinsinawa Mound Center** in Sinsinawa.

Plan your visit: sinsinawa.org/moundcenter /museums. 585 County Road Z, Sinsinawa, WI 53824. (608) 748-4411.

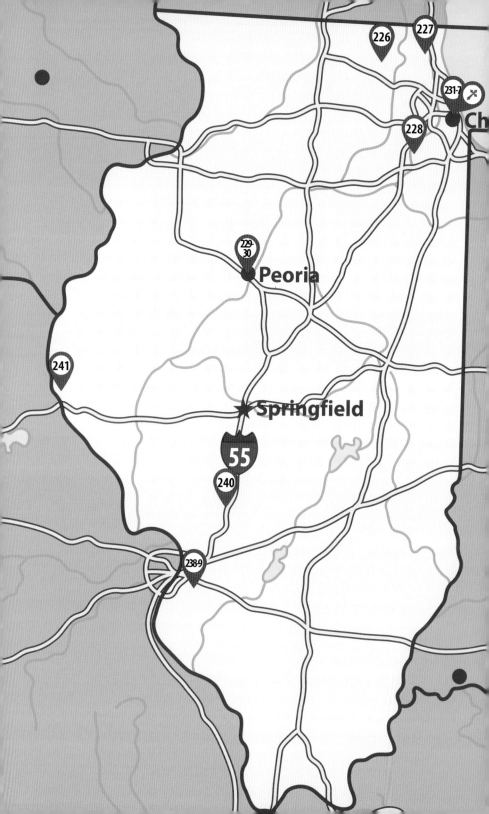

NORTHERN ILLINOIS

It's said that devils hate round churches — there's no place to hide! Devils not only hate the circular **Saints Peter and Paul Catholic Church** in Cary, they can't stand the light. Thousands of "stained-glass windows" — panes of colored glass inset in brickwork — create a kaleidoscope of Son-light that changes hour by hour, day by day. You might experience "contemplative blues" one minute and glorious reds of Pentecost the next.

Plan your visit: peterpaulchurchcary.org. 410 N. First Street, Cary, IL 60013. (847) 516-2636.

If a picture is worth a thousand words, then the eleven-foot-tall mosaic of Saint Maximilian Kolbe (1894–1941) at the **National Shrine of St. Maximilian Kolbe at Marytown** in Libertyville is an encyclopedia of love. The Conventual Franciscan, who was martyred at Auschwitz after offering to take the place of a family man condemned to die, is shown ascending above the starvation bunker in the Nazi concentration camp to his eternal reward. Other Kolbe mosaics depict his life, while the Holocaust exhibit recreates his death-camp cell. At the heart of the shrine is Our Lady of the Blessed Sacrament Chapel, with a five-foot-tall monstrance made from gifts of precious jewelry.

Plan your visit: kolbeshrine.org. 1600 W. Park Avenue, Libertyville, IL 60048. (847) 367-7800.

St. Mary of the Angels Church [234]

If you're looking for a "window to heaven," visit **Annunciation Byzantine Catholic Church** in Homer Glen. Consecrated in 2000, the church, with distinctive domes and topped with Russian crosses, is loaded with hundreds of "windows" — Byzantine icons. The "Bible in icons" is not only beautiful, but the brilliant colors are stories in themselves. Red garments symbolize heaven; blue garments, earth. Jesus and Mary wear both, but in reverse. Jesus' red garment signifies his divinity and the blue cloak his humanity. Mary's blue garment represents her humanity, the red cloak her assumption into heaven.

Plan your visit: byzantinecatholic.com. 14610 S. Will Cook Road, Homer Glen, IL 60491. (708) 645-0241.

Pray before the marble tomb of Venerable Fulton J. Sheen (1895–1979) at Peoria's **Cathedral of St. Mary of the Immaculate Conception** and you can almost hear the Holy Hour devotee say, "The greatest love story of all time is contained in a tiny white host." Ordained a priest in 1919 in this grand Gothic Revival cathedral — styled after St. Patrick's Cathedral in New York City — the Illinois native gained fame as a preacher, author, and television evangelist. In 1953, he won an Emmy Award for Most Outstanding Personality.

Plan your visit: catholicpeoria.com. 607 NE Madison Avenue, Peoria, IL 61603. (309) 673-6317.

 The archbishop's legacy is preserved at the **Archbishop Fulton Sheen Museum,** in the nearby Spalding

Pastoral Center. Artifacts include the beautiful crucifix from his TV stage.

Plan your visit: cdopmuseums.org. 419 NE Madison Avenue, Peoria, IL 61603. (877) 717-4336.

CHICAGO AREA

Pilgrims might blink twice when they visit the **National Shrine of Saint Frances Xavier Cabrini** in Lincoln Park: It's attached to a luxury condominium tower. When Columbus Hospital — founded by Mother Frances Cabrini (1850–1917) in 1905 and where she died twelve years later — was razed in 2001, developers agreed to preserve the shrine chapel. Romanesque in design, the shrine presents the Italian immigrant's life (from her premature birth to canonization miracles) in brilliant ceiling frescoes and Florentine stained glass. Mother Cabrini's recreated convent room includes her metal bed, the wicker chair in which she died, and her statue of the Baby Jesus. (See 21 and 325.)

Plan your visit: cabrininationalshrine.org. 2520 N. Lakeview Avenue, Chicago, IL 60614. (773) 360-5115.

You don't need to go to heaven to find paradise. Visit **Resurrection Catholic Cemetery and Mausoleums** in Justice. Resembling a Greek temple, the 1969 Resurrection Mausoleum glows with the largest stained-glass walls in the world: 22,381 square feet of *dalle de verre* (faceted glass). Dramatic scenes include dinosaurs roaming the Garden of Eden; Christ standing on a ship's prow on a storm-tossed sea; and Pharaoh cracking a whip, accidentally ensnaring himself.

Plan your visit: catholiccemeterieschicago.org/Locations/Details/Resurrection. 7201 Archer Avenue, Justice, IL 60458. (708) 458-4770.

233 Picture this: thousands of people standing in line every Friday to attend a novena! It happened at the Servites' **Our Lady of Sorrows Basilica** in Chicago. The great novena to Our Lady of Sorrows began in 1937, and during World War II, upward of 70,000 folks were attending one of thirty-eight weekly services. The novena is still going. Nicknamed the Joy of Chicago, the 1890 Italian Renaissance beauty will take your breath and sorrows away. Massive murals, a Holy Face Crucifix, and the dramatic ceiling dome usher you into the foyer of heaven.

Plan your visit: ols-chicago.org. 3121 W. Jackson Boulevard, Chicago, IL 60612. (773) 638-0159.

Can a church name be prophetic? Yes! Around 1205, Christ told Saint Francis of Assisi to "repair my church." Francis repaired several dilapidated churches, including the Chapel of St. Mary of the Angels (the Portiuncula). In 1988, **St. Mary of the Angels Church** in Chicago was closed and in disrepair, until Opus Dei priests arrived in 1991 and began restoring the majestic Polish church to its early twentieth-century glory. Angels are everywhere: standing like sentinels on the rooftop perimeter, in a sanctuary mural with Mary, and even on the pulpit. How many can you find?

234

Plan your visit: sma-church.org. 1850 N. Hermitage Avenue, Chicago, IL 60622. (773) 278-2644.

What are the odds of two shrines, in the same city, launching novenas to Saint Jude in 1929 — the year the Great Depression began? Heavenly odds. From these two shrines in Chicago — the Claretian **National Shrine of St. Jude** in Our Lady of Guadalupe Church and the Dominican **Shrine of St. Jude Thaddeus** in St. Pius V Church — devotion to the patron saint of hope swept the nation during an era of great need.

235

236

In the Claretian shrine, you'll find the wonder-working saint at a gorgeous side altar, the chapel filled with petitions.

Plan your visit: shrineofstjude.org. 3200 E. Ninety-First Street, Chicago, IL 60617. (312) 544-8230.

At the Dominican shrine, statues of petitioners — a doctor, a mother with her child, a businessman, and others, collectively representing the peoples of the world — kneel at Saint Jude's feet.

Plan your visit: the-shrine.org. 1901 S. Ashland Avenue, Chicago, IL 60608. (312) 226-0020.

237 "After my death I will let fall a shower of roses," Saint Thérèse of Lisieux promised. Some of those roses are falling at the **National Shrine and Museum of St. Thérèse** in Darien. Etched roses adorn chapel windows, while delicate wooden roses embellish a massive woodcarving — the largest religious woodcarving in America — that tells the story of her soul. The museum not only holds the largest collection of Little Flower artifacts outside France, but the replica of her convent cell includes the very window that overlooked the Carmel rose garden at Lisieux.

Plan your visit: saint-therese.org. 8433 Bailey Road, Darien, IL 60561. (800) 647-1430.

SOUTHERN ILLINOIS

238 Pilgrims don't come to the **National Shrine of Our Lady of the Snows** in Belleville to pray for snow (though they might, come July) but to honor Mary under an ancient title. According to one account, Our Lady appeared to a wealthy Roman couple in A.D. 352 and asked that a church be built on a site that would be covered with snow. On a hot August 5 morning, Esquiline Hill was snow-white! The "miracle hill" is now the site of the Basilica of Saint Mary

Major. Belleville's many devotional areas include a Lourdes grotto, an outdoor altar and amphitheater with a fifty-foot-tall "M," and an eighty-five-foot Millennium Spire rising from a candle shrine at its base.

Plan your visit: snows.org. 442 S. De Mazenod Drive, Belleville, IL 62223. (618) 397-6700.

Holy Family Catholic Church in Cahokia is old — so old that it displays the flags of four countries that once ruled here: Spain, France, Britain, and Colonial America. Built in 1799 (the parish was originally founded by Québécois missionaries in 1699), the French colonial church was constructed of vertical walnut timbers that alternate with thick columns of chinking for a striped appearance. Artifacts include two candlesticks from King Louis XIV of France, a bell from King Louis XV, and the original chalice used by missionaries in 1699 and three centuries later by Pope Saint John Paul II (see 58, Finding Faith in Maryland, 101, 257, 272, and Finding Faith in Colorado), during his 1999 visit to nearby St. Louis, Missouri.

Plan your visit: holyfamily1699.org. 116 Church Street, Cahokia, IL 62206. (618) 337-4548.

Get your kicks on Route 66, but pray at **Our Lady of the Highways Shrine** near Raymond when you go. Constructed in 1959 by a local Catholic Youth Council, the shrine features a Carrara marble statue of Mary and is inscribed with "Mary, Loving Mother of Jesus, Protect Us on the Highway." Along the road arc Burma Shave-style signs displaying the Hail Mary prayer.

Plan your visit: facebook.com /OurLadyOfTheHighways, il66assoc.org/destination /our-lady-of-the-highways-shrine. 22353 W. Frontage Road, Raymond, IL 62560.

(241) The tall grave marker at **St. Peter's Cemetery** in Quincy doesn't begin to tell the epic story of Venerable Augustus Tolton (1854–1897). Born to Missouri slaves, slave boy Augustus and his family ran for freedom to Quincy, where Father Peter McGirr befriended the lad and enrolled him in the parish's all-white school. Rejected by American seminaries because of his color, Augustus studied for the priesthood in Rome and was ordained in 1886 (see 149). When Good Father Gus arrived back home in Quincy, thousands of people, black and white alike, lined the streets, singing Negro spirituals and hoping to catch a glimpse of the man often described as America's first black Catholic priest. (Bishop James A. Healy was of mixed race. See 4.)

Plan your visit: tolton.archchicago.org. 3300 Broadway Street, Chicago, IL 60657. (217) 223-3390.

✣ FINDING FAITH
✝ in Illinois

Can miracles strike twice? It happened at **Holy Family Church** in Chicago. When the Great Chicago Fire that began on October 8, 1871, threatened the 1857 Jesuit church, Father Arnold Damen invoked Our Lady of Perpetual Help and vowed to light seven candles before her image, in perpetuity, if the church were spared. Seven lights still burn today. In mid-1990, Father George Lane and the parish were told to raise $1 million in repair money before midnight on December 31 or the old church would be razed. Like his predecessor, Father Lane invoked Our Lady's help. She delivered — $1,011,000!

One of few structures that survived the Chicago Fire (an estimated 300 lives were lost and 17,000 buildings destroyed), the Victorian Gothic church is a paradise in wood. The high altar — fifty-two feet of elaborate woodcarving — dates from 1865; the intricately carved walnut Communion rail, 1866. The great Mitchell Organ, with its "orchestra" of hand-carved wooden angels playing musical instruments, was installed in 1870. (See 209 and 210.)

Plan your visit: holyfamilychicago.org. 1080 W. Roosevelt Road, Chicago, IL 60608. (312) 492-8442.

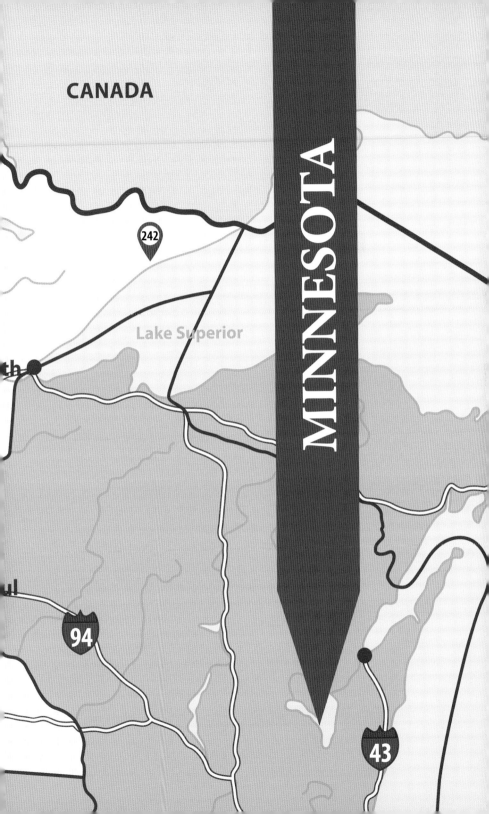

NORTHERN MINNESOTA

 When Venerable Frederic Baraga (see Finding Faith in Michigan) got word in 1846 of a possible epidemic among the Ojibwa tribe in northeastern Minnesota, the missionary and his guide set out in a small boat from Wisconsin's Madeline Island across Lake Superior to Minnesota's North Shore. A wicked storm popped up, and Father Baraga — like Jesus asleep in a storm-tossed boat — laid down and read his breviary. Providence blew the boat over a sandbar and into the mouth of the Cross River. Overlooking Lake Superior, the **Father Baraga Cross** near Schroeder marks the miraculous landing site.

Plan your visit: 56 Baraga Cross Road, Schroeder, MN 55613.

 All eyes are on the **National Shrine of St. Odilia** at Holy Cross Catholic Church in Onamia. Patroness of the Crosier Order, Saint Odilia is famous for healing eye diseases. Besides a major relic of the saint, the shrine boasts stained glass illuminating both her earthly life and her patronage of the Crosiers, as well as a replica of her original reliquary depicting her martyrdom with her ten companions around A.D. 300. The Crosiers hold twice-monthly novenas to Saint Odilia; the annual Solemn Novena runs July 10–18.

Plan your visit: crosier.org. 104 Crosier Drive N., Onamia, MN 56359. (320) 532-3103.

SOUTHERN MINNESOTA

What good can come from a settlement original- ◀ 244
ly called Pig's Eye? The magnificent **Cathedral of
Saint Paul** in Saint Paul! Completed in 1915 and
patterned after Saint Peter's Basilica in Rome, the
Beaux Arts temple on a hill is a dazzling array of
stained glass, marble carvings, pious paintings, and
more. Highlights include the 120-foot-wide dome
topped with a nearly three-stories-tall, copper-clad
lantern; the massive bronze grilles portraying Saint

Paul's life from conversion to martyrdom; and the Shrine of the Nations honoring the ethnic saints of Minnesota's early settlers. The cathedral was designated the National Shrine of the Apostle Paul in 2009.

Plan your visit: cathedralsaintpaul.org. 239 Selby Avenue, Saint Paul, MN 55102. (651) 228-1766.

(245) Angels are watching you at the **Basilica of Saint Mary** in Minneapolis. Some 675 angels — glass, marble, bronze, and wood — adorn this glorious church of colossal proportions. The exterior is nearly one football field long; the apex of the dome, five-sixths of a football field tall. The Beaux Arts gem, erected from 1907 to 1914, was named America's first basilica in 1926. Marian artworks include the facade's in-situ carving of Mary's assumption, a nine-foot *Mater Divinae Gratiae* statue atop a forty-foot baldachin, and a dome with twelve windows depicting the attributes of Mary as found in the Song of Songs.

Plan your visit: mary.org. 1600 Hennepin Avenue, Minneapolis, MN 55403. (612) 333-1381.

(246) As you ascend New Ulm's **Way of the Cross**, you can't help but marvel at the women who built it c. 1904: the Sisters of the Poor Handmaids of Jesus Christ. They rolled up the sleeves of their black habits and pushed umpteen wheelbarrows of cobblestones up the hill to construct the retaining walls, stations of the cross (Bavarian statuary inscribed in

German and English), and Lourdes grotto. The Sorrowful Mother Chapel, taller than it is wide, awaits pilgrims at the top.

Plan your visit: newulm.com/visitors-community /things-to-do/attractions. 1500 Fifth Street N., New Ulm, MN 56073. (888) 463-9856.

If you're church artist Anton Gag painting cherubs, who do you use as models? Your children! That's part of the lore at New Ulm's **Cathedral of the Holy Trinity**. Dedicated in 1893, the Romanesque red-brick church, with a stately clock tower, looks like it was translated directly from Old Germany. Dominating the ceiling apse are Gag's cherubs and a spectacular painting of the Holy Trinity. When a tornado destroyed an earlier church in 1881, folks vowed to pray a weekly Rosary for protection against bad weather, a practice that continues today.

Plan your visit: holycrossafc.org. 605 N. State Street, New Ulm, MN 56073. (507) 354-4158.

Schoenstatt Chapel in Sleepy Eye (see 221).

Plan your visit: schoenstattmn.com. 27762 County Road 27, Sleepy Eye, MN 56085. (507) 794-7727.

Whether you love or hate the Brutalist architecture, there's no doubting who is Lord over the Benedictine monks' **Saint John's Abbey Church** at Collegeville. Designed by Marcel Breuer (see 280), the 1958 concrete temple touts an eleven-story, 100-foot-wide bell banner with a twenty-eight-foot-tall cross. Hundreds of hexagonal stained-glass windows light up the massive north wall of the upper church, while the lower church features a catacomb-like reliquary chapel and dozens of private chapels where, before Vatican II, resident priests said daily Mass. Another must-see: original folios of *The Saint John's Bible*, the abbey's renowned seven-volume, handwritten, illuminated Scriptures.

Plan your visit: saintjohnsabbey.org. 2900 Abbey Plaza, Collegeville, MN 56321. (320) 363-2011.

250 Who can defeat a locust plague? Maria! In 1876, swarms of Rocky Mountain locusts — or grasshoppers, as some called them — invaded the Cold Spring area. The "flying demons" devoured fields and gardens, even stripping the trees bare. When grasshopper eggs began hatching the following spring, Father Leo Winter, OSB, had a divine idea: Ask the German settlers to build a frame chapel honoring Maria Hilf (Mary's Help) to avert the plague. As soon as construction began, the demons took wing. Today's **Assumption Chapel**, popularly called the Grasshopper Chapel, was erected of granite in 1951. (See 286.)

Plan your visit: stboniface.com. 501 Main Street, Cold Spring, MN 56320. (320) 685-3280.

✠ FINDING FAITH
✝ in Minnesota

Rochester's Mayo Clinic is world renowned, but many people don't know the clinic has Franciscan roots. In 1889, Mother Alfred Moes, OSF, began **Saint Marys Hospital,** a twenty-seven-bed facility, in a cornfield near town. The attending staff: Protestant doctors W. W. Mayo and sons William and Charles Mayo. (In 1914, the sons erected a five-story medical office building that became known as the Mayo Clinic.)

The hospital and the clinic expanded many times over the years, but the Franciscan-Mayo bond remained as tight as sutures. The Sisters operated the hospital, and Mayo Clinic doctors served as its staff. In 1986, to better care for their patients, Saint Marys Hospital, Rochester Methodist Hospital, and Mayo Clinic integrated operations. An era ended for Saint Marys, but not the Franciscan spirit. It lives on in the hospital's philosophy and the many Franciscan artworks that grace the hospital complex, known today as Mayo Clinic Hospital, Saint Marys Campus.

Plan your visit: history.mayoclinic.org /timelines/history-timeline.php. 1216 Second Street SW, Rochester, MN 55902.

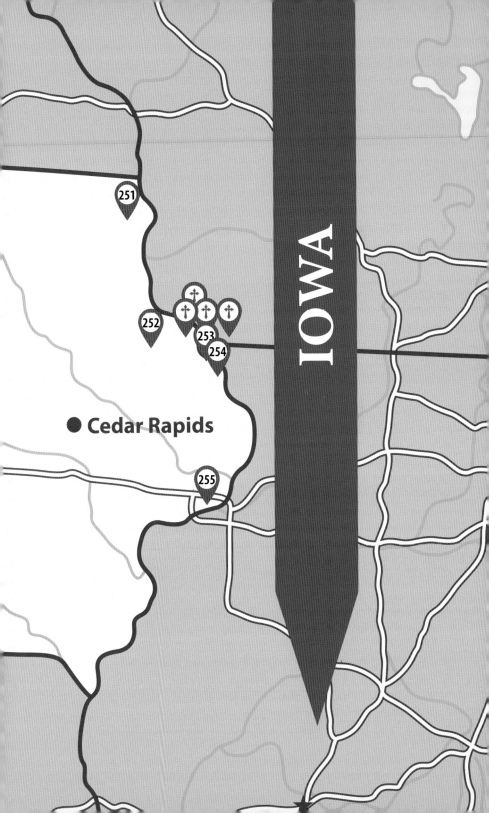

EASTERN IOWA

More than 200 years ago in France, a mother watched as her son, Johann Gaertner, was conscripted into Napoleon's army. "Return my son safely," she prayed, "and I promise to build a chapel." Johann survived, but a depression at war's end stopped her promise. Years passed; Johann and his family emigrated and settled in Iowa. In 1885, at age ninety-two, Johann fulfilled his mother's vow: He erected **St. Anthony of Padua Chapel** at Festina. The quaint stone chapel, with a bell tower and stained glass, seats eight. An annual Mass is held on the Sunday closest to Saint Anthony's feast on June 13.

Plan your visit: facebook.com/St -Anthony-of-Padua-Chapel-Festina-Iowa -111637529523196. 1120 Little Church Road, Festina, IA 52144. (563) 562-3045.

"Build it and they will come," the saying goes. Come they do to the **Basilica of St. Francis Xavier** in Dyersville. Dedicated in 1889, this red-brick gem is hailed as one of the finest examples of Gothic architecture in the Midwest. Like Saint Francis Xavier, apostle of the Far East, the church boldly preaches Christ — from the 212-foot illuminated spires to the glorious apse painting of the Church Triumphant. Because Saint Francis Xavier labored in India, the parish ordered a stained-glass window of him preaching to the "Indians." The artist made them Native Americans!

Plan your visit: xavierbasilica.com. 104 Third Street SW, Dyersville, Iowa 52040. (563) 875-7325.

For extra penance, climb the **Outdoor Way of the Cross** (reportedly America's oldest) up Calvary Hill in St. Donatus, a Luxembourger village. Built in 1861, the Way — fourteen brick alcoves with Parisian lithographs detailing Christ's Passion — runs switchback up the steep hill behind St. Donatus Church. At the summit is the Pietà Chapel, an 1885 stone replica of Luxembourg's Chapelle du Bildchen in Vianden. Watch your step: The hillside lawnmowers are sheep that leave calling cards!

Plan your visit: 97 E. First Street, St. Donatus, IA 52071. (563) 582-7392.

In the mid-1800s, Mathias Fritz, his wife, and their six children left Luxembourg and sailed for America. When rough seas threatened their ship, Fritz made a solemn vow: If God granted them a safe voyage, he would build a stone chapel — a chapel of gratitude that would endure as long as the stone itself. True to his word, Fritz erected **Fritz Chapel**, a three-sided limestone chapel with an open facade, near Bellevue.

Plan your visit: Spruce Creek Road, west of junction with US 52, Bellevue, IA 52031.

Two Saint Margarets grace the history of Davenport's **Sacred Heart Cathedral**. The first church, erected in 1856 and named for Saint Margaret of Scotland, was elevated to a cathedral in 1881. A decade later, a new and larger cathedral was dedicated to the Sacred Heart of Jesus, sparked by a pastor's pilgrimage to Paray-le-Monial in France, where Saint Margaret Mary Alacoque received visions of Jesus' Sacred Heart. The nation's first cathedral dedicated to the Sacred Heart (today there are no fewer than fourteen), the Gothic Revival structure with open interior and extensive woodwork is strikingly unique and beautiful.

Plan your visit: shcdavenport.org. 422 E. Tenth Street, Davenport, IA 52803. (563) 324-3257.

WESTERN IOWA

When the legendary Father Edmund Hayes, who **256** had struck it rich in California gold and oil and Nevada silver, arrived in tiny Imogene in 1888, he found a white frame church. Thirty years later, **St. Patrick Catholic Church** — a mini-cathedral erected of black brick in Romanesque/Late Gothic Revival style — was bursting with beauty and lore. The Italian altars arrived in thousands of pieces and took two years to assemble; the Venetian mosaic stations of the cross, one year. Father Hayes returned the stained-glass image of Saint Patrick three times before he was content with the face (some say it's his face!). Commodious pews "accommodated" his hour-long sermons.

Plan your visit: stpatrickchurchimogeneiowa .weebly.com. 304 Third Street, Imogene, IA 51645. (712) 623-2744.

Relive Pope John Paul II's historic 1979 visit to **257** Iowa at Living History Farms near Urbandale. Constructed in 1980 in Carpenter Gothic style, the **Church of the Land** marks the spot where the future saint (see 58, Finding Faith in Maryland, 101, 239, 272, and Finding Faith in Colorado) delivered his message on land stewardship and feeding the world's hungry to 350,000 pilgrims. The stained-glass window, based on the magnificent quilted banner that graced the papal platform, features a cross with four fields representing Iowa's seasons and crops.

Shrine of the Grotto of the Redemption [260]

Plan your visit: lhf.org/aboutus/saint-pope-john
-paul-ii-visit. 11121 Hickman Road, Urbandale,
IA 50322. (515) 278-5286.

258 To see the quilt in person, visit the **Catholic Pastoral Center** in Des Moines.

Plan your visit: dmdiocese.org. 601 Grand Avenue, Des Moines, IA 50309. (515) 243-7653

259 You'll feel the love at **Trinity Heights** in Sioux City. Towering over one side of the sixteen-acre retreat is a thirty-foot stainless steel statue of the Immaculate Heart of Mary, Queen of Peace, her right hand pointing toward a thirty-three-foot statue of the Sacred Heart of Jesus on the opposite side. Between the hearts is St. Joseph Center, home of an incredibly detailed carving of the Last Supper. Created by Iowa sculptor Jerry Traufler, the twenty-two-foot-long masterpiece is one of a few life-size Last Supper carvings in the world.

Plan your visit: www.trinityheights.com. 2511
33rd Street, Sioux City, IA 51108. (712) 239-8670.

260 When Father Paul Dobberstein made a vow, his word was rock-solid. According to one account, two weeks before his ordination in 1897, the German native contracted pneumonia and barely clung to life. He begged Mother Mary's intercession and vowed to build a grotto if he lived. A composite of nine separate grottoes covering a city block, the **Shrine of the Grotto of the Redemption** at West Bend proclaims in stone the glorious Redemption story — from the Garden of Eden to the Annunciation to the Crucifixion. More than 100 train-car-loads of petrified wood, stalactites and stalagmites, semi-precious stones, and more were used to build the shrine, heralded as the Eighth Wonder of the World.

Plan your visit: westbendgrotto.com. 208 First Avenue NW, West Bend, IA 50597. (515) 887-2371.

✝ FINDING FAITH
in Iowa

Join the "nun run" to Dubuque. Not only does the Dubuque area have one of the highest concentrations of religious sisters' motherhouses per capita in the country (there are four), it's also "habit forming." Collectively, about 9,600 sisters have professed final vows — the equivalent of a good-sized Iowa town!

Founded in 1843, the **Sisters of Charity of the Blessed Virgin Mary** trace their roots to Irish immigrant-teacher Mary Frances Clarke. Final professed sisters: 4,290.

Plan your visit: bvmsisters.org. 1100 Carmel Drive, Dubuque, IA 52003. (563) 588-2351.

Just across the Mississippi River in Sinsinawa, Wisconsin, Venerable Samuel Mazzuchelli, OP (see 222 and Finding Faith in Wisconsin), founded the **Sinsinawa Dominicans** in 1847. Final professed sisters: nearly 3,500.

Plan your visit: sinsinawa.org/moundcenter/museums. 585 County Road Z, Sinsinawa, WI 53824. (608) 748-4411.

Established in 1874, the **Sisters of the Presentation of the Blessed Virgin Mary** track their Irish heritage to hedge school teacher Venerable Nano Nagle. Final professed sisters: 438.

Plan your visit: dubuquepresentations.org. 2360 Carter Road, Dubuque, IA 52001. (563) 588-2008.

Exiled from Germany, Mother Xavier Termehr and her flock founded the **Sisters of St. Francis** in 1878. Final professed sisters: 1,377.

Plan your visit: osfdbq.org. 3390 Windsor Avenue, Dubuque, IA 52001. (563) 583-9786.

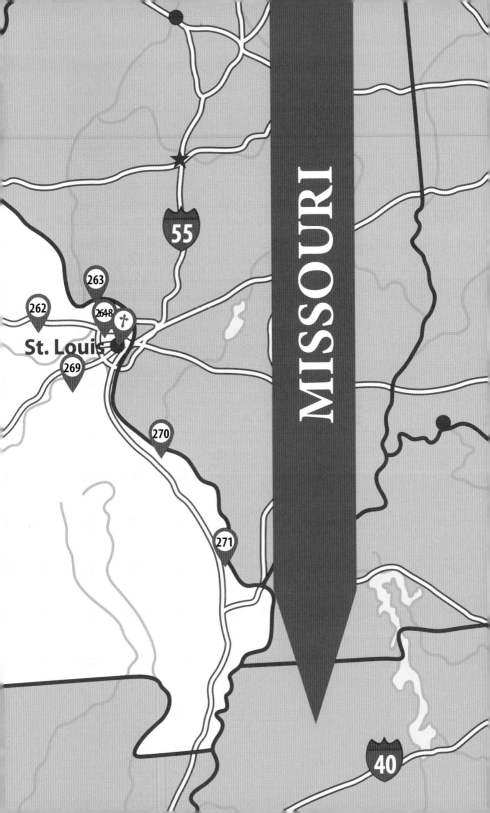

EASTERN MISSOURI

 Father Francis O'Duignan had a dream: Build a shrine to Saint Patrick. Fate (and faith) led him in 1935 to tiny Saint Patrick, reportedly the world's only town named for the saint, where he spent decades typing and mailing appeal letters to people with Irish surnames. In 1956, the **Shrine of Saint Patrick** went up. Patterned after Saint Patrick's Memorial Church of Four Masters in Donegal, Ireland, the stone church touts a round bell tower, green marble altars, and Dublin stained glass inspired by the Book of Kells.

Plan your visit: saintpatrickshrine.com. 2 Erin Circle, Saint Patrick, MO 63466. (660) 727-3472.

 St. Martin's Church in Starkenburg (near Rhineland) is steeped in miracles. When weeks of rain in 1891 threatened wheat crops, folks vowed to make annual processions to Our Lady's Chapel — a log chapel with a "White Lady" statue (so named because she was unpainted) — if rains ceased. The next day was sunny and bright. During a drought in 1894, the faithful again flocked to the chapel and lit candles for rain. One night the altar caught fire, but a different Marian statue, her veil held by a waxen wreath, escaped harm. When the little "miracle chapel" became a pilgrimage site, the parish erected a larger chapel, the **Shrine of Our Lady of Sorrows**. The grounds include the quaint log chapel, Mount Calvary, and the Grotto of Lourdes.

Plan your visit: historicshrine.com. 197 Highway P, Starkenburg, MO 65069. (573) 236-4390.

In 1951, the flooded Mississippi River, which had **263** already swallowed up several towns upstream, threatened Portage Des Sioux. Father Edward B. Schlattmann, pastor of St. Francis of Assisi Church, called upon his parish's Legion of Mary to invoke Our Lady's protection. When the river crested two weeks later, the town stayed high and dry. In thanksgiving, boaters and townsfolk erected **Our Lady of the Rivers Shrine**, a towering white fiberglass statue of Mary near the confluence of the Mississippi, Missouri, and Illinois rivers.

Plan your visit: ourladyoftheriversshrine.org, greatriverroad.com/portage-des-sioux. 1553 River View Drive, Portage Des Sioux, MO 63373.

When Mother Rose Philippine Duchesne, RSCJ **264** (1769–1852), a French native, landed in Saint Charles in 1818, she called it "the remotest village in the US." Yet here she founded the Academy of the Sacred Heart of Jesus, the first free school west of the Mississippi. Her spirit lives on at the centuries-old academy and adjacent **Shrine of St. Rose Philippine Duchesne**, where her remains rest. Pilgrims may also visit the parlors of an early brick convent ("the house where charity dwells," as the saint called it) and the little cell where she died. (See 265, 302, and 303.)

Plan your visit: duchesneshrine.org. 619 N. Second Street, St. Charles, MO 63301. (636) 946-6127, ext. 1801.

265 **Old St. Ferdinand Shrine** in Florissant has "heart": Not only does it house a wax effigy and relics of Saint Valentine beneath the altar, but it's also filled with stories of Saint Rose Philippine Duchesne, a Religious Sister of the Sacred Heart. The red-brick shrine dates from 1821 and the adjacent convent, 1819. It's said that Mother Duchesne, who lived at the convent for many years, slept in a closet under the hallway stairs to be closer to the chapel. Other buildings include the 1840 rectory and 1888 schoolhouse. (See 264, 302, and 303.)

Plan your visit: oldstferdinandshrine.com. 1 Rue St. Francois, Florissant, MO 63031. (314) 837-2110.

266 "Be who you are and be that well," Saint Francis de Sales once said. The **Saint Francis de Sales Oratory** in Saint Louis does it so well that it's dubbed the Cathedral of South Saint Louis. The 1907 German Gothic masterpiece — designed after Germany's Ulm Minster, the tallest church in the world — touts a 300-foot spire, five-story high altar, and front portal said to mirror the famous Gothic portal of the Cathedral of Munich. The spectacular artistry inside, from frescoes painted by German artist Fridolin Fuchs (see 152 and 352) to German immigrant Emil Frei's stained glass (see 388), will transport you straight to heaven.

Plan your visit: institute-christ-king.org /stlouis-home. 2653 Ohio Avenue, St. Louis, Missouri 63118. (314) 771-3100.

National Shrine of Mary, Mother of the Church [272]

The **Cathedral Basilica of Saint Louis** in St. Louis isn't just another cathedral (St. Louis is called the Rome of the West, after all!): It boasts one of the largest collections of mosaics in the world. Crafted by twenty artists over seventy-six years (1912–1988), the mosaics cover 83,000 square feet, and comprise 41.5 million glass tesserae and more than 7,000 colors. Scenes range from Elias' fiery chariot being taken up to heaven; to the Passover; to the life of Saint Louis IX, King of France (the city's patron saint). The 1908 cathedral is also hailed for its Romanesque exterior and Byzantine interior.

Plan your visit: cathedralstl.org. 4431 Lindell Boulevard, St. Louis, MO 63108. (314) 373-8200.

268 The **Abbey Church** at the Benedictine monks' Saint Louis Abbey in Creve Coeur (in the St. Louis metropolitan area) is fit for a king: It's shaped like a crown. (Its namesake, Saint Louis IX, was the king of France.) Completed in 1962, the visually stunning church was erected of three tiers of whitewashed, thin-poured concrete parabolic arches, with the top tier forming the bell tower. Artworks include a fourteenth-century sculpture of the Madonna and Child, and a seventeenth-century holy water font in Della Robbia style.

Plan your visit: stlouisabbey.org, stanselmstl.org. 530 S. Mason Road, St. Louis, MO 63141. (314) 878-2120.

269 The **Black Madonna Shrine and Grottos** in Pacific is a grotto paradise. From 1937 to 1960, Franciscan Missionary Brother Bronislaus Luszcz, a Polish native, built acres of rock walls and grottoes, turning "junk" into sacred art. Light streaming through colored glass jars adds a surreal touch in the Gethsemane Grotto, while flowers crafted from light fixtures adorn the St. Joseph Grotto. Cake molds produced the concrete bunnies and lambs in the St. Francis Grotto. Also on the grounds is the open-air Chapel of the Hills, featuring a mosaic wall with an icon of the Black Madonna, the work of artist Frederick Henze.

Plan your visit: franciscancaring.org. 265 St. Joseph Hill Road, Pacific, MO 63069. (636) 938-5361.

270 You'll find a litany of devotional sites at **Saint Mary's of the Barrens** in Perryville. Renowned for its seven-story Angelus Bell Tower, the grand 1827 church houses seven side chapels (each with its own patron saint) and the National Shrine of Our Lady of the Miraculous Medal. Shrine highlights include the gleaming white altar incorporating the medal's design, stained glass depicting Our Lady's apparitions to Saint Catherine Labouré (1806–1876), and a dome painting of Catherine distributing miraculous medals to fellow Parisians. Outdoor sites include the Grotto of Our Lady of the Miraculous Medal, the Mound of Our Lady of Victory, and the Rosary Walk.

Plan your visit: amm.org. 1805 W. Saint Joseph Street, Perryville, MO 63775. (800) 264-6279.

271 Want to visit an American medieval church? Come to **Old St. Vincent Church** in Cape Girardeau. More than 130 plaster faces inspired by medieval mystery and morality plays, portraying the characters Good and Evil, and Youth and Old Age, decorate the English Gothic church inside and out. The red-brick legend, consecrated in 1853, is also known for its "marble pillars" (plaster-encased trees) and "rock walls" (canvas-like fabric painted to resemble rocks). Take time to examine the ten-foot crucifix: Jesus is nailed to the cross with four — not the usual three — nails.

Plan your visit: oldstvincents.org. 131 S. Main Street, Cape Girardeau, MO 63703. (573) 335-9347.

WESTERN MISSOURI

Wherever you go at the **National Shrine of Mary,** **Mother of the Church** in Laurie, Our Lady will find you. A fourteen-foot stainless steel statue of Mary — portrayed as a teen girl with flowing hair and welcoming arms — stands within a fountain and rotates 360 degrees. A tribute to Mother Mary and all mothers around the world, the black granite Mothers' Wall of Life is engraved with thousands of mothers' names, including actress and Catholic convert Jane Wyman and Emilia Kaczorowska, mother of Pope Saint John Paul II (see 58, Finding Faith in Maryland, 101, 239, 257, and Finding Faith in Colorado).

Plan your visit: mothersshrine.com. 176 Marian Drive, Laurie, MO 65037. (573) 374-6279.

Enter **Saint Francis Xavier Catholic Church** in Kansas City and you might feel a little like Jonah in the belly of a whale. Erected of concrete from 1948 to 1950, the Jesuit church was built in the shape of a fish (an ancient Christian symbol) and fitted with sea-blue windows. Standing outside "the fish church" is a humongous statue of "fisher of men" Saint Francis Xavier, a sixteenth-century Jesuit missionary to India and Japan.

Plan your visit: sfx-kc.org. 1001 E. Fifty-Second Street, Kansas City, MO 64110. (816) 523-5115.

In the 1890s, when Benedictine monks of Conception Abbey painted the Beuronese murals at today's

Basilica of the Immaculate Conception in Conception, nobody dreamed they were preserving art. The murals replicated the famous Beuronese murals at Emmaus Abbey in Prague, Czechoslovakia, which was bombed in World War II. The hieratic murals do more than tell a story; they invite viewers into the scenes. In *The Annunciation* mural, Mary's upraised hands evoke wonder, while in *The Descent from the Cross*, you feel Jesus' dead weight as he's lowered into the arms of a muscular young man.

Plan your visit: conceptionabbey.org/monastery /basilica. 37174 State Highway VV, Conception, MO 64433. (660) 944-3100.

✤ FINDING FAITH
✝ in Missouri

Need a miracle? Go to the **Shrine of St. Joseph** in St. Louis! The 1844 red-brick church, with its Baroque facade and lavish interior, is a mighty font of miracles — even a miracle that got a saint canonized. In 1864, Ignatius Strecker was working his factory job when he accidentally struck his chest with a pointed piece of iron. Doctors soon gave him up for dead. Hearing of a parish mission about then-Blessed Peter Claver (see 116), Strecker dragged himself to the church, where he was blessed with and kissed a relic of the Jesuit priest. Strecker's miraculous recovery propelled Claver to sainthood in 1888.

Two years after Strecker's miracle, a massive cholera epidemic hit St. Louis; hundreds were dying daily. Led by Father Joseph Weber, parishioners pledged $4,000 to erect a monument honoring Saint Joseph if he interceded for their lives. From that day forward, not one person from any family who signed the pledge contracted the dreaded scourge. Inscribed on the monument — the Altar of Answered Prayers — are the words *Ite ad Joseph* ("Go to Joseph").

Plan your visit: shrineofstjoseph.org. 1220 N. Eleventh Street, St. Louis, MO 63106. (314) 231-9407.

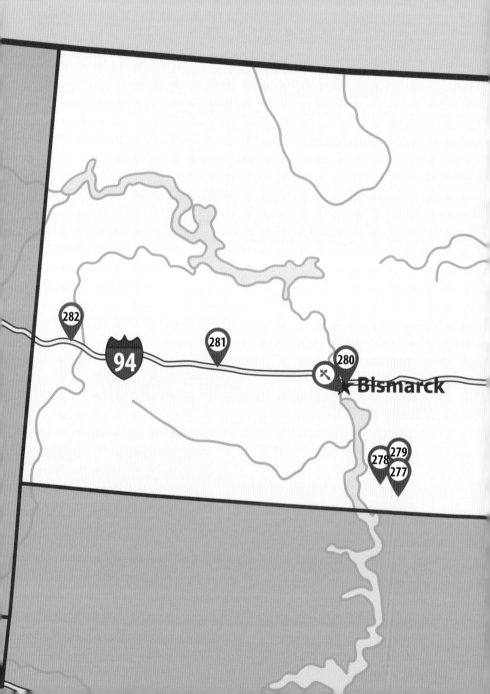

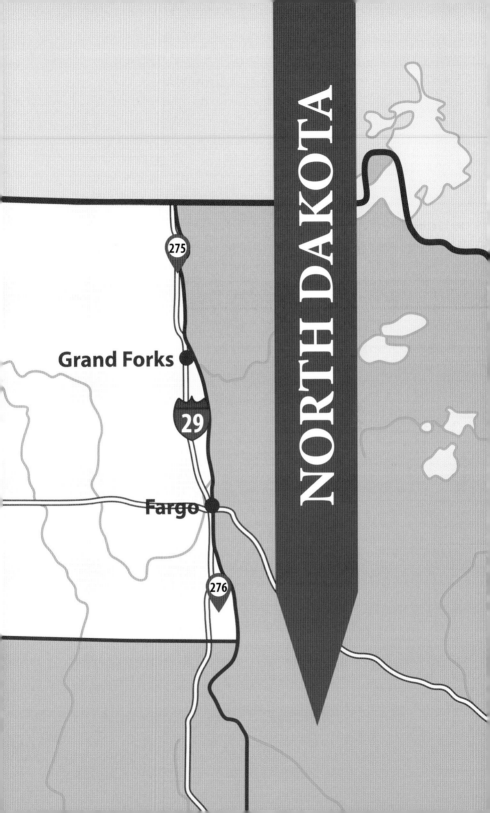

EASTERN NORTH DAKOTA

 When eight pioneer farmers — four of them named Joe — build a wooden wayside chapel in Old World Polish tradition, they dedicate it to Saint Joseph, of course! Constructed in 1907, **St. Joseph's Chapel** near Warsaw is just big enough for an altar, a priest, and two altar boys (note the quaint steeple and cupolas). Summer Masses ask God's blessings on local crops.

Plan your visit: sh-ss.org. Exit 168 off Interstate 29, two miles east and one mile north. 6207 CR 2, Oslo, ND 58771. (701) 248-3589.

 Mother Mary was surely with the Carmelite nuns when they founded Wahpeton's **Carmel of Mary** in 1954. Not only was 1954 a Marian year, the monastery is located by the M-shaped Wild Rice River. Marian tributes include a striking mural of Our Lady of Mount Carmel and the outdoor Shrine of Our Lady of the Prairies. Celebrating both the Bread of Life and the local "wheat basket," the white Mary statue holds a real sheaf of wheat. An annual pilgrimage is held around August 15.

Plan your visit: carmelofmary.org. 17765 Seventy-Eighth Street SE, Wahpeton, ND 58075. (701) 642-2360.

 You'll fly on angel wings at **St. Mary's Catholic Church** in tiny Hague. Built by German-Russian pi-

oneers in 1929, the Romanesque Revival brick gem is decked with angels — more than 100 of them! (You might need your guardian angel's help to find them all.) Heralded as one of North Dakota's most beautiful churches, St. Mary's rivals Old World cathedrals with its turret-like towers, ceiling paintings, Daprato statuary, and spectacular stained glass. The crown jewel? The white marble high altar, adorned with a blond-haired Mary statue and lighted halo.

Plan your visit: emmonscatholics.org. 210 Fourth Street S., Hague, ND 58542. (701) 336-7172.

 If the tower of Strasburg's **Sts. Peter and Paul Church** looks short, it is. According to lore, when German-Russian settlers were erecting the 1909 brick structure, the younger men wanted to spend more money for a taller tower. The elders, however, feared the young'uns would build and build until they had another tower of Babel! Step inside and you're off to heaven: intricately carved snow-white altars, ceiling paintings by German Count Berthold von Imhoff, and old-time confessionals with "eavesdropping" statues sitting on top. Ethnic wrought-iron crosses mark graves in the church cemetery.

Plan your visit: emmonscatholics.org. 503 N. Second Street, Strasburg, ND 58573. (701) 336-7172.

 Make a joyful noise unto the Lord at **Prairie Bells: Grotto of the Holy Family** near Linton. Dedicated in 1994, the park-like fieldstone grotto was erected by the extended Vetter farm family and friends.

A life-size Holy Family statue decorates the inside, while three old church bells in the fifty-foot bell tower beg to be rung. An audio recording tells the story.

Plan your visit: sixteen miles east of Linton on State Highway 13 and one mile north, Linton, ND 58552.

From afar, the ten-story bell banner of Bismarck's **280**
Annunciation Monastery resembles a giant sail. Designed by renowned architect Marcel Breuer (see 249), the concrete "sail" is more than a local landmark. The open cross signifies the Risen Christ (and lets the prairie winds sail through), while the three bells call the Benedictine Sisters to prayer. At the winter solstice, the cross — as though portending the Savior's birth and crucifixion — casts a shadow on Our Lady of the Annunciation Chapel.

Plan your visit: annunciationmonastery.org. 7520 University Drive, Bismarck, ND 58504. (701) 255-1520.

WESTERN NORTH DAKOTA

If **Assumption Abbey** in Richardton sounds fa- **281**
miliar, there's good reason. Author Kathleen Norris wrote about the abbey and her spiritual quest in *The Cloister Walk* and *Dakota: A Spiritual Geography.* Constructed by Benedictine monks in the early 1900s, the Romanesque red-brick St. Mary's Church serves up a visual feast: lofty stenciled arches, dozens of stained-glass and clerestory wheel windows,

elaborate wood-carved choir stalls, and a unique guardian angel statue — depicted as a mature man who has worked hard in his angelic life.

Plan your visit: assumptionabbey.com. 418 Third Avenue W., Richardton, ND 58652. (701) 974-3315.

 If you have your own town, why not your own church? That's the Badlands story of **St. Mary's Catholic Church** in Medora, founded in 1883 by French Marquis de Mores and named for his wife, Medora. Wealthy and devoutly Catholic, Medora erected a small brick church with Gothic windows — a gift to Medora from Medora. Seating sixty-five, the church is still in use and part of Medora's historic walking tour.

Plan your visit: triparishnd.org. 305 Fourth Street, Medora, ND 58645. (701) 872-4153.

✠ FINDING FAITH
in North Dakota

The Spirit descended upon them, and up went Bismarck's **Cathedral of the Holy Spirit**. While the Spirit led, "God's acre" built the church. In 1940, Bishop Vincent J. Ryan asked farmers to donate the profit from one acre of land (or a proportional amount for other workers) to fund the church. Painted in dove white, the monolithic concrete landmark is unique for another reason: It may be the only Art Deco cathedral in the world.

Ten large art-glass windows (each window has eight panels, for eighty scenes in all) tell, with symbols and Scripture, the Holy Spirit's role in salvific history. Beginning with Genesis 1:2 ("the Spirit of God moved over the waters"), the windows travel through the Old and New Testaments, the Middle Ages, the discovery of America, and conclude with the Church in North Dakota — represented by a tipi, a cross, and wheat stalks.

Plan your visit: cathedralparish.com. 519 Raymond Street, Bismarck, ND 58501. (701) 223-1033.

EASTERN SOUTH DAKOTA

 Monsignor Anthony Helmbrecht had a dream for small-town Hoven: Erect a church so grand the bishop would move there. Patterned after a 1,000-year-old Bavarian cathedral, and seating 850, **St. Anthony of Padua Church** took four years to build (1917–1921) and cost a then-princely $300,000. The bishop didn't come, but flocks of tourists do. Nicknamed the Cathedral of the Prairie, the brick Romanesque structure dazzles with its 147-foot twin spires and Bavarian stained glass infused with Bavarian humor. In one window, Saint Joseph appears as a carpenter, sporting a Bavarian hat!

Plan your visit: saintanthonyofpadua.wordpress .com. 546 Main Street, Hoven, SD 57450. (605) 948-2451.

 For a touch of Fátima, visit the **Mid-America Fatima Family Shrine** in Alexandria: It contains soil and rock from the site of Our Lady's apparitions at Fátima, Portugal. Father Robert J. Fox (1927–2009), founder of the Fatima Family Apostolate, began the 1987 outdoor shrine with royalties from his many books. Featuring a host of devotional areas, the shrine is "kid-spirational." They love hugging a seated Jesus statue or pretending to be "Star Wars" Saint Michael the Archangel slaying a serpent. St. Mary of Mercy Church is next door.

Plan your visit: Fifth Street and Juniper Street, Alexandria, SD 57311. (605) 239-4578.

The **Cathedral of Saint Joseph** in Sioux Falls is uniquely "peopled" with people art. Ceiling bas-reliefs depict the apostles (ordinary people when Christ called them), while three large rose windows portray "everyday saints" — people going about their daily lives. A nurse and a teacher appear in Mary's rose window, a wheat farmer and a hunter in Saint Joseph's window. Paying homage in the Christ the King window are native peoples from around

285

the world. The Renaissance Revival structure dates from 1916.

Plan your visit: stjosephcathedral.net. 521 N. Duluth Avenue, Sioux Falls, SD 57104. (605) 336-7390.

 One July Sunday in 1874, a noisy cloud descended over Jefferson: grasshoppers! Within hours the crops were stubble. The plague returned the next year. But when spring planting neared in 1876, Father Pierre Boucher of St. Peter Catholic Church took up spiritual arms. He led Catholics and Protestants in an eleven-mile procession around the area, praying and planting tall wooden crosses. The hoppers fled. Three **Grasshopper Crosses** still guard the town — two in the country and one near the church. (See 250.)

Plan your visit: 402 Main Street, Jefferson, SD 57038. (605) 966-5716.

 Save a portion for God, a priest advised Ed and Jean English in 1957 when they bought a large parcel of land near Yankton. They did: forty-five acres. On a bluff overlooking Lewis and Clark Lake, the couple began the **House of Mary Shrine** and crowned the hilltop with three enormous crosses. The rustic setting, with its prairie grasses and wildflowers, nestles oodles of statues and shrines, a heart-shaped Rosary Pond, St. Joseph's Chapel, and the Little House of Mary.

Plan your visit: thehouseofmaryshrine.org. 142 Drees Drive, Yankton, SD 57078. (605) 668-0121.

Does history repeat itself? At Yankton's Sacred Heart Monastery, stained-glass windows in the **Bishop Marty Memorial Chapel** portray parallel scenes from Jesus' life and the lives of Benedictine saints. In one window, Jesus raises the widow of Nain's son from the dead, and Saint Benedict raises a peasant's dead son. In another, Jesus walking on water rescues a sinking Peter, and Saint Maurus runs across a lake to pull Saint Placidus by the hair to safety. Benedictine Sisters founded the monastery in the 1880s.

Plan your visit: yanktonbenedictines.org. 1005 W. Eighth Street, Yankton, SD 57078. (605) 668-6000.

WESTERN SOUTH DAKOTA

"Let the children come to me," Jesus said. In the **Children's Memorial Garden** at Terra Sancta Retreat Center in Rapid City, three child statues, their robes flying, run with glee to a Jesus statue with open arms. Sculpted by Tom White, the life-size bronze statues inspire families to both remember their deceased children and celebrate their eternal reunion with God.

Plan your visit: terrasancta.org. 2101 City Springs Road, Rapid City, SD 57702. (605) 716-0925.

290 When Native American catechist and Servant of God Nicholas Black Elk (1863–1950) died, it's said that "miracle lights" filled the night sky over Pine Ridge Indian Reservation: The Oglala Lakota holy man was home. A Catholic convert, the evangelist led an estimated 400 Native Americans to the baptismal waters and was godfather to more than one hundred. In 2016, Harney Peak in South Dakota's Black Hills National Forest — the nation's highest peak east of the Rocky Mountains — was renamed **Black Elk Peak**. A lookout tower at the summit offers a sweeping view of four states.

Plan your visit: fs.usda.gov/recarea/blackhills /recarea/?recid=80906. South of Hill City. (605) 673-9200.

✚ FINDING FAITH
in South Dakota

When Father John Hatcher, SJ, former pastor at **St. Charles Borromeo Church** in St. Francis, part of the St. Francis Mission on the Rosebud Indian Reservation, asked the parish council what color they wanted to paint the church exterior, they couldn't decide. So he asked the youth group. They chose wisteria! Fondly dubbed the Purple Church and hailed as one of South Dakota's most beautiful churches, the unique exterior is a prelude to the artistic paradise waiting inside.

Constructed of poured concrete (hauled in buckets in those days) and completed in 1922, the Romanesque structure is filled to its rafters with Catholic and Lakota symbolism. Tipi poles represent Lakota hospitality, while Joseph Light's splendid sanctuary mural honors Our Lady and the North American Jesuit Martyrs. Note the sacred circle, with four colors, on the ceiling: White signifies the north, the source of snow; red, east, the red dawn and sunrise; yellow, south, for the heat that it brings; and black, west, where thunder clouds originate.

Plan your visit: sfmission.org. 350 S. Oak Street, St. Francis, SD 57572. (605) 747-2361.

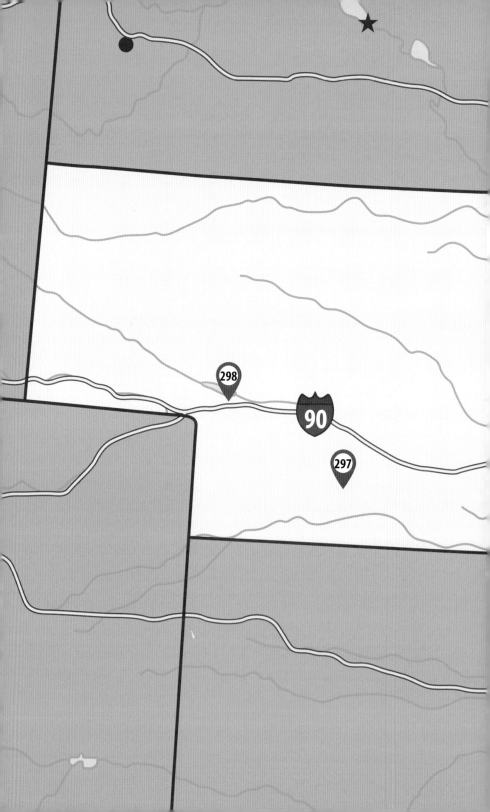

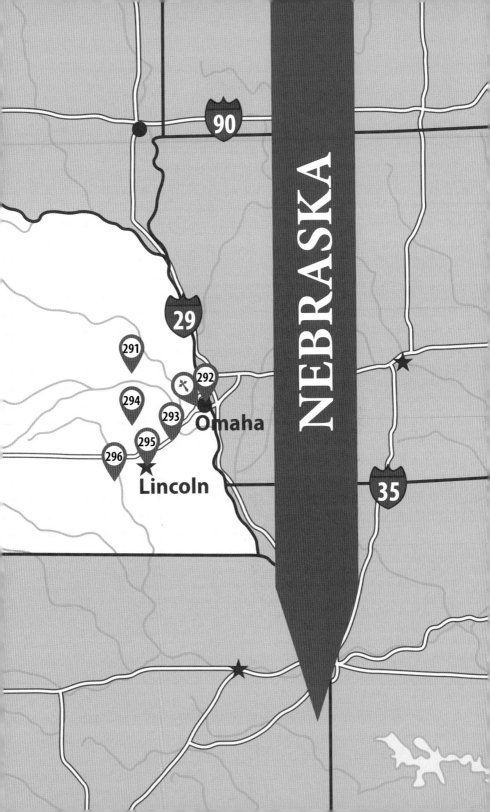

EASTERN NEBRASKA

 Join the Missionary Benedictine monks and pray with your eyes at **Christ the King Priory and Saint Benedict Center** in Schuyler. Unlike *lectio divina* (Latin for "holy reading"), which uses Scripture to encounter God, *visio divina* ("holy seeing") uses sacred art. *Praying with the Arts* (pick up a brochure for locations and descriptions) includes artwork ranging from a Peruvian-pottery Last Supper, to seventeenth-century Russian icons, to a *Maasai Bible* (biblical scenes depicted with elongated features in the Maasai tribal tradition of East Africa). More must-sees: the handwritten, illuminated *Saint John's Bible* (Heritage Edition) and Marian statues from around the world.

Plan your visit: christthekingpriory.com. 1123 Road I, Schuyler, NE 68661. (402) 352-2177.

 You'll sing the praises of **Saint Cecilia Cathedral** in Omaha. It took fifty-four years (1905–1959) and three million bricks — count them! — to erect this magnificent Spanish Renaissance Revival temple on the Nebraska prairie. Highlights include sixteenth-century stained-glass windows from Spain's Cathedral of Pamplona, a Spanish colonial art collection, and a mystical crucifix in the sanctuary. According to lore, sculptor Albin Polasek was baffled about how to carve Christ's face when a carpenter arrived looking for work. Captivated by the man's face, Polasek carved Christ looking up to heaven. The carpenter was never

seen again.

Plan your visit: stceciliacathedral.org. 701 N. Fortieth Street, Omaha, NE 68131. (402) 551-2313.

 In the 1990s, four Catholics felt individually inspired to erect a travelers' chapel along Interstate 80 in Nebraska. When the four connected through a series of divine events, they began planning the glass-walled, Prairie-style **Holy Family Shrine** at Gretna. Every building feature, from the tomblike visitors' entrance, to the forty-five-foot-tall wooden trusses simulating wheat, to the twin streams of water flowing into the chapel, is spiritually evocative. Drive by at night and the illuminated chapel appears out of this world.

Plan your visit: hfsgretna.org. 23132 Pflug Road, Gretna, NE 68028. (402) 332-4565.

 Who's your help if you aspire to be a priest? The Blessed Mother! As a seminarian, Father Benedict Bauer, OSB, vowed that, if ordained, he would build a shrine in her honor. And he did at **Assumption Catholic Church** in Dwight. The tiny brick Chapel of Our Lady of Perpetual Help, dedicated in 1934, seats four. Other devotional areas include the Mother of Grace Shrine, the Grotto of Agony in the Garden of Gethsemane, and the Grotto of Saint Jude Thaddeus.

Plan your visit: dwightassumption.weebly.com. 336 W. Pine Street, Dwight, NE 68635. (402) 566-2765.

Everything at the **Cathedral of the Risen Christ** in Lincoln — from its name to spectacular artworks — proclaims, "He is risen!" Constructed in 1964–1965, the Ecclesiastical Modern church is a joyous swirl of color and light. Sixty-nine stained-glass windows, including the stories-tall Crystal Screen, portray the redemption story. One window might test your biblical IQ: Why is Jesus wearing a gardener's hat and carrying a spade? Dominating the sanctuary is a nearly fourteen-foot-tall cross with a carved wooden statue of the Resurrected Christ.

Plan your visit: cathedraloftherisenchrist.org. 3500 Sheridan Boulevard, Lincoln, NE 68506. (402) 488-0948.

Schoenstatt Chapel in Crete (see 221).

Plan your visit: cormariae.com. 340 State Highway 103, Crete, NE 68333. (402) 826-3346.

WESTERN NEBRASKA

On October 7, 1944, the feast of Our Lady of the Rosary, Father Henry Denis — a Pole incarcerated at Germany's Dachau concentration camp — was mentally praying the Rosary during roll call and didn't hear his name and number. Failure to step forward when called was a Nazi crime punishable by death. The young priest went to his work detail and began preparing himself for execution later that day. Providentially, he was spared, and in thanksgiving he vowed to build Our Lady a shrine if he survived the death camp. After the war, Father

Denis immigrated to the United States and was assigned, in 1949, to **St. Germanus Catholic Church** in Arapahoe. Seven years later, he fulfilled his vow. Surrounded by statues of angels, sheep, and the three shepherd children, Our Lady of Fatima Shrine exudes a heavenly calm and peace.

Plan your visit: arapahoe-ne.com/attractions /shrine.htm. 912 Chestnut Street, Arapahoe, NE 68922. (308) 697-3722.

298 Can I get an "Amen"? **The Little Church** in Keystone is a testament to ecumenical harmony. Built in 1908 in a pioneer town too small for two churches, the eighteen-by-forty-foot white clapboard building seats seventy-five and features two altars: a Catholic altar at one end and a Protestant altar at the other. Reversible pews allowed churchgoers to face the altar of their faith.

Plan your visit: visitnebraska.com/keystone /little-church-keystone. Keystone Lake Road to McCarthy Street, Keystone, NE 69144. (800) 658-4390.

✠ FINDING FAITH
in Nebraska

A tour of **Boys Town** will warm your heart. The Hall of History tells the fascinating story of Servant of God Edward Flanagan (1886–1948), the young Irish native who began a home for boys in Omaha in 1917. As the number of boys swelled, Father Flanagan bought Overlook Farm, near Omaha, in 1921. Renamed Boys Town, the incorporated village has its own fire and police departments, schools, and post office. In 1979, Boys Town opened its doors to girls.

Other tour highlights include the Garden of the Bible with more than 150 biblical plants, the Father Flanagan House, the Leon Myers Stamp Center (the world's largest ball of stamps), and the Gothic-inspired Dowd Memorial Chapel of the Immaculate Conception, where Father Flanagan was laid to rest.

Plan your visit: boystown.org. Visitors Center at 13628 Flanagan Boulevard, Boys Town, NE 68010. (800) 625-1400.

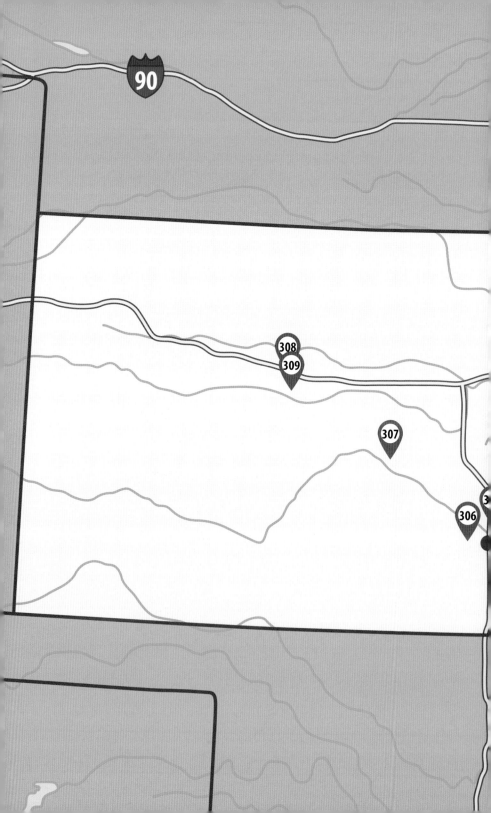

EASTERN KANSAS

 When you enter **St. Mary's Church** in rural St. Benedict (near Seneca), you're walking into paradise. Erected by German and Irish pioneers, the 1893 Late Romanesque limestone church is so breathtakingly beautiful it was named one of the 8 Wonders of Kansas Art. Artwork includes seventy-nine angels, nearly 3,000 square feet of artistic windows, fourteen large oil paintings (don't miss Mary's assumption over the high altar), and friezes and stenciling galore. Even the cast iron columns are decorated to high heaven.

Plan your visit: stmarystbenedict.org. 9208 Main Street, St. Benedict, KS 66538. (785) 336-3174.

 Benedictine College in Atchison has a good friend in Mary. One night in 1856, Father Henry Lemke, OSB, founder of adjacent St. Benedict Abbey (see 301), was walking home from a sick call when he got caught in a torrential thunderstorm. Disoriented, the former Lutheran begged Mary's help. Meanwhile, a "lady in white" appeared to a girl in a nearby cabin and asked her to put a lantern in the window. The priest saw the light and found refuge. Abbey monks founded the college near that spot in 1858 — the same year a "lady in white" appeared to Bernadette in Lourdes, France. Marian tributes include Mary's Grotto, a two-story-tall Our Lady of Grace Fountain, and Guadalupe Hall, crowned with twelve stars.

Plan your visit: www.benedictine.edu. 1020 N. Second Street, Atchison, KS 66002. (800) 467-5340.

Go boating with Christ at **St. Benedict's Abbey Church** in Atchison. Dubbed the Ship of the Prairie, the limestone church, completed in 1957, was designed to resemble a boat. The tower is the mast; the nave's plank-like pews, rowing benches. The entrance is the bow; artist Jean Charlot's 610-square-foot fresco *The Trinity and Episodes of Benedictine Life*, the stern. Above the altar, at the helm, is a striking double crucifix. On one side, Christ's head is lifted in life; on the other, bowed in death.

301

Plan your visit: kansasmonks.org, kansastravel .org/stbenedictsabbey.htm. 1020 N. Second Street, Atchison, KS 66002. (913) 367-7853.

For decades, French-born Saint Rose Philippine Duchesne (1769–1852) dreamed of evangelizing the American Indians. Finally, at age seventy-two, her dream came true: She began a school in 1841 for Potawatomi Indians at St. Mary's Mission near Centerville. Her legacy (the Indians called her Woman Who Prays Always) and the Potawatomi Trail of Death — a 660-mile resettlement march from Indiana to Kansas — are memorialized at the mission site, now called **St. Rose Philippine Duchesne Memorial Park**. (See 264, 265, and 303.)

302

Plan your visit: kansastravel.org /stphilippinepark.htm. 8487 W. 1525 Road, Centerville, KS 66014.

Saint Rose Philippine Duchesne once said, "It will be done if it be God's will, even if it takes 100 years." It was 100 years from her 1841 arrival in Linn County to establish an Indian school until Sacred Heart Catholic Church, the county's first Catholic church, was built in Mound City in 1941. Inside the church, the **Shrine of St. Rose Philippine Duchesne** honors the saint in stained glass, statuary, and paintings that portray her life with the Potawatomi Indians. (See 264, 265, and 302.)

303

Plan your visit: miamilinncatholics.org. 729 W. Main Street, Mound City, KS 66056. (913) 755-2652.

Tales of the Good Thief, Servant of God Emil J. Kapaun (1916–1951), fill **St. John Nepomucene Catholic Church** in tiny Pilsen (near Lincolnville). Born to Czech immigrant farmers, Pilsen's native son served as a United States Army chaplain during the Korean War. Captured in November 1950, God's holy man developed sticky fingers. Invoking Saint Dismas, the good thief at Calvary, he snuck into supply sheds and pilfered food for his starving comrades. Pilsen's Good Thief died in a prison hospital in May 1951. The Father Kapaun Museum and a larger-than-life statue tell his remarkable story.

304

Plan your visit: fatherkapaun.org, hfpmc.org. Remington Road and 275th Street, Marion, KS 66861. (620) 382-3369.

Basilica of St. Fidelis [308]

305 There's "joy in the mourning" at **Ascension Cemetery** in Bel Aire. Mounted atop a twenty-seven-foot-tall column, a twelve-foot bronze statue of *The Ascending Christ* soars to heaven — a healing balm inspiring hope in mourners that their loved ones are likewise returning to God. Sculpted by Rip Caswell, the muscular Jesus statue is flanked by twelve pillars representing the Twelve Apostles, with a reflecting pool in front.

Plan your visit: catholiccemonterieswichita.org /ascension. 7200 E. Forty-Fifth Street N., Bel Aire, KS 67226. (316) 722-1971.

WESTERN KANSAS

306 **St. Mark the Evangelist Catholic Church** in Colwich is a German timepiece. The 1903 Romanesque Revival edifice was built by German settlers using blueprints from Old Germany and building materials from a dismantled watch factory in nearby Wichita. It's also a font of answered prayer. During World War II, a German priest led the congregation in praying a Sunday Rosary for parish soldiers in harm's way. All forty-seven survived. In gratitude, folks erected a Lourdes grotto. The Sunday Rosary continued during the Korean and Vietnam wars — every soldier returned home alive.

Plan your visit: stmarkks.org. 19230 W. Twenty-Ninth Street N., Colwich, KS 67030. (316) 796-1604.

Martyred on the Kansas plains in 1542, Padre Juan de Padilla — one of America's first martyrs — is remembered with the granite **Padilla Cross** near Lyons. In 1541, the Franciscan priest accompanied Coronado to "Quivira," in his fabled search for gold in today's Kansas. No gold was found, and the expedition returned to New Mexico. A year later, Padre Padilla returned to evangelize the Quivira Indians. When he left them to convert other tribes and enlarge his "tent of souls for the Lord," he was slain with arrows.

Plan your visit: kansas-kofc.org/index.php/site /general/641. Three miles west of Lyons on US Highway 56. N 38° 20.853 W 098° 16.591. (620) 257-2320.

From afar, the 141-foot twin towers of the **Basilica of St. Fidelis** in Victoria look like giant exclamation marks. Step inside "the cathedral of the plains," as William Jennings Bryan once hailed the 1909 Romanesque church, and the wows continue. Erected by German-Russian settlers, the massive limestone church, seating 1,100 (nearly the town's entire population), boasts forty-six elaborate stained-glass windows, Austrian hand-carved stations of the cross, fourteen Vermont granite pillars, and five wooden altars painted to imitate marble. The basilica is so grand and so beautiful it was named one of the 8 Wonders of Kansas.

Plan your visit: stfidelischurch.com. 900 Cathedral Avenue, Victoria, KS 67671. (785) 735-2777.

309 If you like to church-hop, come to **Ellis County**. Built by German homesteaders from Russia and Bukovina (a region in Eastern Europe), a string of ten historic churches, including the Basilica of St. Fidelis (see 308), decorate small towns off Interstate 70 between Russell and Hays. Known for their ethnic cemetery crosses, the churches are "steepled" in lore. Why is Holy Cross Church in Pfeiffer — one of the 8 Wonders of Kansas Architecture — dubbed the Two-Cent Church? How did the tiny town of Catharine get its name? (Think Russia.)

Plan your visit: visithays.com/163/Churches. (800) 569-4505.

✠ FINDING FAITH
in Kansas

How long is a promise? Forever, in Greenbush! In 1869, Father Phillip Colleton, SJ, was riding his horse on the prairie when he got caught in a fierce thunderstorm with pounding hail. Taking refuge under his saddle in some bushes, he promised to erect a church on that spot if he lived. In 1871, a small wooden St. Aloysius Church went up. The promise doesn't end there.

When an 1877 storm destroyed the church, a second church was built in 1881. A third and larger church was dedicated in 1907, and the 1881 church became a hall. When the third church burned in 1982, the 1881 church — the second church — was renovated and became the fourth church. When the fourth church closed in 1993, folks banded together to preserve the structure, now called **St. Aloysius Historic Site**, and to keep Father Colleton's promise alive.

Plan your visit: saintaloysius.weebly.com. 947 W. Highway 47, Girard, KS 66743.

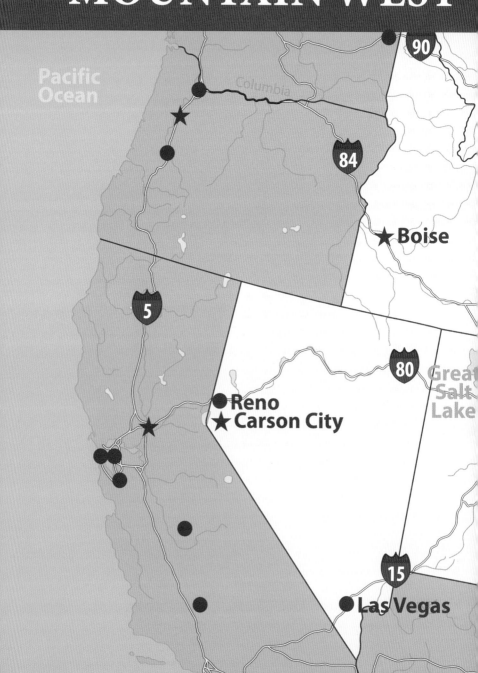

MOUNTAIN WEST

Pacific
Ocean

Columbia

90

84

★ **Boise**

5

80

Great
Salt
Lake

● **Reno**
★ **Carson City**

★

15

● **Las Vegas**

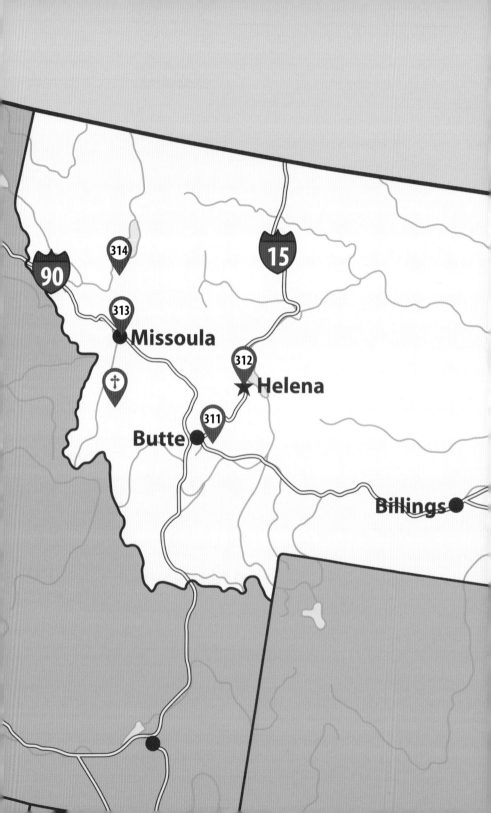

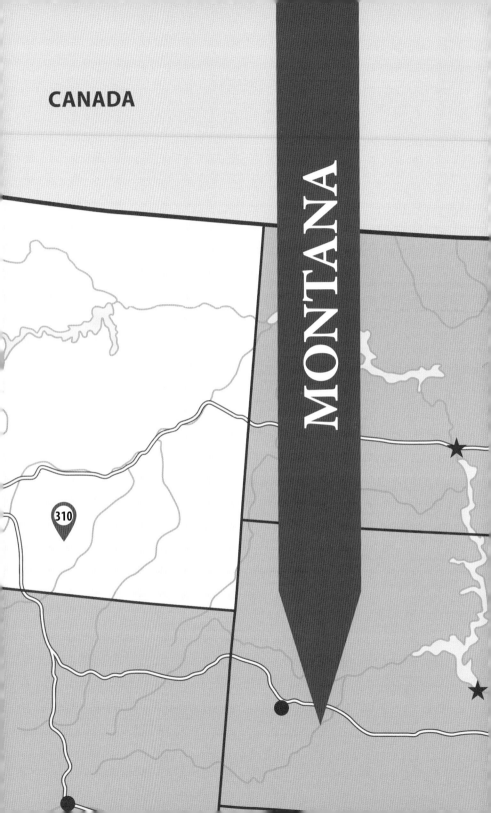

CANADA

MONTANA

310

EASTERN MONTANA

Tabernaculum means "tent" in Latin, and the tent-shaped **St. Labre Chapel** in Ashland, on the Northern Cheyenne Reservation, is a house worthy of the Lord. Inspired by tipis of the Plains Indians, the stone chapel features a great wooden beam that cants skyward through the "smoke hole" at the top. Beautiful stained-glass windows, resembling feathers floating to heaven, adorn the inside.

Plan your visit: southeastmontana.com/st-labre -mission. Tongue River Road, Ashland, MT. (406) 784-4516.

WESTERN MONTANA

Overlooking Butte, **Our Lady of the Rockies** — the nation's third tallest statue — was born of a miracle. In 1979, Butte resident Bob O'Bill vowed to make a five-foot statue of Our Lady for his yard if his dying wife recovered from cancer. She did. But O'Bill's statue grew into a ninety-foot mountaintop icon! Standing on the Continental Divide at 8,510 feet, the brilliant white statue is lit at night: a beacon of hope to travelers, on Interstates 15 and 90, that everything — even a miracle — is possible with prayer.

Plan your visit: ourladyoftherockies.net. Butte Plaza Mall, 3100 Harrison Avenue, Butte, MT 59701. Guided tours only. 406-782-1221.

It's a wonder the twin spires of the **Cathedral of St.**

St. Francis Xavier Church [313]

Helena in Helena are still standing! According to lore, a madcap pilot bet that he could fly his small plane between the 230-foot-tall spires. He made it, just barely. Modeled after Austria's famous Votive Church in Vienna, the 1908 Gothic-style church boasts fifty-nine Bavarian stained-glass windows depicting biblical events and events in Church history. Note the window of Pope Saint Pius X giving first Communion to children, a tribute to his 1910 decree that lowered the age of first Communicants from twelve to seven.

Plan your visit: sthelenas.org. 530 N. Ewing Street, Helena, MT 59601. (406) 442-5825.

Erected of red brick in 1891–1892, Missoula's **St. Francis Xavier Church** is "egg-ceptionally" beautiful — and for good reason. As the story goes, for eighteen months eggs arrived by the gross at the Jesuit church to make the tempera that Brother Joseph Carignano, SJ (see 314), needed to paint the sixty-six murals. A visual catechism, the Renaissance-style murals depict Bible stories and saints that seem to glow with inner divine light. Brother Joseph also painted the stations of the cross, in oil on canvas.

Plan your visit: sfxmissoula.org. 420 W. Pine Street, Missoula, MT 59802. (406) 542-0321.

A cook at **St. Ignatius Mission** in St. Ignatius, Brother Joseph Carignano, SJ (see 313), also "served up" paradise. From 1904 to 1905, the self-taught Italian artist painted fifty-eight murals — biblical scenes ranging from the manna in the desert to the miracle of the loaves and fishes, as well as dozens of saints — on the church walls and ceiling. In the apse, an enormous triptych portrays in exquisite detail the three life-changing visions of Saint Ignatius of Loyola. Located on the Flathead Indian Reservation, the red-brick church dates from 1891.

Plan your visit: stignatiusmission.org. 300 Beartrack Avenue, St. Ignatius, MT 59865. (406) 745-2768.

✠ FINDING FAITH
in Montana

Touted as "where Montana began," **Historic St. Mary's Mission** in Stevensville is filled with firsts. Founded in 1841 by Jesuit legend Father Pierre De Smet (see 323 and 389), the mission is reportedly the first permanent settlement in Montana. The mission's cattle brand, a "Cross on a Hill," was one of the first brands in the state. Montana's first physician, surgeon, and pharmacist was Jesuit-of-all-trades Father Antonio Ravalli (see 315). Another first: his cabin/infirmary with a "ride-up" window, where he mixed his own compounds and dispensed medicine.

Italian-born Father Ravalli also had an artistic flair. Using the fruits of Mother Earth, he transformed the present log chapel — erected in 1866 for the Salish Indians — into a pioneer cathedral. He used vermillion clay for the red wall accents and berry juice for the blue robe of his hand-carved Mary statue. He also crafted a crucifix from the handle of a shepherd's crook.

Plan your visit: saintmarysmission.org. 315 Charlo Street, Stevensville, MT 59870. (406) 777-5734.

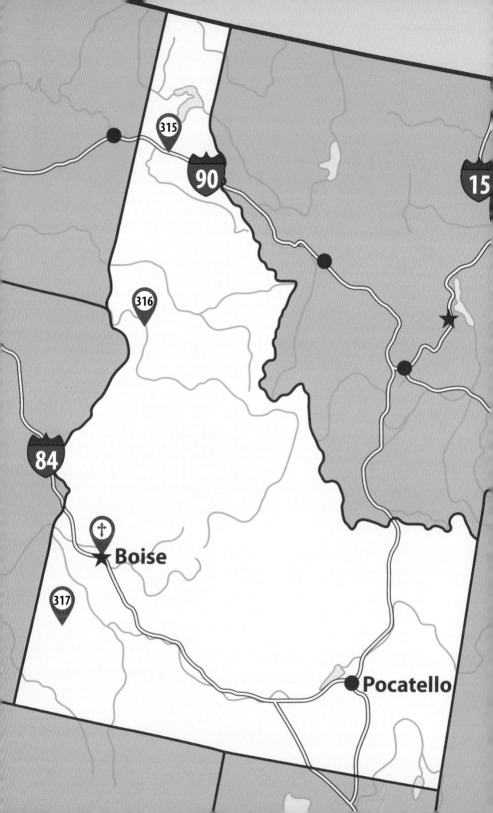

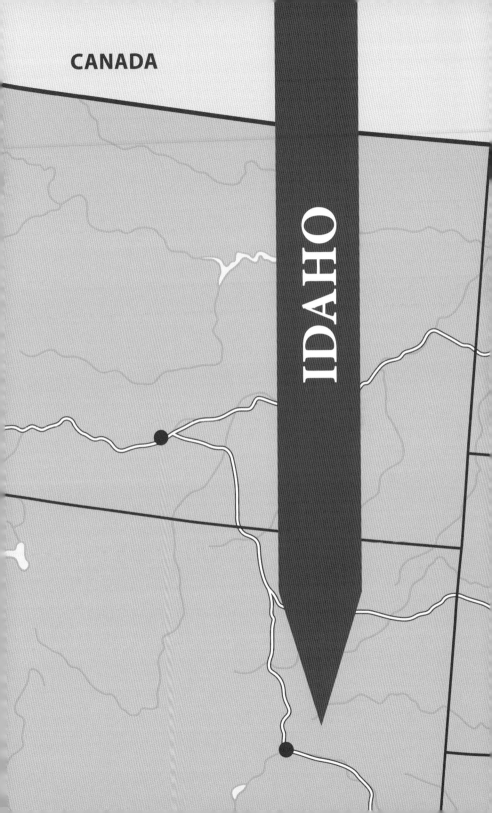

NORTHERN IDAHO

315 When Jesuit Father Antonio Ravalli (see Finding Faith in Montana) designed the **Mission of the Sacred Heart** (popularly called Cataldo Mission) for the Coeur d'Alene Indians near Cataldo, he ingeniously blended the grandeur of Old World cathedrals with frontier materials. The 1850s Greek Revival log church shines with chandeliers made from tin cans, wooden ceiling panels stained blue with huckleberry juice, and wallpaper crafted from newspaper. Idaho's oldest standing building, the House of the Great Spirit, is part of Coeur d'Alene's Old Mission State Park. An annual Mass is held August 15.

Plan your visit: parksandrecreation.idaho.gov /parks/coeur-d-alenes-old-mission. Exit 39 off Interstate 90, Cataldo, ID 83810. (208) 682-3814.

316 Rising like incense over the rolling Camas Prairie, the ninety-seven-foot twin towers of the Benedictine Sisters' **Monastery of St. Gertrude** near Cottonwood are visible for miles. Erected in 1919–1924, the Romanesque Revival chapel of blue porphyry rock is equally striking inside. Ceiling paintings depict the twelve emblems of the Apostles' Creed, while the huge painting over the altar, one of eight paintings, including *Creator Spiritus* (based on a Hubble telescope photo), changes with liturgical events. A museum preserves the Sisters' story and the fascinating legends of local characters, including former Chinese slave and American pioneer Polly Bemis.

Plan your visit: stgertrudes.org. 465 Keuterville Road, Cottonwood, ID 83522. (208) 962-3224.

SOUTHERN IDAHO

Upon this rock in Silver City, a church was built and ◀ 317 nothing could prevail against it, not even money-hungry men. Legend has it that when mining petered out in the 1920s, speculators wanted to buy the town's Episcopalian church and turn it into a roadhouse. The Episcopal bishop wouldn't hear of it and sold the church to the Catholic bishop for one dollar. Dedicated to **Our Lady of Tears**, the white-frame Gothic Revival church stands resolutely on a bluff overlooking the ghost town below. Periodic summer Masses offered.

Plan your visit: nampacatholic.church, westernmininghistory.com/special/churches/5608. 43°01'06.6"N 116°43'50.4"W. (208) 466-7031.

✙ FINDING FAITH
in Idaho

Something's missing at Boise's **Cathedral of St. John the Evangelist**: towers. As the story goes, the coffers dried up and the towers stopped short. Fifteen years in the building (1906–1921), the Romanesque Revival church was erected of Boise sandstone. But the jewel-box interior (to the delight of tourists) isn't always what it seems. Many "stained-glass" windows are colored glass with painted faces and hands, the "painted ceiling" a false ceiling done on canvas. It's said the gargoyles, holding up the bearing arches, are doing penance for their sins.

Boise is also home to a large Catholic Basque population, one of the highest concentrations of Basques outside of Spain. Famous saints of Basque heritage include Ignatius of Loyola and Francis Xavier.

Plan your visit: boisecathedral.org. 707 N. Eighth Street, Boise, ID 83702. (208) 342-3511.

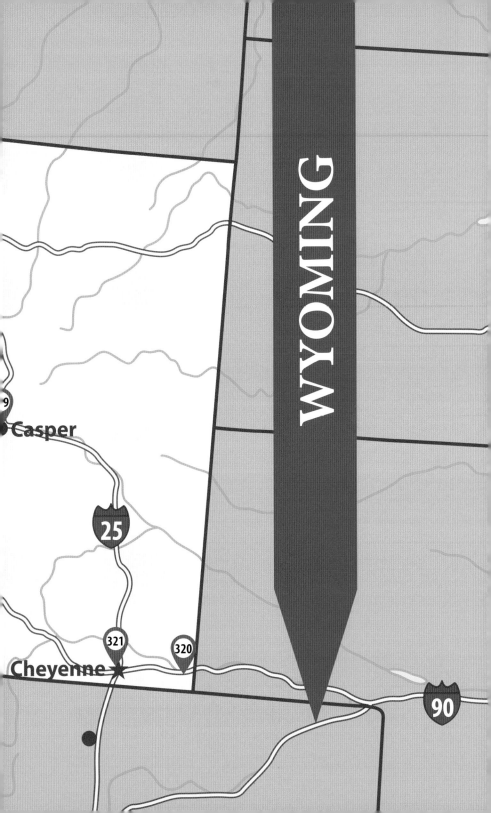

EASTERN WYOMING

 Want to read the Bible in one afternoon? You can at **Holy Name Catholic Church** in Sheridan. Just follow the twenty-four clerestory windows that tell in splendid stained glass the story of salvation. See the Seven Days of Creation, Noah's Ark riding out the Great Flood, David toppling Goliath, the Nativity, Judas clutching a bag of silver and a hangman's noose at the Last Supper, and the triumphant Resurrection of Christ.

Plan your visit: holynamesheridan.org. 260 E. Loucks Street, Sheridan, WY 82801. (307) 672-2848.

 Take in the Light at **Our Lady of Fatima Catholic Church** in Casper. Originally a World War II chapel at Casper Air Base, the converted church is filled with glorious light: stained glass depicting the Luminous Mysteries of the Rosary (possibly the country's first Luminous Mystery windows). Sunlight is God's light, and the windows were created in such a way that "Sonlight" emanates from the images of Jesus. Gracing the grounds is a twenty-two-foot statue of the Sacred Heart of Jesus, his red heart illuminated at night.

Plan your visit: fatimaincasper.org. 1401 CY Avenue, Casper, WY 82604. (307) 265-5586.

 You can't miss **Our Lady of Peace Shrine** near Pine Bluffs. Mounted on a tall pedestal, the towering white statue with open arms stands thirty feet high and weighs 180 tons. Ted and Marjorie Trefren erected the shrine in 1998 after a European pilgrimage to Marian apparition sites. Other statues include Our Lady of Lourdes, the child Mary with her mother Saint Anne, and Mary as a mother with the Child Jesus.

Plan your visit: ourladyofpeaceshrine.com. Exit 401 off Interstate 80, Pine Bluffs, WY 82082. 41°10'56.9"N 104°03'14.7"W. (307) 631-4606.

Cheyenne's **Cathedral of St. Mary** has a lofty claim: Altitude-wise, it's one of the highest cathedrals in the country. True to its name, the cathedral esteems Mary. European stained-glass windows in the nave portray both her life and the life of her Son, while the choir loft glows with a unique stained-glass adaptation of Raphael's *Sistine Madonna*. Unlike Raphael's masterpiece, halos appear over Mary and the Child Jesus, and the Basilica of Saint Peter rises in the background. The English Gothic church dates from 1907.

321

Plan your visit: stmarycathedral.com. 2107 Capitol Avenue, Cheyenne, WY 82001. (307) 635-9261.

WESTERN WYOMING

St. Stephens Indian Mission, on the Wind River Reservation in St. Stephens, honors the Great Spirit. The mission was founded in 1884 when Jesuit Father John Jutz pitched a tent and offered Mass, as Arapaho Chief Black Coal and his family watched. The current stark-white church, c. 1928, is decorated inside and out with brightly colored Indian designs. Note the stations of the cross portrayed with Indian figures and the sanctuary crucifix mounted on tipi poles.

322

Plan your visit: saintstephensmission.com. 33 St. Stephens Road, St. Stephens, WY 82524. (307) 856-7806.

323 Nearly two centuries have passed, but Father Pierre De Smet, SJ, remains a tall legend in the Daniel and Pinedale areas. On July 5, 1840, the Great Black Robe, as Indians called him, offered Wyoming's first Mass at a rendezvous with 2,000 trappers, fur traders, and Indians in attendance. The **De Smet Monument**, a three-sided stone-and-wood chapel, commemorates the historic event. An annual Mass is held on the second Sunday in July. (See Finding Faith in Montana and 389).

Plan your visit: ourladyofpeacewy.com. Inquire in Daniel for directions (GPS not recommended). Buffalo, WY 82834. (307) 367-2359

324 Behold the beauty of the **Chapel of the Sacred Heart** in Grand Teton National Park. Nestled among whispering pines and overlooking Jackson Lake, the log chapel was built in 1937 and seats 115. Open the doors and you'll be drawn to the sanctuary with its log altar and stained-glass wheel window of the Sacred Heart. A mission of Our Lady of the Mountains Church in Jackson, the chapel holds weekend summer Masses.

Plan your visit: olmcatholic.org. One mile south of Jackson Lake Dam. 43°50'43.6"N 110°36'10.0"W. (307) 733-2516.

✠ FINDING FAITH
in Wyoming

How fortunate for the priests of **St. Anthony of Padua Catholic Church** in Cody that they aren't circuit-riding preachers on horseback. Area-wise, the parish is the largest in the lower forty-eight states! Spanning more than 6,000 square miles — an area greater than Connecticut and Rhode Island combined — the parish also serves two permanent missions and a summer mission.

On a typical summer weekend, one priest travels 140 miles to say Mass at St. Theresa of the Child Jesus Church in Meeteetse and Our Lady of the Valley Church in Clark. A second priest travels 256 miles and stays overnight in Yellowstone National Park to say Mass at three different sites within the park. A third priest stays home and says Mass in Cody.

Plan your visit: stanthonycody.org. 1333 Monument Street, Cody, WY 82414. (307) 587-3388.

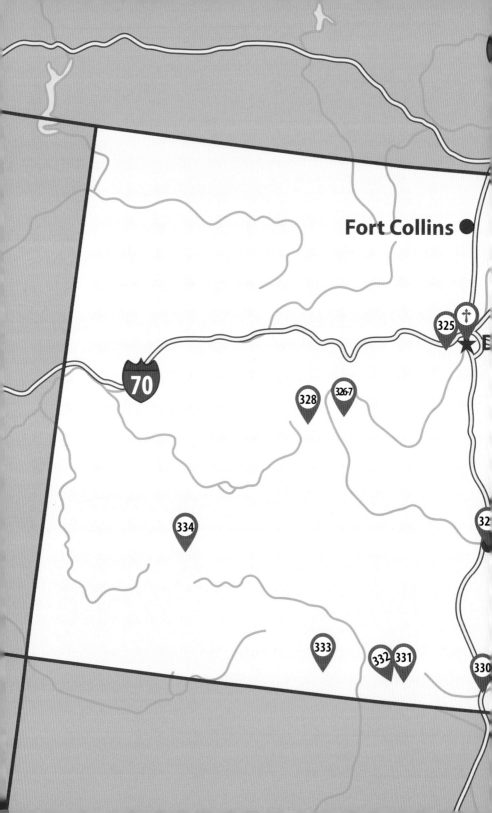

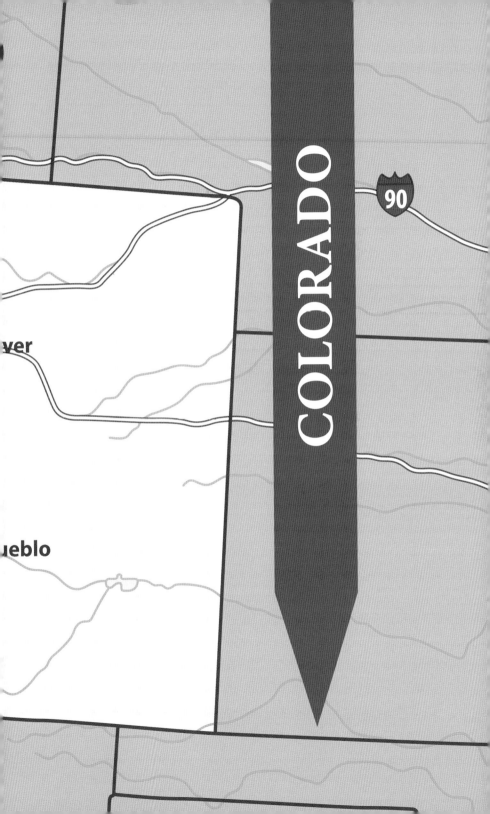

NORTHERN COLORADO

You might call the **Mother Cabrini Shrine** in Golden the Lourdes of Colorado. In 1912, when Mother Frances Cabrini's Missionary Sisters of the Sacred Heart of Jesus complained of thirst, the future saint said, "Lift that rock over there and start to dig. You will find water fresh enough to drink and clean enough to wash." They found the miraculous spring, and it's never stopped running. Other shrine attractions: the Stairway of Prayer (373 steps to the Mount of the Sacred Heart), Rosary Garden, and Cabrini Museum. (See 21 and 231.)

Plan your visit: mothercabrinishrine.org. 20189 Cabrini Boulevard, Golden, CO 80401. (303) 526-0758.

You're almost in heaven at **Annunciation Catholic Church** in Leadville, where the country's highest steeple — at 11,000 feet — could be a landing strip for angels! The steeple also boasts a legendary 1885 bell, a 3,000-pounder called St. Mary. As the story goes, when villagers petitioned the town fathers to halt the bell ringing (it woke them up), the pastor published their names for all to see. St. Mary is still ringing today.

Plan your visit: holyfamilyleadville.com, diocs. org/Parishes/Holy-Family. 609 Poplar Street, Leadville, CO 80461. (719) 486-1382.

While in Leadville, step inside **St. Joseph Catholic Church** and admire the wall-to-ceiling murals, hailed as some of the finest Slovene folk art in America.

◀ 327

Plan your visit: holyfamilyleadville.com, diocs.org /Parishes/Holy-Family. Corner of Maple Street and W. Second St, Leadville, CO 80461. (719) 486-1382.

It's a "Rocky Mountain (spiritual) high" at **St. Mary Catholic Church** in Aspen. Built by silver miners in the early 1890s, the two-story red-brick affair is architecturally curious: The parish offices are located on the lower level, and the church is on the upper level. Twelve icons portraying modern-day holy people — including "saint on skis," Blessed Pier Giorgio Frassati — line the star-speckled apse. Bonus trivia: According to legend, Christ's cross was made of aspen wood. When the tree learned of its holy victim, its leaves began to quake and have never stopped.

Plan your visit: stmaryaspen.org. 533 E. Main Street, Aspen, CO 81611. (970) 925-7339.

SOUTHERN COLORADO

 Take a mini-pilgrimage to Lisieux, France, at the **Shrine of St. Therese** in Pueblo. Completed in 1994, the shrine incorporates architectural elements — from cloister to arches to towers — of Thérèse's Carmelite monastery, while the dormer windows recall her family home. Five faceted windows depicting Thérèse's favorite flowers also represent her virtues: lotus, triumph over evil; olive, peace; daisy, innocence; violet, humility; and rose, joy.

Plan your visit: shrine-sttherese-pueblo.org. 300 Goodnight Avenue, Pueblo, CO 81004. (719) 542-1788.

According to legend, one blizzardy morning in 1908, a doctor was walking home after an all-night shift at Trinidad's old Mount San Rafael Hospital when

he saw a flickering light on a hill. Thinking some-
one was hurt, he went to the light and found a candle burning at the feet of a 250-pound Mary statue!
Where did she come from? Nobody knows, but one
title for Mary is Our Lady of Light. Sometime later,
the Spanish-style **Ave Maria Shrine** was erected on
that hilltop. An enormous rosary adorns the facade.

Plan your visit: trinidadcatholic.org. 412 Benedicta
Avenue, Trinidad, CO 81082. (719) 846-3369.

You'll be immersed in Christ's Passion at the **Shrine
of the Stations of the Cross** in San Luis. Sculpted
by Humberto Maestas, the dramatic, near-life-size
bronze stations (observe the minutely detailed facial
expressions) follow a switchback trail up *La Mesa de
la Piedad y de la Misericordia* (the Hill of Piety and
Mercy). At the summit is *La Capilla de Todos los San-
tos* (the Chapel of All Saints), a unique adobe with
towers and domes, and the Fifteenth Station — a
breathtaking portrayal of Christ's resurrection.

Plan your visit: sdcparish.org. Off State Highway 159, San Luis, CO 81152. 37°12'04.9"N
105°25'47.8"W. (719) 992-0122.

A miracle built **San Acacio Mission Church** in the
hamlet of San Acacio. According to one account,
when a band of Utes was about to attack the village in
1853, Spanish settlers began praying furiously to San
Acacio (Spanish for Saint Agathius, a centurion beheaded c. A.D. 303) and vowed to build him a church
if rescued. The Utes suddenly halted and then fled

faster than lightning: A soldier in the sky was guarding the village below! The adobe church is the oldest standing church in Colorado.

Plan your visit: sdcparish.org. Off State Highway 142, 37°12'22.6"N 105°30'01.3"W. (719) 992-0122.

333 According to tradition, Our Lady of Guadalupe selected the site of Colorado's oldest parish. Spanish settlers were traveling through the Conejos area in the mid-1800s when one of the burros began to balk. Nothing, not coaxing nor beatings, could make the burro go. When a small statue of Our Lady was discovered in the burro's pack, the Spaniards vowed to erect a church on that spot. The burro then moved. Today's **Our Lady of Guadalupe Church**, built in 1926, features a beautiful altar with an image of Our Lady.

Plan your visit: ologp.com. 6633 County Road 13, Antonito, CO 81120. (719) 376-5985.

334 Say your prayers and you might hit gold. In the 1950s, when mining hit rock bottom in Silverton, folks at St. Patrick Catholic Church erected the **Christ of the Mines Shrine** — a twelve-ton, sixteen-foot Carrara marble Jesus statue on Anvil Mountain — and prayed. A few months later, a new tunnel was opened and gold poured out!

Plan your visit: silvertoncolorado.com. 258 Fifteenth Street #252, Silverton, CO 81433. (800) 752-4494.

✠ FINDING FAITH
in Colorado

Buffalo Bill prayed here. So did the Unsinkable Molly Brown. Pope Saint John Paul II (see 58, Finding Faith in Maryland, 101, 239, 257, and 272) offered Mass here during World Youth Day 1993. That's just the beginning of the "mile-high" tales at Denver's **Cathedral Basilica of the Immaculate Conception**. Today's pilgrims flock to the turn-of-the-twentieth-century French Gothic temple to honor another legend: freed slave and Servant of God Julia Greeley, whose remains now rest here.

Born in Missouri between 1833 and 1848 (Julia didn't know her age), Denver's Angel of Charity worked menial jobs by day but pulled a little red wagon by night, making secret deliveries of food, clothing, medicine, and coal to people in need. It's said that she even gave away her own burial plot. When Julia died on June 7, 1918, she was between seventy and eighty-five years of age.

Plan your visit: denvercathedral.org. 1535 Logan Street, Denver, CO 80203. (303) 831-7010.

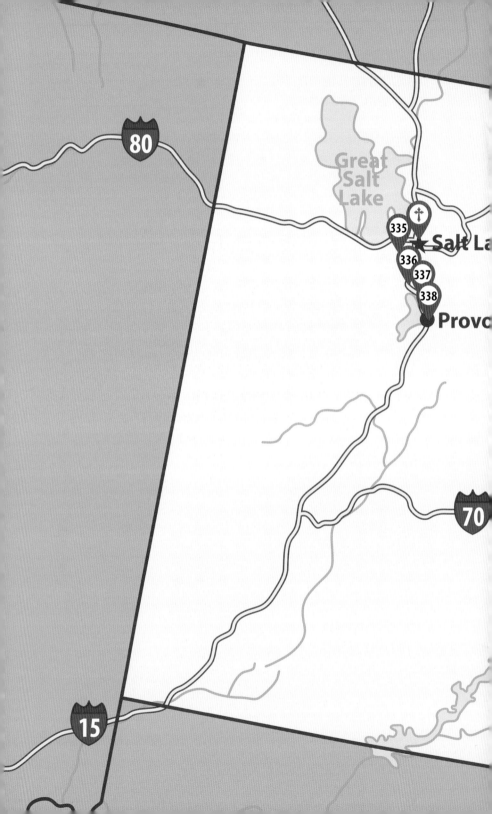

335 Weld nearly ten miles of steel rods together and what do you get? An eight-foot-tall metal sculpture of Saint Francis of Assisi. Mounted on a pedestal on the grounds of **Saint Francis Xavier Catholic Church and School** in Kearns, Michael Peery's "monumental Francis" — with upturned head and outstretched arms — radiates joy in the Lord. Steel rods form the saint's gown and head; chains, his hair and beard.

Plan your visit: sfxkearns.org. 4501 W. 5215 S., Kearns, UT 84118. (801) 968-2123.

336 Oval-shaped, with a cross at the bow, **St. Joseph the Worker Catholic Church** in West Jordan, constructed in 2010 of board-formed concrete, resembles a ship on heavenly seas. The portholes: twelve

glass windows of various colors representing the Twelve Apostles. Across the courtyard, another "vessel" — the day chapel dubbed the Ark for its unique shape and altar skylight — provides spiritual shelter amid life's daily storms.

Plan your visit: sjtwchurch.org. 7405 S. Redwood Road, West Jordan, UT 84084. (801) 255-8902.

Want to go on pilgrimage? Come to **St. Francis of Assisi Catholic Church** in Orem. A labyrinth in the foyer begins your journey, while artist James Mc-Gee's "faith-traveler" mural awaits in the sanctuary. Spanning cultures and time periods, the two-story masterpiece portrays diverse seekers — from a Holy Land Crusader, to a young mother with children in tow, to a businessman (note the smartphone) — navigating a mountainous path toward the light. A massive crucifix with an eight-foot corpus aptly intersects their path. The Spanish Mission-style church was dedicated in 2012.

Plan your visit: oremstfrancis.org. 65 E. 500 N., Orem, UT 84057. (801) 221-0750.

When you climb the **Escalante Cross Trail** overlooking Spanish Fork, you're retracing a historic expedition. On July 29, 1776, Franciscan explorers Atanasio Domínguez and Silvestre Escalante left Santa Fe, New Mexico, to find an overland route to Monterey, California. Reaching Spanish Fork

Canyon in late September, the padres ascended a hill and named the area Our Lady of Mercy of the Timpanogotzis (a local Indian tribe). The thirty-seven-foot Escalante Cross on Dominguez Hill, located in Spanish Oaks Campground, went up in 1981.

Plan your visit: hikingproject.com/trail/7063634 /escalante-cross-trail. 2939 S. Spanish Oaks Drive, Spanish Fork, UT 84660. (801) 804-4600.

✦ FINDING FAITH
in Utah

When the saints go marching in, they gather at the **Cathedral of the Madeleine** in Salt Lake City. Multitudes of saints, from Agnes to Venantius, appear in carvings, stained glass, and even the tympanum over the main doors. The colossal sanctuary murals, the eye-catching works of Felix Lieftuchter (see 108 and Finding Faith in Ohio), depict Christ Crucified, flanked by Old Testament figures and more saints. According to lore, Lieftuchter used local Mormons as his models; their Latter-Day descendants are known to come here looking for their "Catholic ancestors."

The country's only cathedral dedicated to Saint Mary Magdalene (Madeleine in French), this 1900 Romanesque structure is also one of the most colorful. Inspired by the Spanish Gothic of the Late Middle Ages, the dramatic polychrome interior is out of this world. Purple fluted columns, starry blue ceiling, splashes of red and gold — there's hardly an inch not glowing with vivid color.

Plan your visit: utcotm.org. 331 E. South Temple, Salt Lake City, UT 84111. (801) 328-8941.

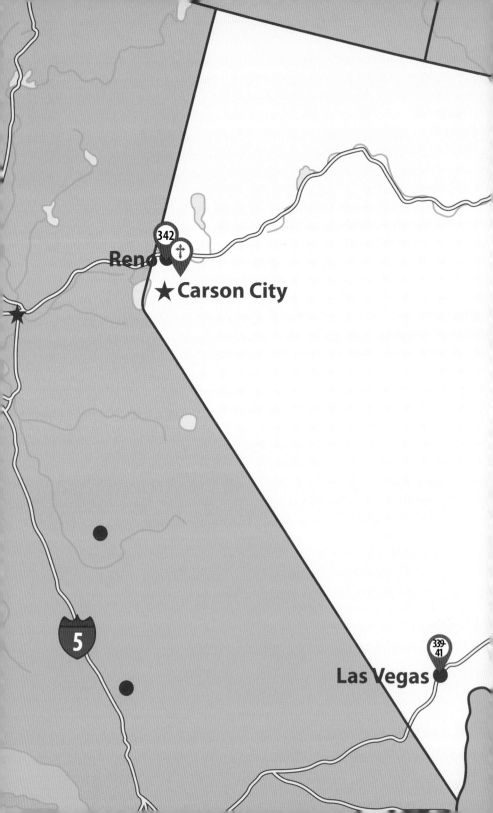

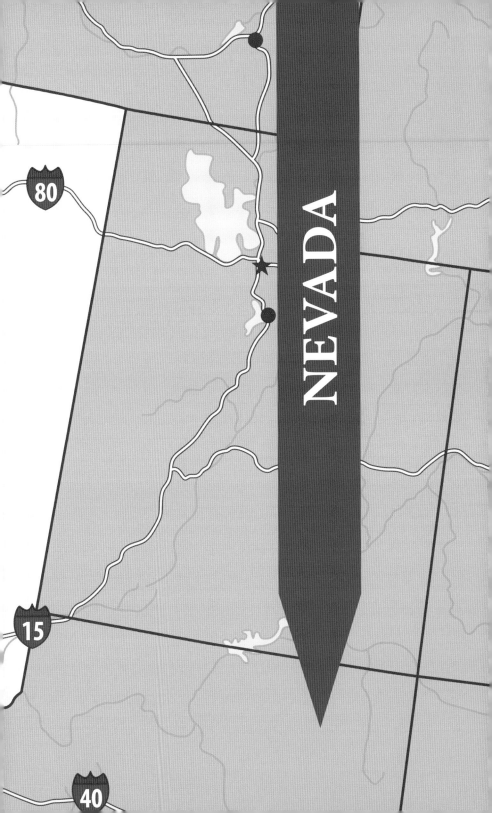

EASTERN NEVADA
LAS VEGAS

 Your guardian angel is always with you, even in Sin City! Erected in 1963 on the Strip, the A-shaped **Guardian Angel Cathedral** is, well, angelic. It's said the ceiling was angled to resemble angel wings, while artist Edith Piczek's stories-tall guardian angel mosaic keeps watch over the main doors. Her sister Isabel created the unique A-shape stained-glass windows with the stations of the cross. (See 341 and 342.) Every weekend thousands of tourists (and their angels) flock here for Mass.

Plan your visit: gaclv.org. 302 Cathedral Way, Las Vegas, NV 89109. (702) 735-5241.

 Dwarfed by big-name hotels, the **Roman Catholic Shrine of the Most Holy Redeemer**, dedicated in 1993, has a big name of its own: Jesus! Outside, a Jesus statue seated on a rock beckons tourists to come unto him and have their photos taken. Inside, bronze-like tableaus, the figures seemingly suspended in air, portray Jesus' life. You'll marvel at Gabriel flying through Mary's window in the Annunciation scene and Jesus washing Peter's feet in a vertical Last Supper.

Plan your visit: mostholyredeemer.tripod.com. 55 E. Reno Avenue, Las Vegas, NV 89119. (702) 891-8600.

 When Bishop Lawrence Scanlan built the city's first Catholic church in 1910, he wanted it named for

Joan of Arc. It didn't matter that she wasn't yet canonized (she would be in 1920), he still had a blazing good reason. He was riding a horse through town one hot summer day — so hot that he felt like he was being burned at the stake! **Historic Saint Joan of Arc Roman Catholic Church** features spectacular artworks, including Isabel and Edith Piczek's (see 339 and 342) sanctuary mural of Joan's martyrdom and exterior mosaic of the Eight Beatitudes.

Plan your visit: stjoanlv.org. 315 S. Casino Center Boulevard, Las Vegas, NV 89101. (702) 382-9909.

WESTERN NEVADA

You can't help but contemplate the great sanctuary mural at Reno's 1907 Neoclassical **St. Thomas Aquinas Cathedral**. Executed by artist-sisters Edith and Isabel Piczek (see 339 and 341), *Adoration of the Lamb of God, Our Lord in the Blessed Eucharist* depicts saints from both the Old Law (Moses, Ruth, and David, among others) and the New Law (from Clare of Assisi to Paschal Baylon to Pope Pius X). Other church highlights: stained-glass windows of Nevada's "faith pioneers," including Fray Francisco Garcés navigating a raging Colorado River in a raft, and copper-clad front doors with embossed angels and censers.

342

Plan your visit: stacathedral.com. 310 W. Second Street, Reno, NV 89503. (775) 329-2571.

✠ FINDING FAITH
in Nevada

When trouble strikes, fight back! That's the Wild West spirit of **Saint Mary in the Mountains Catholic Church** in Virginia City, an old silver mining town. The first church, built of wood in 1860, blew down. A subsequent brick church burned in the Great Fire of 1875. The Comstock Lode was running with silver at the time, and an even grander Gothic church went up: European stained glass, dazzling chandeliers, an elaborate high altar, California redwood pews with doors, and a double staircase to the choir loft.

Trouble struck again in 1957 when the Mad Monks — as townsfolk dubbed these Cistercian monks — took over the historic church and began stripping the ornate interior, claiming it was a distraction to prayer. The furious community banded together and drove the monks out. Restored to its holy heyday, Saint Mary's houses a must-see museum filled with surprising artifacts.

Plan your visit: travelnevada.com /discover/26201/saint-mary-mountains -catholic-church. 111 E Street, Virginia City, NV 89440. (775) 847-9099.

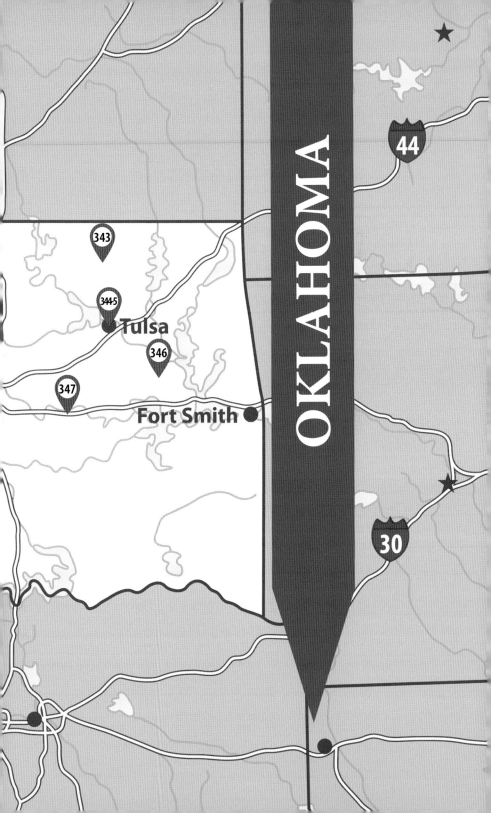

EASTERN OKLAHOMA

When parishioners of **Immaculate Conception Catholic Church** in Pawhuska, on the Osage Reservation, gaze at their world-famous Osage Window, they're looking at a family portrait. Crafted in Germany, the spectacular window, spanning nearly ten by twenty-five feet, depicts Father John Schoenmakers, SJ, bringing the Gospel to the Osage Nation. Subjects (all in tribal dress) include Chief Bacon Rind and his wife, Julia; Chief Arthur Bonnicastle; and Chief Saucy Calf. Some say gold dust is what makes the window so beautiful. Dubbed the Cathedral of the Osage, the brick church dates from 1910.

Plan your visit: icccpawhuska.org. 1314 Lynn Avenue, Pawhuska, OK 74056. (918) 287-1414.

Your sins are forgiven you — in person and in stained glass at **Holy Family Cathedral** in Tulsa. "Windows of mercy" include *The Prodigal Son; Jesus Knocking at Our Door; The Penitent Woman; Jesus, the Good Shepherd*; and Scriptural passages dealing with sin and forgiveness. In one image, the Crucified Jesus and a chalice appear with the words, "Behold the price of sin." Opened in 1914, the Gothic-style church boldly proclaims the Gospel: Three spires representing the Holy Family soar 251 feet to the heavens and are crowned with ten-foot-tall crosses.

Plan your visit: holyfamilycathedralparish.com. Eighth Street and Boulder Avenue, Tulsa, OK 74119. (918) 582-6247.

There's no mistaking Tulsa's **Christ the King Catholic Church**. Reputedly the world's first church named for Christ the King, after Pope Pius XI instituted the liturgical feast in 1925, the Gothic-Byzantine-Art Deco gem — wider than it is long — looks and feels kingly. The high walls and pinnacles are reminiscent of a king's palace; the front steps, a moat. Inside, Art Deco stained glass portrays Old Testament kings and Christian king-saints offering their crowns in homage to the King of kings.

Plan your visit: christthekingcatholic.church. 1520 S. Rockford, Tulsa, OK 74120. (918) 584-4788.

French Benedictine monks searched the country over for a new monastery site before settling on a ranch in the Ozark Mountains near Hulbert. Their first dwelling: a humble stable with horse stalls converted into monk cells. Founded in 1999, **Our Lady of Clear Creek Abbey**, with a Romanesque-style church, harkens to Old World monasteries. Early morning Masses (in Latin) are offered simultaneously by priests at the main altar and little side altars along the church walls.

Plan your visit: clearcreekmonks.org. 5804 W. Monastery Road, Hulbert, OK 74441. (918) 772-2454.

In December 1947, Father George V. Johnson was pacing the aisle of St. Wenceslaus Church in Prague, fretting. The oil boom was over. Where would he find money for a new church? When he eyed a statue of the Infant Jesus of Prague, he blurted out, "Why don't you do something?" The Infant did! Money rolled in and a new church went up. Located inside the church, the **National Shrine of the Infant Jesus of Prague** (don't miss the Infant's wardrobe of gowns) is world famous for answered prayer.

Plan your visit: shrineofinfantjesus.com. 304 Jim Thorpe Boulevard, Prague, OK 74864. (405) 567-3080.

WESTERN OKLAHOMA

The Oklahoma City bombing on April 19, 1995 **348** killed 168 people, injured many hundreds more, and destroyed or extensively damaged scores of buildings, including **St. Joseph Old Cathedral**. Miraculously, the sanctuary lamp remained lit during the blast. Overcoming evil with good, the parish restored the 1902 Gothic temple. Located on church grounds (adjacent to the Oklahoma City National Memorial), the sculpture *And Jesus Wept* recalls that fateful day. Based on John 11:35, a white statue of Jesus faces away from the bombing site, one hand covering his grief-stricken face.

Plan your visit: sjocokc.org. 307 NW Fourth Street, Oklahoma City, OK 73102. (405) 235-4565.

The **Shrine of Our Lady of Fatima** in tiny Bison **349** is a celebration of Marian feasts. On September 8, 1951 (the feast of the Nativity of the Blessed Virgin Mary), parish men hauled limestone to the site; construction began on October 11 (the original feast of the Maternity of the Blessed Virgin Mary); and the shrine was dedicated on December 8 (the feast of the Immaculate Conception). The enclosed shrine, with faceted glass depicting Fátima's "Miracle of the Dancing Sun," is located on the grounds of St. Joseph Catholic Church.

Plan your visit: fatimashrine-bison.com. 101 First Street, Bison, OK 73720. (405) 853-4425.

✢ FINDING FAITH
in Oklahoma

"The shepherd cannot run," Blessed Father Stanley Rother (1935–1981) wrote before he was murdered on July 28, 1981, at his mission rectory in Santiago Atitlán, Guatemala. Pilgrims, however, do "run" to holy sites in and around Oklahoma City to venerate America's firstborn beatified martyr. **Holy Trinity Catholic Church** in Okarche was Father Rother's "ground zero of faith." It was here the farm boy was baptized and celebrated his first Mass. Highlights include displays with photos and artifacts, and a life-size statue of Father Rother greeting a barefoot Guatemalan girl.

Plan your visit: holytrinityok.org. 211 W. Missouri Avenue, Okarche, OK 73762. (405) 263-7930.

Father Rother's in good company at **St. Eugene Catholic Church** in Oklahoma City. Presented in stained glass are his life and the life of fellow priest-martyr Blessed Miguel Pro, SJ (1891–1927), executed during Mexico's Cristero War.

Plan your visit: steugenes.org. 2400 W. Hefner, Oklahoma City, OK 73120. (405) 751-7115.

The final resting place of Oklahoma's native son, the **Blessed Stanley Rother Shrine** in Oklahoma City is expected to be completed in 2022. The planned shrine church, seating 2,000 and designed in Spanish Mission style, will echo Father Rother's mission church in Guatemala. A museum will tell his remarkable story.

Plan your visit: archokc.org/shrine. SE 89th and Shields Boulevard, Oklahoma City, OK 73149. (800) 721-5651.

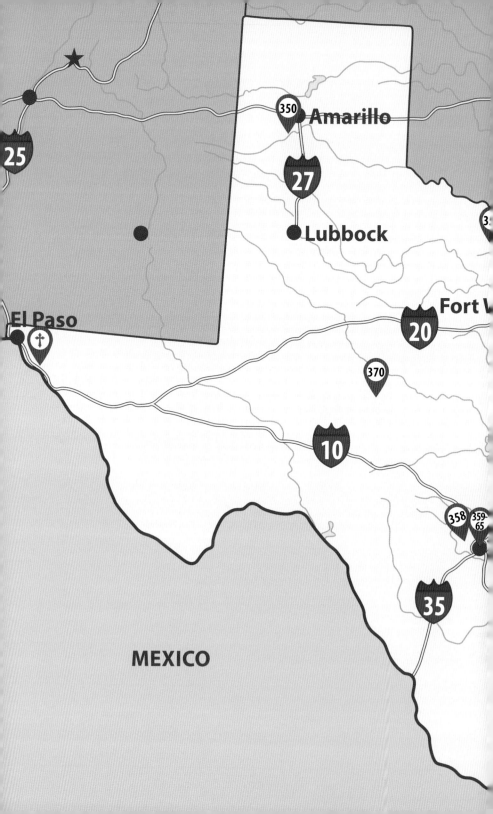

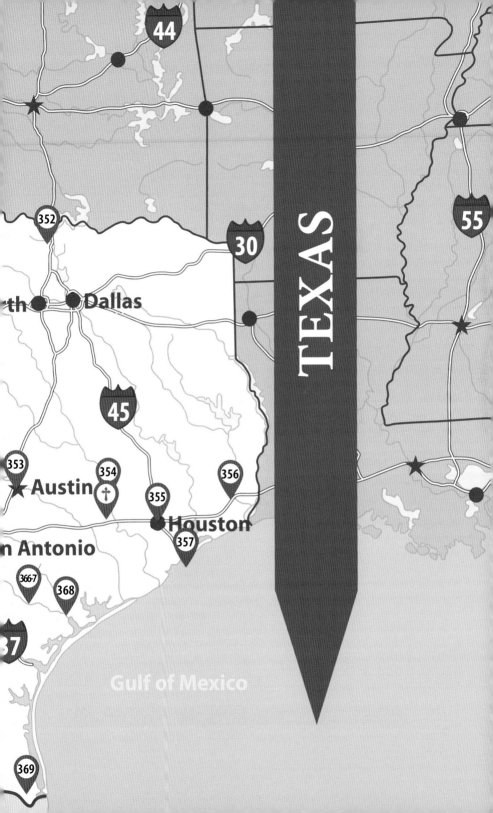

NORTH TEXAS

 Built in 1929 on a Depression-era budget, **St. Mary's Catholic Church** in Umbarger was white as a barn inside. White walls. White stations of the cross. Until 1945, when the pastor had a divine idea: Recruit Italian POW-artists interned at nearby Camp Hereford to decorate the church. In exchange, parish women would feed the men. The German vittles were so good the POWs returned week after week, transforming the "white barn" into a seventh heaven. An angel mural. Three large sanctuary paintings of Mary. A wood-carved Last Supper. There's hardly an inch the POWs didn't touch.

Plan your visit: stmarysumbarger.com. 22830 Pondaseta Road, Umbarger, TX 79091. (806) 499-3531.

 "Their prayers were answered." Those words on a plaque at **St. Mary's Grotto** in tiny Windthorst preach a mighty sermon. During World War II, sixty-four area men went off to fight. While folks at home fervently prayed to Our Lady of Perpetual Help to protect their kin, soldiers sent back a portion of their military pay to fund a grotto. Miraculously, every soldier returned home alive. The 1949 hillside grotto, about thirty feet wide with a twenty-foot-tall opening, sits below St. Mary's Church.

Plan your visit: stmarysstboniface.org. 101 Church Street, Windthorst, TX 76389. (940) 423-6687.

St. Peter's Catholic Church [352]

Pass under the street-wide archway announc-
ing **St. Peter's Catholic Church** in small-town
Lindsay, and you'll enter a house of God like no
other. Built by German settlers in 1918, the neo-
Romanesque church is a dazzling array of Byzantine
abstract and geometric designs — from diamond-
shaped tiles, to striped walls, to colorful Greek
crosses on the ceiling. Other remarkable features in-

352

clude the Beuronese-style stations of the cross, replicas of a once-renowned set in Stuttgart, Germany. Study the eleventh station: Jesus is looking at the viewer just before being nailed to the cross. German native Fridolin Fuchs (see 152 and 266) did much of the artwork. On the grounds you'll find four chapels and a grotto.

Plan your visit: stpeterlindsay.org. 424 W. Main Street, Lindsay, TX 76250. (940) 668-7609.

CENTRAL AND EAST TEXAS

(353) **Schoenstatt Chapel** in Austin (see 221).

Plan your visit: schoenstatt.us. 225 Addie Roy Road, Austin, TX 78733. (512) 330-0602.

(354) Not *everything* is bigger in Texas, at least not **St. Martin's Catholic Church** near Warrenton. Seating twenty, St. Martin's wasn't always so teeny. As the story goes, it spanned thirty-six by sixty-eight feet when built in 1888. What happened to the incredibly shrinking St. Martin's? In 1915, the pastor dismantled the church and used the lumber to erect a parochial school in nearby Fayetteville. Enough boards were left over to put up the quaint roadside attraction. Mass is said monthly for intentions left on the altar.

Plan your visit: stjohnfayetteville.com. 3490 S. Highway 237, Fayetteville, TX 78940. (979) 378-2277.

You'll find a touch of medieval England at Houston's **355** **Cathedral of Our Lady of Walsingham**, founded by former Anglicans and now headquarters of the Personal Ordinariate of the Chair of St. Peter. In 1061, Our Lady asked Lady Richeldis to build a Holy House — a replica of Mary's home in Nazareth — in Walsingham. Inspired by fourteenth-century churches in the Walsingham area of Norfolk, the cathedral honors the famous English pilgrimage site. Attractions include the sky-high outdoor shrine of Our Lady and the tiny Holy House Chapel, located inside the church. (See 106.)

Plan your visit: olwcatholic.org. 7809 Shadyvilla Lane, Houston, TX 77055. (713) 683-9407.

Are bilocations for real? You'll say yes after viewing **356** a spectacular mural at **St. Anne Catholic Church** in Beaumont. The mural portrays Spain's Venerable María of Ágreda, a seventeenth-century cloistered Conceptionist nun, teaching the Jumano Indians of West Texas the Catholic faith. The outer border, taken from an altar cloth that María personally embroidered, includes her recollections of the West Texas landscape. How can this be? She never physically left Spain! (See 370 and 381.)

Plan your visit: stannebmt.org. 2715 Calder Avenue, Beaumont, TX 77702. (409) 832-9963.

The mother church of Texas (the original Dio- **357** cese of Galveston encompassed the entire state), **St. Mary's Cathedral Basilica** in Galveston was erected in 1847 with a gift of 500,000 bricks from Belgium and patterned after King's College Chapel in Cambridge, England. The church is also riddled with history and bullet holes. After the 1863 Civil War Battle of Galveston, it's said that Bishop Claude Dubuis remarked, "Only on dry days can we say Mass within its walls." Tradition holds that a rooftop statue of Mary Star of the Sea, with lighted crown, once guided sailors into Galveston Bay.

Plan your visit: holyfamilygb.com. 2011 Church Street, Galveston, TX 77550. (409) 762-9646.

SOUTH TEXAS

 Schoenstatt Chapel in Helotes (see 221).

Plan your visit: mountschoenstatt.org. 17071 Low Road, Helotes, TX 78023. (210) 695-1400.

Our Lady appears not once but twice at **Lourdes Grotto and Tepeyac de San Antonio**, located on the grounds of the Missionary Association of Mary Immaculate in San Antonio. Constructed in 1941 of reinforced concrete, the stories-high grotto is hailed as the country's most precise reproduction of the French grotto. Atop the grotto, Tepeyac de San Antonio honors Our Lady of Guadalupe's apparitions to Juan Diego at Tepeyac Hill near Mexico City. **◀359**

Plan your visit: oblatemissions.org/5-2. 5712 Blanco Road, San Antonio, TX 78216. (210) 342-9864.

San Antonio's **Basilica of the National Shrine of the Little Flower** is a family affair: It holds a large portrait of Saint Thérèse of Lisieux painted by her blood sister and Carmelite nun Céline (Sister Geneviève of the Holy Face). Built during the Great Depression, the Beaux Arts church is a stained-glass paradise of Carmelite saints and lore (don't miss Elijah's chariot of fire). In the Tomb Chapel, a replica of Thérèse's reliquary chapel in Lisieux, France, more stained glass presents seventeen events in the saint's life, including sneaking into the Roman Colosseum with Céline (see *The Story of a Soul*, Chapter VI). **◀360**

Plan your visit: littleflowerbasilica.org. 1715 N. Zarzamora Street, San Antonio, TX 78201. (210) 735-9126.

Basilica of the National Shrine of the Little Flower [360]

361 Remember the Alamo — and remember it began as a Spanish Franciscan mission! Originally called **Mission San Antonio de Valero**, the Alamo, built in **362** 1718 and secularized in 1793, was one of five Spanish colonial missions founded in today's San Antonio. **363** Each mission is strikingly unique. An "Eye of God" (circular window) greets you at **Mission Concepción**; a keyhole-shaped door arch at **Mission Espada**. **Mission San José** is known for a fabled "Rose **365** Window"; **Mission San Juan Capistrano**, for its two-tiered bell arch. All five missions are UNESCO World Heritage sites.

Plan your visit: archsa.org/caminosanantonio. (210) 734-1648; worldheritagesa.com. (210) 207-2111.

366 It's a "twist of faith" in Goliad: The State of Texas owns a Catholic mission (see 367) and the Catholic Church (the Diocese of Victoria) a presidio. But **Presidio La Bahia** (1749) isn't any old fort. This is where the Texas Revolution began! Dedicated to Our Lady of Loreto, the presidio chapel boasts a curious fresco: The archangel Gabriel appearing to Mary has a six-toed left foot.

Plan your visit: presidiolabahia.org. 217 Loop 71 Highway 183, Goliad, TX 77963. (361) 645-3752.

367 Across the road at Goliad State Park, **Mission Espíritu Santo** (1749) opens doors to the past. The "door of the neophyte" was a door into the Faith, while the smaller "door of the dead" led to the graveyard. When the sun's rays hit a "crown of mirrors" on the altar, a halo appears over the crucifix.

Plan your visit: tpwd.texas.gov/state-parks/goliad. 108 Park Road 6, Goliad, TX 77963. (361) 645-3405.

Schoenstatt Chapel in Rockport (see 221). 368

Plan your visit: schoenstatt-texas.org. 134 Front Street, Rockport, TX 78382. (361) 729-2019.

Sometimes one miracle begets another. That's the story of the **Basilica of Our Lady of San Juan del Valle National Shrine** in San Juan. In 1623, in San Juan de los Lagos, Mexico, a traveling acrobat's daughter fell while practicing her act and was killed. When a statue of Our Lady was placed on the girl, she came back to life. On October 23, 1970, fifty priests were concelebrating Mass at the Texas shrine when a deranged pilot crashed into the roof. Miraculously, no one inside was hurt! Artworks include the enormously tall exterior mosaic, *Christ Presents His Mother*.

Plan your visit: olsjbasilica.org. 400 N. Virgen de San Juan Boulevard, San Juan, TX 78589. (956) 787-0033.

WEST TEXAS

 The Lady in Blue appears again, this time in statues along the **Concho River Walk** in San Angelo. Sculpted by Vic Payne, the larger-than-life bronze figures depict Spain's Venerable María of Ágreda (see 356 and 381) with two Jumano Indians, a brave and a young girl. The cloistered mystic is said to have bilocated hundreds of times from Spain to bring the Jumanos the Gospel of Christ. According to legend, as a sign of her final bilocation, the Flying Nun left behind a meadow of bluebonnets — known today as the state flower of Texas.

Plan your visit: sanangelodiocese.org/lady-in-blue. Near Oakes Street Bridge, San Angelo, TX 76903 (325) 651-7500.

✝ FINDING FAITH
in Central and East Texas …

It's a steeplechase (of the church kind) to the **Painted Churches of Schulenburg** in the Texas Hill Country. Typical country churches on the outside, their interiors are fonts of German-Czech folk art and pioneer ingenuity.

The humblest of the four churches, **Sts. Cyril and Methodius Catholic Church** (1912) in Dubina is also the merriest. Ascending the Gothic arches are colorful angel murals, but one angel-musician, who is said to play off-key, is missing her bowstrings. Instead of tuning her up, the artist tuned her out!

Seating once followed an Old World custom at Ammansville's **St. John the Baptist Catholic Church** (1918). Men sat to the right of the center aisle; women, to the left. Even the statues and stained-glass windows are segregated. Nicknamed the Happy Church, St. John's interior is painted pink.

Comfort takes a back seat at **St. Mary Roman Catholic Church** in High Hill (1906). When more seating was needed, pews were ingeniously shaved off a few inches and squeezed together to make way for more pews. The gorgeous "marble" columns are carved of wood, as are the exquisite gold-trim altars.

Folks at Praha's **St. Mary's Catholic Church** (1895) transcend problems by looking up. Exuding a surreal sense of calm, the tongue-and-groove wooden ceiling is painted in dreamy flora and fauna, some native to Texas. Ceiling artist Gottfried Flury painted backdrops for opera houses.

Plan your visit: schulenburgchamber.org. (866) 504-5294, (979) 743-4514.

... and West Texas

If not for the Rio Grande flood of 1829, **El Paso Mission Trail** near El Paso would be in Mexico, not Texas. The flood cut a new river channel and put the historic adobes on the future American side of the river. Present-day Socorro Mission (c. 1840), with a Pueblo step-like facade, boasts carved wooden beams and a fabled statue of Saint Michael the Archangel. As the story goes, in the 1830s, the Mexican statue was traveling via oxcart through Socorro to New Mexico when the wheels suddenly refused to turn. When the statue was given refuge in the church, the wheels turned once again.

Plan your visit: visitelpasomissiontrail.com. 328 S. Nevarez Road, El Paso, TX 79927. (915) 859-7718.

Ysleta Mission at Ysleta was founded for the Tigua Indians who fled New Mexico's Pueblo Revolt of 1680. The present 1907 church, with a distinctive bell tower, holds a 1722 wood-carved statue of *Santo Entierro* (Christ Interred), the 1722 date stamped onto its feet. Crafted in centuries-old Spanish colonial style, Margarito Mondragón's *All Saints* reredos depicts patron saints of the Tigua Pueblo.

Plan your visit: ysletamission.org. 131 S. Zaragoza Road, El Paso, TX 79907. (915) 859-9848.

A walking tour of San Elizario will take you to the town plaza and the stark-white **Presidio Chapel of San Elizario**. After a 1935 fire, the 1870s adobe was renovated and a colorful pressed-tin ceiling added. In true presidio style, one wall honors local soldiers who died for our country. Our Lady's grotto stands outside.

Plan your visit: visitelpasomissiontrail.com. 1556 San Elizario Road, El Paso, TX 79849. (915) 851-2333.

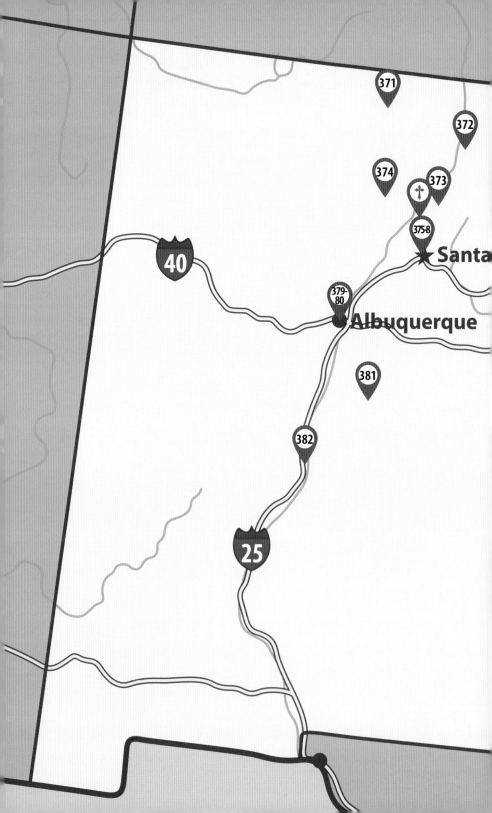

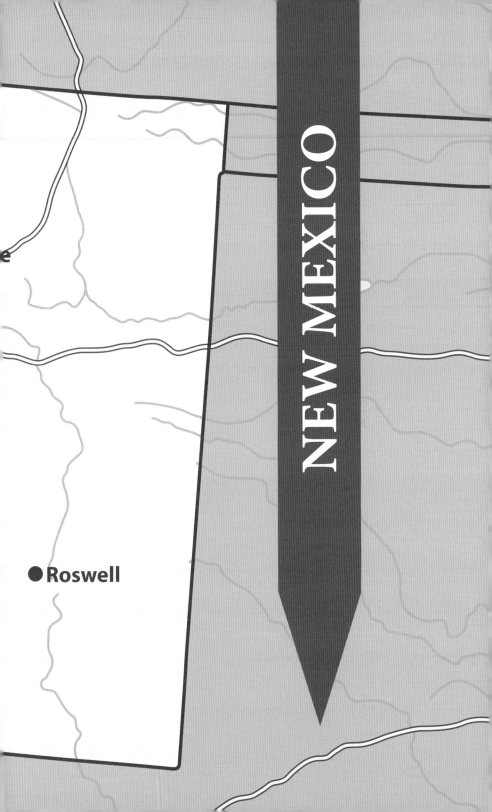

NORTHERN NEW MEXICO

 Never discount the power of "Help!" prayers! Around the turn of the twentieth century, Josefa Gallegos Burns lost control of her horse and buggy coming down a steep hill into Los Ojos. "Help!" she screamed. Farmers and shepherds in the fields below heard the piercing cries, saw the runaway buggy, and began praying furiously. Suddenly, the buggy righted itself. In gratitude, Josefa's family erected the hillside **Grotto of Our Lady of Lourdes**, on the same road that nearly took her life.

Plan your visit: elvallecatolico.org. on NM Highway 514 descending into Los Ojos, NM 87551. (575) 588-7473.

 "Preach always; use words when necessary," an old adage tells us. **San Francisco de Asís Church** in Ranchos de Taos, erected of adobe in 1815, does just that: from the white crosses atop the twin belfries to the oft-painted and photographed cruciform shape (visible outside from the back) to Henri Ault's 1896 "mystery painting," *The Shadow of the Cross*. In daylight, a life-size Jesus stands on the shores of the Sea of Galilee; in darkness, a cross appears over his left shoulder.

Plan your visit: taos.org/what-to-do/arts-culture /spanish-culture/san-francisco-de-asis-church. 60 St. Francis Plaza, Ranchos de Taos, NM 87557. (575) 758-2754.

Monastery of Christ in the Desert [374]

Santo Niño de Atocha Chapel in Chimayo has **373** an endearing tradition: the practice of offering baby shoes to Santo Niño (the Christ Child). According to lore, Santo Niño wanders the countryside at night healing the sick, wearing out his shoes along the way. In both petition and gratitude, the faithful keep Santo Niño shod. Severiano Medina built the quaint 1857 adobe in thanksgiving for healing received.

Plan your visit: holychimayo.us. 6 Santuario Drive, Chimayo, NM 87522. (505) 351-9961.

374 Silence is beautiful at the Benedictine monks' **Monastery of Christ in the Desert**, located deep in a canyon north of Abiquiu. Getting here is part adventure, part prayer: The thirteen-mile forest road curls in and around mountainous hills and seemingly dangles at times like a precipice over the Chama River below. Founded in 1964, the monastery is famous for both its adobe chapel set against red-rock cliffs and Byzantine-style tabernacle shrine. When the afternoon sun engulfs the gold-leaf-embellished shrine, it suddenly seems ablaze in divine glory.

Plan your visit: christdesert.org. Off US Highway 84 near Mile Marker 227, 36°22'49.9"N 106°40'19.4"W. Check the website for road conditions before setting out. (575) 613-4233.

375 When Santa Fe's famed **Loretto Chapel** was nearing completion in 1878, the Sisters of Loretto noticed a "slight" defect: no staircase to the choir loft! Because the loft was so high, a regular staircase would take too much room. The Sisters began a novena to Saint Joseph. On the ninth day, a stranger arrived looking for work. Armed with a few carpenter tools, he built a spiral staircase of wood. Making two 360-degree turns, the staircase with thirty-three steps has no central support and appears to be floating on air. Who built the Miraculous Staircase? Many believe it was Saint Joseph himself.

Plan your visit: lorettochapel.com. 207 Old Santa Fe Trail, Santa Fe, NM 87501. (505) 982-0092.

The **Santuario de Guadalupe** in Santa Fe is an "old soul." The nation's oldest extant shrine of Our Lady of Guadalupe (erected of adobe in the late 1700s) boasts a floor-to-ceiling 1783 Mexican oil painting of Our Lady's apparitions to Juan Diego. Look closely and you'll see stitches. The painting was cut in strips, carried by mules up *El Camino Real de Tierra Adentro* (The Royal Road of the Interior Lands), and stitched back together. A larger-than-life Guadalupe statue graces the grounds, a rock from her second apparition site at her feet.

Plan your visit: santuariodeguadalupesantafe.com. Guadalupe and Agua Fria Streets, Santa Fe, NM 87501. (505) 983-8868.

How fortuitous that **San Miguel Chapel** in Santa Fe is dedicated to Saint Michael the Archangel, defender of the Faith! The chapel needed a lot of defending over the years. Hailed as the country's oldest church structure still in use, the chapel — built of adobe c. 1610 — partially survived the 1680 Pueblo Revolt and a mid-Victorian "makeover." In 1865, French Christian Brothers covered the centuries-old Spanish colonial reredos with five layers of white house paint! The reredos was later restored to its former glory.

Plan your visit: sanmiguelchapel.org. 401 Old Santa Fe Trail, Santa Fe, NM 87501. (505) 983-3974.

The mother church of the Wild West, Santa Fe's **Cathedral Basilica of St. Francis of Assisi** is filled to its Romanesque arches with lore. Bishop Jean-Baptiste Lamy, immortalized in Willa Cather's *Death Comes for the Archbishop*, built the 1869 stone cathedral over and around a 1714 adobe church. Enshrined in a side chapel is the country's oldest Marian statue, *La Conquistadora* (Our Lady of Conquering Love). How old is she? Nobody knows, but the wooden *bulto a vestir* (statue dressed in clothes) was carved in Spain and brought here in 1626 (the parish dates from 1610). It's said the statue began to weep during the Pueblo Revolt of 1680.

Plan your visit: cbsfa.org. 131 Cathedral Place, Santa Fe, NM 87501. (505) 982-5619.

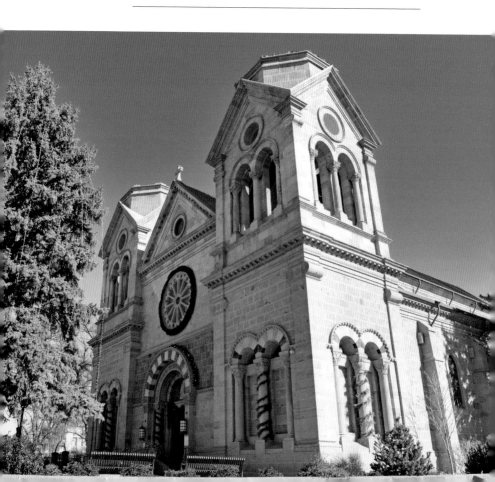

SOUTHERN NEW MEXICO

San Felipe de Neri Church in Old Town Albuquerque transcends time. Erected in 1793 (the parish dates from 1706), the church's five-foot-thick adobe walls and small high windows protected against warring Indians during Spanish Franciscan colonial days, while latter-day French and Italian clergy added the Gothic Revival towers, a pitched roof, and a pressed tin ceiling. Some say the Stars of David on the sanctuary arch honor New Mexico's crypto-Jews — Spanish Jewish colonists who converted to Catholicism but secretly retained Jewish practices.

379

Plan your visit: sanfelipedeneri.org. 2005 N. Plaza NW, Albuquerque, NM 87104. (505) 243-4628.

It's a Wild, Wild West story at the **Sister Blandina Convent** (next door to San Felipe de Neri Church, see 379). Dubbed the Fastest Nun in the West, Servant of God Blandina Segale, SC (1850–1941), staved off a mob lynching, stopped Billy the Kid from robbing a stagecoach, and built hospitals and schools in Colorado and New Mexico. Despite being told it couldn't be done, in 1881 she erected this two-story adobe convent, now a gift shop and museum.

380

Plan your visit: sanfelipedeneri.org. 2005 N. Plaza NW, Albuquerque, NM 87104. (505) 243-4628.

Cathedral Basilica of St. Francis of Assisi [378]

381 When a band of Jumano Indians arrived at Isleta Pueblo near Albuquerque in the 1620s and asked for "the waters," the Spanish Franciscans were astounded. Where had they learned about baptism? From the Lady in Blue's visits to Gran Quivira, part of today's **Salinas Pueblo Missions National Monument** near Mountainair. Also known as the Flying Nun, Venerable María of Ágreda (1602–1665) — wearing a blue cape over her cream-colored habit — reportedly bilocated more than 500 times from her cloistered convent in Ágreda, Spain, to teach the Gospel and tenets of the Faith to Indians in what is now Texas and New Mexico. (See 356 and 370.)

Plan your visit: nps.gov/sapu/index.htm. 105 S. Ripley Avenue, Mountainair, NM 87036. (505) 847-2585.

382 What's in a church name? At **San Miguel Church** in Socorro, a tale of divine protection. Around 1800, as one story goes, marauding Apache Indians were preparing to attack Iglesia de Nuestra Señora del Socorro (Our Lady of Help Church), a Spanish colonial adobe, when they suddenly retreated. A gigantic being with wings and a shiny sword was hovering over the entrance! The church was renamed San Miguel (Saint Michael the Archangel), to honor the warrior-angel in the sky.

Plan your visit: sdc.org/~smiguel. 403 El Camino Real, Socorro, NM 87801. (575) 835-2891.

✝ FINDING FAITH
in New Mexico

When believers follow the light, miracles happen. On Good Friday in 1810, Bernardo de Abeyta was doing penance when he saw a light coming from the ground near the Santa Cruz River in Chimayo. Digging in the dirt, he found a wooden crucifix of *Nuestro Señor de Esquipulas* (also known as the Black Christ, a devotion originating in Esquipulas, Guatemala). The crucifix was taken to a nearby church, but it miraculously reappeared back in the hole. When this happened twice again, **El Santuario de Chimayo** — a small adobe chapel — was erected over the sacred site.

Called the Lourdes of America, El Santuario is renowned for wondrous healings and answers to prayer. Pilgrims scoop up "holy dirt" (it's been blessed) from the hole and rub it on ailing body parts. On Good Friday, tens of thousands of pilgrims journey here by foot to venerate the Black Christ (the green cross with green shoots represents Christ's victory over death). The Good Friday walk is the largest religious pilgrimage in the country.

Plan your visit: holychimayo.us. 15 Santuario Drive, Chimayo, NM 87522. (505) 351-9961.

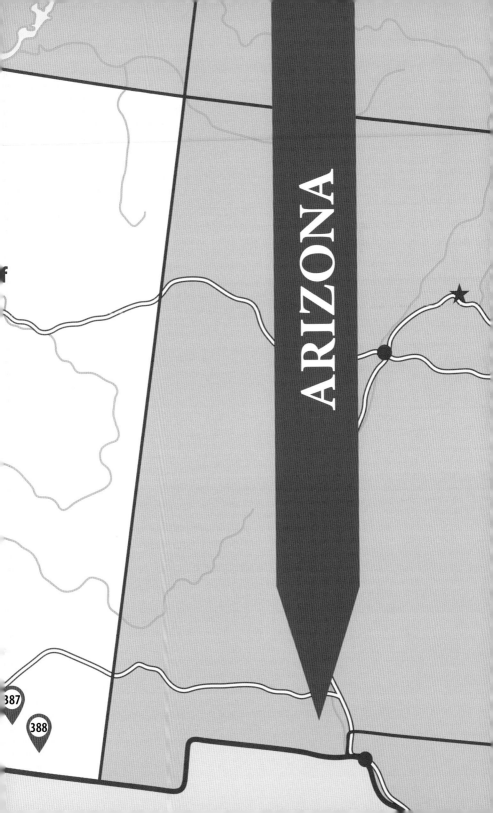

383 Ascending from red rocks, the stunning **Chapel of the Holy Cross** near Sedona has a curious effect on souls: You'll want to ascend too! Constructed of reinforced concrete in 1955–1956, the desert sanctuary, conceived by Catholic sculptor Marguerite Brunswig Staude, deliberately pulls eyes to the ninety-foot cross that serves as both the chapel's physical and spiritual foundation. Step outside and study the famous red rocks with mystical shapes. Can you find the Madonna and Child? The Praying Nuns?

Plan your visit: chapeloftheholycross.com. 780 Chapel Road, Sedona, AZ 86336. (928) 282-7545.

384 Test your Franciscan trivia knowledge at **St. Mary's Basilica** in Phoenix. Dedicated in 1915, the Mission Revival-style church, with Romanesque interior, is a *portiuncula* (little portion) of Franciscan saints. How many saints in statues and stained glass can you identify? Who was saved by a dog? Who had a golden tongue? Who was a nobleman's mistress? (Her body remains incorrupt today.) What's the difference between a halo and a mandorla?

Plan your visit: saintmarysbasilica.org. 231 N. Third Street, Phoenix, AZ 85004. (602) 354-2100.

385 There's no mistaking **Vietnamese Martyrs Catholic Church** in Phoenix. Dedicated in 2010, the strikingly unique church, with a pagoda-style roof, curved eaves, carved marble dragons, and tiers of

crosses, looks like it was translated from Vietnam. Attired in traditional Vietnamese gowns, a beautiful statue of Our Lady of La Vang with the Christ Child (note his tiny red slippers) adorns the interior.

Plan your visit: cttdvnphx.org, dphx.org/parish /vietnamese-martyrs-parish-phoenix. 2915 W. Northern Avenue, Phoenix, AZ 85051. (602) 395-0421.

 There's a backstory for every work of art, but none quite like the sanctuary mural at **Assumption of the Blessed Virgin Mary Church** in Florence. Painted c. 1945, the mural provides a backdrop of dreamy clouds and cherubs for a blue-robed Mary statue. The artist? A prison inmate named Monet.

Plan your visit: assumptionofmary.org. 177 E. Eighth Street, Florence, AZ 85132. (520) 868-5940.

 Tombstone — the Town Too Tough to Die — has one tough Catholic church. Dedicated on January 1, 1881, ten months before the legendary shootout at the OK Corral, **Sacred Heart of Jesus Catholic Church** still stands. Part of Tombstone's historic tour, the quaint adobe structure originally housed a rectory on the top floor and the church on the bottom floor.

Plan your visit: tombstonescatholicchurch.org. 592 E. Safford Street, Tombstone, AZ 85638. (520) 457-3364.

Bring your binoculars when you tour Bisbee's **St. Patrick Catholic Church**. The two tiers of Emil Frei's (see 266) Victorian-style stained glass are minutely detailed, from facial expressions to halos (no two halos are alike). There are unique touches as well. In the Nativity scene, a shepherd plays bagpipes and one "Wise Man" may actually be a woman. Built by Welsh and Irish copper miners, the 1915 Gothic Revival brick church sits 200 feet above the floor of Tombstone Canyon — proof that there really is life after death!

388

Plan your visit: stpatsbisbee.com. 100 Quality Hill Road, Bisbee, AZ 85603. (520) 432-5753.

✣ FINDING FAITH
in Arizona

If scallops are a pilgrimage symbol, you're in for a fascinating journey at **Mission San Xavier del Bac**, near Tucson. They're everywhere! Erected by Franciscans in 1783–1797, the gleaming white Spanish Baroque church — dubbed the White Dove of the Desert — is filled to its five domes with spectacular murals and captivating detail. The ornamental reredos looks like carved wood but is fired brick with gilded stucco and plaster, while the nave's painted curtains and faux doors add more drama. There's even an ominous warning carved into the facade. It's said that when the cats catch the mice, the world will come to an end!

Plan your visit: sanxaviermission.org. 1950 W. San Xavier Road, Tucson, AZ 85746. (520) 294-2624.

The pilgrimage (and scallops) continues at **Mission San José de Tumacácori**, part of Tumacácori National Historic Park at Tumacácori. Founded by Venerable Jesuit Eusebio Kino (1645–1711) (see 99) in 1691, Mission San José was assigned to the Franciscan order when the Jesuits were expelled from Mexico in 1767. Father Kino is credited with establishing more than twenty missions and *visitas* (visiting stations) across Mexico and the American Southwest, including Mission San Xavier del Bac above. Tumacácori attractions include the Spanish Baroque church, *convento* (priest's residence and community area), and round mortuary chapel.

Plan your visit: nps.gov/subjects /travelspanishmissions/index.htm. Off Interstate 19 at 1895 E. Frontage Road, Tumacácori, AZ 85640. (520) 377-5060.

PACIFIC WEST

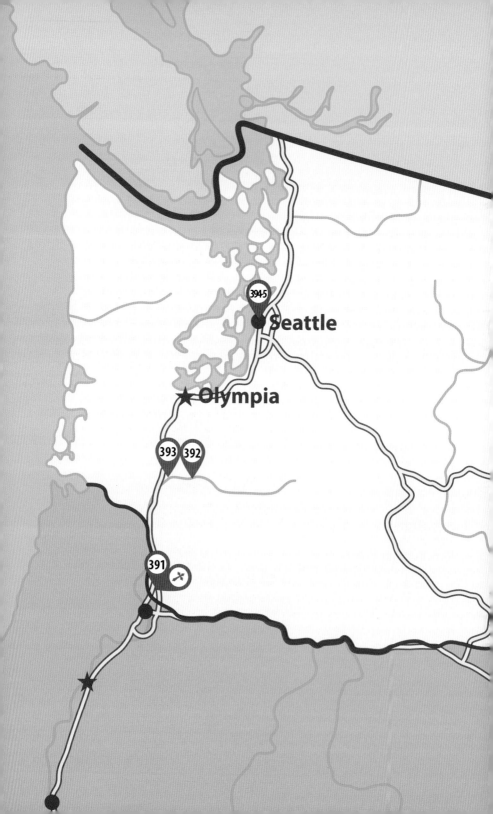

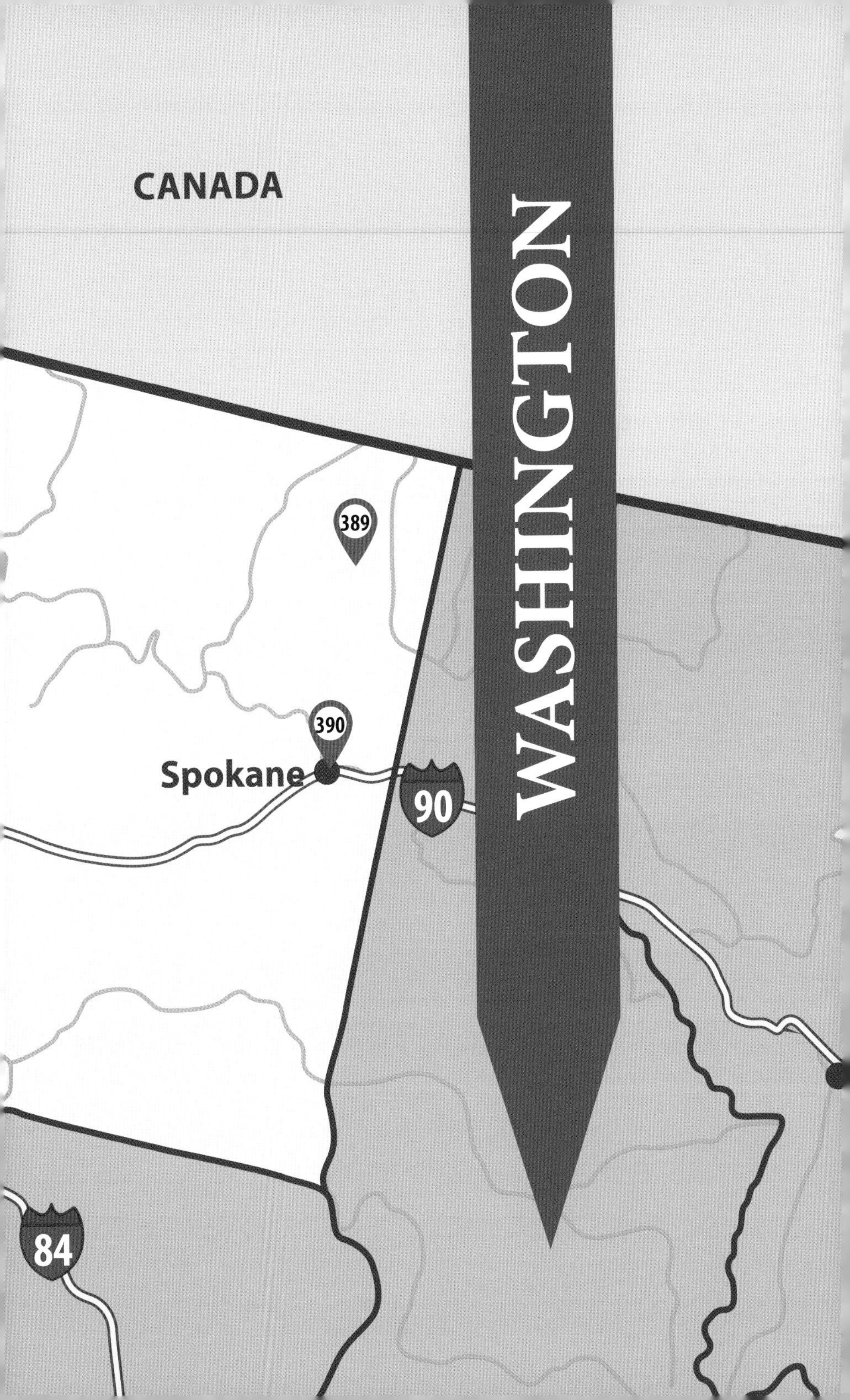

CANADA
WASHINGTON
389
390
Spokane
90
84

EASTERN WASHINGTON

Soak up Jesuit history at **Manresa Grotto**, a cave **389** on the Kalispel Indian Reservation near Cusick, where Father Pierre De Smet, SJ, offered Mass in the 1840s. The legendary Black Robe named the grotto after the famous cave in Manresa, Spain, where Jesuit founder Saint Ignatius of Loyola prayed. Overlooking the Pend Oreille River, the cave church is fitted with stone seats and a stone altar. (See Finding Faith in Montana and 323.)

Plan your visit: pocoparishes.org/kalispel. 6196 Le-Clerc Road N., Cusick, WA 99180. (509) 447-4231.

Does prayer work? Ask the folks at **St. Aloysius** **390** **Church** in Spokane. They've been praying the annual Novena of Grace, held in mid-March, since the late 1920s. According to one account, the novena, in honor of Jesuit Saint Francis Xavier, traces its origins to 1615 in Goa, India, when a boy crippled from birth begged the saint's intercession and was healed. The Romanesque-adapted church features fabulous stained-glass windows of Jesuit saints and Our Lady of the Miraculous Medal trampling a green dragon.

Plan your visit: stalschurch.org. 330 E. Boone Avenue, Spokane WA 99202. (509) 313-5896.

WESTERN WASHINGTON

Pilgrims take delight at the **Proto-Cathedral of** **391** **St. James the Greater** in Vancouver. Like Spain's

Camino de Santiago (Way of Saint James), the cathedral boasts a *compostela*, a "field of stars" on a stellar blue ceiling. The 1884 Gothic Revival gem, with an elaborate Belgian-made high altar, served as the see for the Diocese of Nesqually until 1907, when the see was moved to Seattle (today's Archdiocese of Seattle). But St. James the Greater didn't become any lesser; the church's legacy lives on in fascinating tours and relics. Don't miss the "Catholic Ladder" outside the rectory (see 393).

Plan your visit: protocathedral.org. 218 W. Twelfth Street, Vancouver, WA 98660. (360) 693-3052.

392 Crowning a steep hill near Mossyrock, a seventy-foot white **Cross of Divine Mercy** preaches forgiveness in sevens. The foundation is seven feet deep and seven feet square, with seven steps representing the Seven Sorrows of Mary. Inscribed at the base are Jesus' words to "forgive seventy times seven." A hiking trail, lined with stations of the cross, connects a chapel at the bottom of the hill with the concrete cross at the top. Flower growers Henry and Hildegarde De-Goede erected the 1996 monument in thanksgiving for their many blessings in life.

Plan your visit: degoedebulb.com. 409 Mossyrock Road W., Mossyrock, WA 98564. (360) 983-9000.

393 Ascend the ladder to heaven at Toledo's **St. Francis Xavier Mission** (also called Cowlitz Mission).

Founded in 1838, the old mission holds an outdoor replica of the "Catholic Ladder," a totem pole-like device created by Father François Norbert Blanchet (later the first archbishop of today's Archdiocese of Portland) to teach the Bible and Catholic faith to Indian tribes. A guide explains the ladder's marks and symbols, from the creation of the world to the crucifixion. A ladder replica is also found at the Proto-Cathedral of St. James the Greater in Vancouver (see 391).

Plan your visit: wlpcatholic.org. 139 Spencer Road, Toledo, WA 98591. (360) 864-4126.

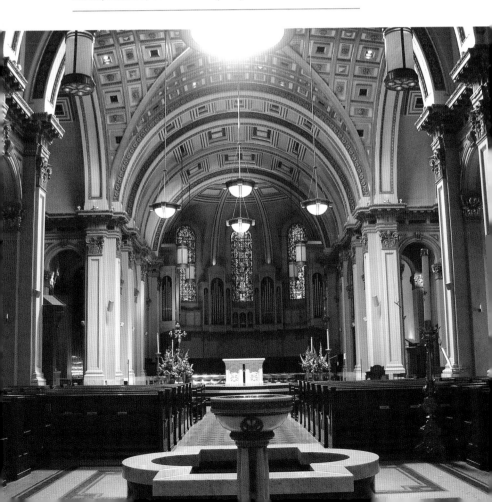

394 The road to sainthood often begins with godly parents. At **Calvary Cemetery** in Seattle, a "Capuchin-brown" granite monument honors Irish immigrants Bernard and Ellen Casey and their son, Blessed Father Solanus Casey, OFM Cap. (See 181.) A bronze Solanus statue overlooks their graves on one side, while the reverse is inscribed with two of his favorite sayings, "Thank God ahead of time" and "Blessed be God in all His designs." Nine of the couple's sixteen children are also buried here.

Plan your visit: mycatholiccemetery.org. 5041 Thirty-Fifth Avenue NE, Seattle, WA 98105. (206) 522-0996.

395 Love a good mystery? Come to Seattle's 1905 **St. James Cathedral.** Gracing the cathedral chapel is a 1456 Renaissance painting by Florentine artist Neri di Bicci. Titled *Madonna and Child with Six Saints*, the *sacra conversazione* (holy conversation) paints the Child standing in Mary's lap, flanked by saints imagined "in conversation" with Mary and Jesus. Where did the nearly 600-year-old gilded painting come from? Nobody knows, but it's been hanging in the chapel for decades.

Plan your visit: stjames-cathedral.org. 804 Ninth Avenue, Seattle, WA 98104. (206) 622-3559.

✝ FINDING FAITH
in Washington

When Esther Pariseau (1823–1902) entered Montreal's Sisters of Providence in 1843, her carpenter-father told the Mother Superior, "She can handle a hammer and saw as well as her father." And then some, as time would tell! Arriving in Vancouver in 1856, Esther — now Mother Joseph — erected eleven hospitals, seven academies, five Indian schools, and two orphanages across Washington Territory (today's northern Oregon, Idaho, Montana, and Washington).

Built in 1873 in Colonial Revival style, Vancouver's three-story brick **Providence Academy** still stands, a testament to Mother Joseph's aesthetic vision and superb workmanship. Tours include tales of the nun jumping on beams or climbing rafters, part of her stringent quality control. One of the first architects in the Pacific Northwest, Mother Joseph is honored with a bronze statue at the National Statuary Hall in the United States Capitol (see 99).

Plan your visit: thehistorictrust.org /providence-academy. 400 E. Evergreen Boulevard, Vancouver, WA 98660. (360) 992-1800.

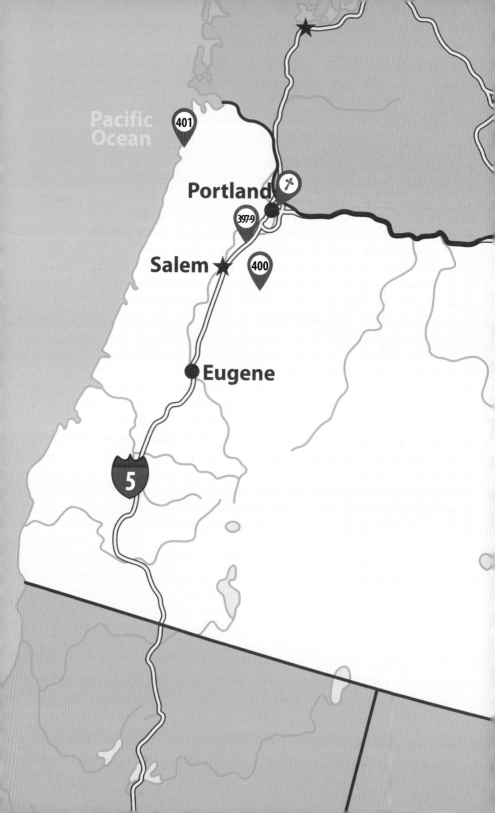

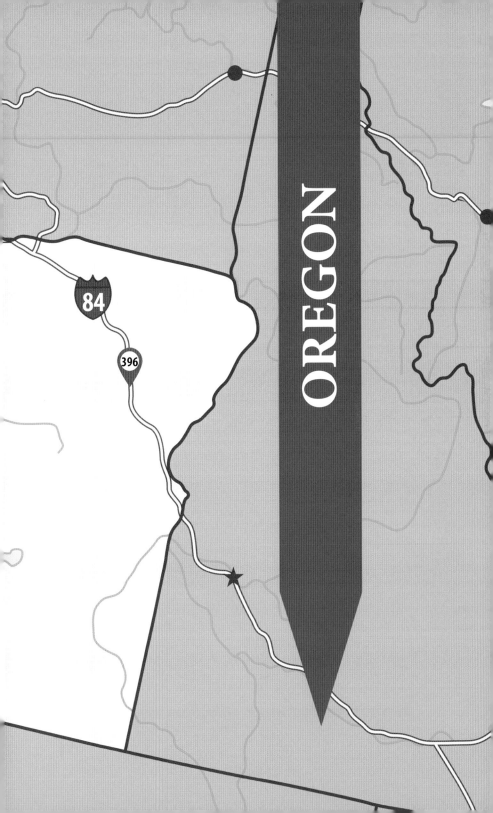

EASTERN OREGON

When Bishop Charles O'Reilly, the first shepherd of the Diocese of Baker, arrived at his see in Baker City in 1903, four renegade priests were waiting with a gun. He wasn't wanted in these parts! The "John Wayne bishop" was undeterred and erected, of volcanic tuff, the Gothic-style **St. Francis de Sales Cathedral**. Eyes can't resist the brilliant blue apse with a mural of Jesus in a red robe, attended by two angelic murals. One angel holds a towel imprinted with Jesus' face; the other, a crown of thorns and three nails.

Plan your visit: saintfranciscathedral.com. 2235 First Street, Baker City, OR 97814. (541) 523-4521.

WESTERN OREGON

For a touch of the angelic, visit **St. Mary Catholic Church** in Mount Angel. High in the nave, *Te Deum* angel murals offer the ancient hymn of praise, while a choir of stained-glass angels, based on Fra Angelico's paintings, sings in the loft. Dubbed the Gothic Jewel of the Willamette Valley, the 1910 German church was constructed of hand-pressed bricks made on site. The blue ceiling signifies Himmel ("Heaven"); the stenciled strawberries, thistles, and roses around windows and arches, the Joyful, Sorrowful, and Glorious Mysteries of the Rosary.

Plan your visit: stmarymtangel.org. 575 E. College Street, Mount Angel, OR 97362. (503) 845-2296.

398 The Benedictine Sisters of **Queen of Angels Monastery** in Mount Angel have come a long way. When the Swiss foundresses arrived in 1882, their home was an abandoned saloon. Today, the Main Building, a four-story brick affair dedicated in 1888, is renowned for its elegant design and exterior detail. Pilgrims can walk the quiet paths, visit Mary's grotto, or pray in Queen of Angels Chapel. Hundreds of majestic trees fill the grounds; a giant sequoia, designated an Oregon Heritage Tree, graces the monastery entrance.

Plan your visit: benedictine-srs.org. 840 S. Main Street, Mount Angel, OR 97362. (503) 845-6141.

Take your angel for a stroll at **Mount Angel Abbey** in Saint Benedict, founded by Swiss Benedictine monks in 1882. The hilltop walking tour includes the Romanesque-style abbey church, a guardian angel statue that survived a devastating abbey fire, the monks' tiny 1883 cemetery chapel, outdoor stations of the cross with Munich statuary, and the abbey museum, a collection of eclectic artifacts ranging from holy medals to porcine hair balls.

Plan your visit: mountangelabbey.org. 1 Abbey Drive, Mount Angel, OR 97362. (503) 845-3030.

On December 28, 1979, Vincent J. Etzel of Sublimity had a vision of Jesus and Mary and their Sacred Hearts. After pondering the vision, the bachelor-farmer asked that a shrine of the Sacred Hearts of Jesus and Mary be built after his death, with his money. Resembling a miniature country church with a spire, **Sacred Hearts Shrine** was dedicated in 2009. Lit from within at night, the shrine's stained-glass windows of the Sacred Heart of Jesus and the Immaculate Heart of Mary glow with love for all.

Plan your visit: saintboniface.net. 375 SE Church Street, Sublimity, OR 97385. (503) 769-5664.

Charming **St. Mary by the Sea Catholic Church** in Rockaway Beach celebrates a unique claim: It's reportedly closer to the ocean than any Catholic church in the lower forty-eight states. Dedicated in 1927, the ocean-facing church simulates a ship inside. The "vessel" is paneled like a ship's cabin, ship wheels adorn the side altars, and the carved holy water fonts are shaped like Spanish galleons. Nautical artworks include a seascape painting of Mary.

Plan your visit: stmarybythesea.com. 275 S. Pacific Street, Rockaway Beach, OR 97136. (503) 355-2661.

✚ FINDING FAITH
in Oregon

In the early 1890s, young Ambrose Mayer learned his mother lay near death after giving birth. Terrified, the lad ran to his church in Kitchener, Ontario, and promised to undertake a "great work" for the Church if she lived. She did. In 1923 the lad — now Servite friar Father Mayer — bought land in Portland and began his promise. A grotto approximately thirty feet wide, thirty feet deep, and fifty feet high was carved into the base of a 110-foot basalt cliff and fitted with a replica of Michelangelo's *Pietà*.

Nearly a century later, the Grotto — formally called the **National Sanctuary of Our Sorrowful Mother** — is indeed a "great work." The sixty-two-acre retreat includes Our Lady's Grotto, Chapel of Mary with the Via Matris (Way of Our Sorrowful Mother), and forested stations of the cross on the plaza level, with the clifftop Meditation Chapel, tiny St. Anne's Chapel (filled with Madonna paintings), and Peace and Rose Gardens on the upper level.

Plan your visit: thegrotto.org. NE Eighty-Fifth Avenue and Sandy Boulevard, Portland, OR 97294. (503) 254-7371.

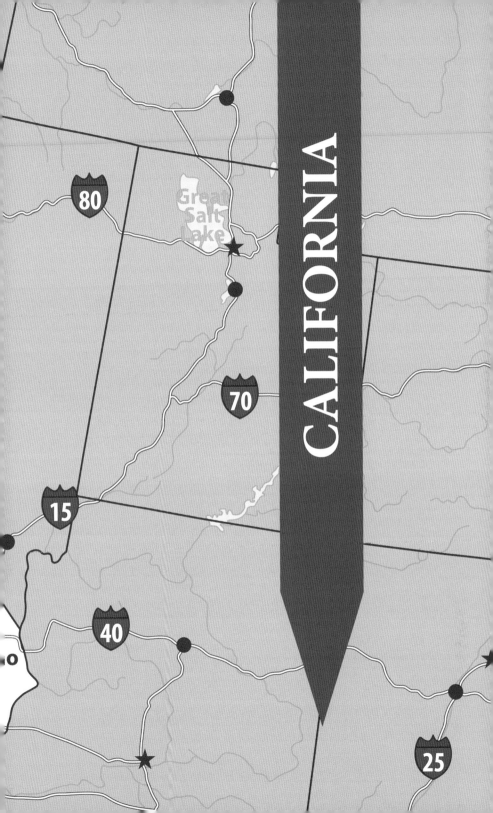

NORTHERN CALIFORNIA

There's nothing minuscule about Mary's love at **Our Lady of Sorrows Shrine** near Colusa: The twin towers of the ten-by-fourteen-foot chapel turn inward, like a mother's arms enfolding a child. Commemorating the area's first Mass in 1856 and hailed as a unique example of folk architecture, the 1883 brick chapel is just big enough for an altar and the presiding priest.

Plan your visit: ourladyoflourdescolusa.com. Eight miles south of Colusa on State Highway 45 (Sycamore Slough Road), Colusa, CA 95932. (530) 458-4170.

When people began arriving for the dedication of Sacramento's **Cathedral of the Blessed Sacrament** on June 30, 1889, artists were still painting the frescoes. That's only one of the stories surrounding the cathedral and its builder, Bishop Patrick Manogue (1831–1895). The burly six-foot, three-inch Irish native, who financed his seminarian education in France by prospecting for gold, and named his first Indian converts Adam and Eve, settled more than one brawl with a pious punch! Patterned after the Église de la Sainte-Trinité in Paris, the cathedral boasts an exact eight-by-ten-foot reproduction of Raphael's painting *The Sistine Madonna*.

Plan your visit: cathedralsacramento.org. 1019 Eleventh Street, Sacramento, CA 95814. (916) 444-3071.

Cathedral of the Blessed Sacrament [403]

You'll find a history lesson in art at **Mission Dolores Basilica** (1913), next door to Mission San Francisco de Asís (see Finding Faith in California) in San Francisco. Stained-glass windows depict the twenty-one California missions with their founding dates, while outside the museum, a tile mural speculates on history itself. What if the Spanish Crown hadn't financed the California expedition? What if Father Serra (see Finding Faith in California) had never set foot in California? What if the Faith had never been planted in San Francisco? *¿Quién sabe?* the mural asks in Spanish. Who knows?

◀404

Plan your visit: missiondolores.org. 3321 Sixteenth Street, San Francisco, CA 94114. (415) 621-8203.

The most Irish church in America? **Saint Patrick Church** in San Francisco! Reconstructed after the Great Earthquake of 1906 (the parish was founded during the gold rush in 1851), the Victorian Gothic landmark touts marble walls and pillars that represent Ireland's patriotic colors: green, white, and gold. Tiffany stained-glass clerestory windows tell the story of Ireland's pre-Christian days, while the lower windows present the patron saints of Ireland's thirty-two counties.

Plan your visit: stpatricksf.org. 756 Mission Street, San Francisco, CA 94103. (415) 421-3730.

 If you know the way to San José, visit **Five Wounds Portuguese National Church**. The 1916 church got its start when Monsignor Henrique Ribeiro bought, for $200, the Pavilion of Portugal built for San Francisco's 1915 Panama-Pacific International Exposition. He turned its wood, stained glass, and decorative medallions into a glorious temple with six side altars. When Mussolini banished Father Luigi Sciocchetti from Italy, the ecclesiastical artist immigrated to California and painted the sanctuary murals.

Plan your visit: fivewoundschurch.org. 1375 E. Santa Clara Street, San José, CA 95116. (408) 292-2123.

 You can't wear this "Madonna medal": She's thirty-two feet tall and stands on a twelve-foot landscaped mound! Sculpted by Charles C. Parks (see Finding Faith in Delaware and 194), the 7,200-pound, stainless steel statue of the **Immaculate Heart of Mary**

outside Our Lady of Peace Church in Santa Clara is a pilgrim magnet. And no wonder: It's the only major Marian shrine on the West Coast between the Grotto in Portland, Oregon (see Finding Faith in Oregon) and the Basilica of Our Lady of Guadalupe in Mexico City. Our Lady's gown, constructed of welded strips of stainless steel, shimmers in the light, earning her the title Awesome Madonna.

Plan your visit: olop-shrine.org. 2800 Mission College Boulevard, Santa Clara, CA 95054. (408) 988-4585.

CENTRAL CALIFORNIA

Indian neophytes weren't the only ones attending Mass at **Mission San Juan Bautista** at San Juan Bautista. The church mice came too. Inset in a rear church door is a little door that lets cats inside to do their holy work. Founded in 1797 and the fifteenth of California's twenty-one missions, San Juan Bautista is also known for its "divine illumination." Around the time of the winter solstice, sunlight beaming through the front window engulfs the altar in a momentary glow of light. A sailor who jumped ship at Monterey painted the colorful reredos, c. 1818, in exchange for room and board.

Plan your visit: oldmissionsjb.org. 406 Second Street, San Juan Bautista, CA 95045. (831) 623-2127.

Saint Michael the Archangel defends us in daily battle, but it's the "Eye of God" that keeps watch over **Mission San Miguel Arcángel** (1797) at San

Miguel. Adorning the floor-to-ceiling reredos, the decorative "Eye" surely elevated minds to things above and kept the young'uns in line! Unpretentious looking on the outside, the mission — the sixteenth in the California mission chain — is a painted paradise inside. The vibrantly colored frescoes are original and were painted by the Salinan Indians. Note the huge frescoes of abalone shells. Highly treasured by Indians, abalone shells were also used for baptisms.

Plan your visit: missionsanmiguel.org. 775 Mission Street, San Miguel, CA 93451. (805) 467-3256.

 It's a steep, steep climb up a big, big hill to Shandon's **Serra Chapel**, also called Chapel Hill. But what a

view and what a chapel! Built by Judge William Clark (1931–2013), a Shandon rancher and an advisor to President Ronald Reagan, the chapel was born of a miracle. In 1988, as the story goes, Clark was nearly killed when the plane he was piloting crashed shortly after takeoff, barely missing a fuel tank. Erected in Mission style, the chapel is touted for its picturesque bell tower and Spanish ceiling. The chapel is open during Sunday Mass; call for schedule.

Plan your visit: saintrosechurch.org, cal-catholic .com/worth-driving-to-serra-chapel-shandon -calif. Off McMillan Canyon Road, 35°40'40.5"N 120°24'22.4"W. (805) 238-2218.

SOUTHERN CALIFORNIA

Want to visit a queen? Come to **Mission Santa Barbara** in Santa Barbara. Founded in 1786 and called the Queen of the California Missions, the Spanish colonial church built by the Chumash Indians boasts walls six feet thick, chandeliers with "lightning bolt" escutcheons (Saint Barbara is patroness against lightning), and colonial artworks. The only California mission with twin towers, the facade mimics an ancient Roman temple. The grounds include a nine-room museum, a cemetery (more than 4,000 Chumash are buried here), and a historical garden featuring mission-era plants and trees.

Plan your visit: santabarbaramission.org. 2201 Laguna Street, Santa Barbara, CA 93105. (805) 682-4713.

412 What could $1 million build in 1927? The sensational **St. Andrew Catholic Church** in Old Town Pasadena. The Romanesque campanile and facade replicate Santa Maria in Cosmedin, a twelfth-century Roman church; the interior, Rome's Basilica of Santa Sabina, c. A.D. 422. Like Santa Sabina's marbles from many lands, St. Andrew's has marble pillars of many colors. It's said that Venetian artist Carlo Wostry spent five years painting the church's murals, including the legend of Saint Andrew and the stations of the cross that run like a banner around the nave. Lit at night, the soaring campanile can be seen near and far.

Plan your visit: saintandrewpasadena.org. 311 N. Raymond Avenue, Pasadena, CA 91103. (626) 792-4183.

413 **St. Timothy Catholic Church** in Los Angeles (Rancho Park/Cheviot Hills area) has a flair for the dramatic. Parishioner-artisans at MGM and Fox studios crafted the pews, executed many of the church's replica paintings of well-known masterpieces (don't miss *Madonna of the Goldfinch*), and turned parishioners' gold and silver jewelry into an exquisite tabernacle. The side-altar statues of Mary and Joseph guest-starred in the 1946 flick *The Jolson Story*. The crowning glory of the 1949-built Spanish Renaissance church? The antique Spanish altarpiece, bought at auction.

Plan your visit: sttimothyla.org. 10425 W. Pico Boulevard, Los Angeles, CA 90064. (310) 474-1216.

Demons tremble when "How Great Thou Art" is played on the world-renowned Hazel Wright Memorial Organ at **Christ Cathedral** in Garden Grove. With nearly 16,000 pipes, the organ can shatter glass! Constructed entirely of glass and steel, the iconic landmark — the former Crystal Cathedral of televangelist Reverend Robert H. Schuller (the Diocese of Orange acquired the thirty-four-acre campus in 2012) — stands twelve stories tall and claims 10,660 panes of mirrored glass. Other campus buildings include the Tower of Hope with a ninety-foot neon-lit cross, and the Crean Tower with a fifty-two bell carillon. Outdoor devotions include the Stations of Mercy, eleven stations extolling a work of mercy ranging from "Welcome the Stranger" to "Bury the Dead."

Plan your visit: christcathedralcalifornia.org. 13280 Chapman Avenue, Garden Grove, CA 92840. (714) 971-2141.

Queen of Life Catholic Chapel has a unique home: a business office park in Irvine. Established by Catholic philanthropist Timothy Busch and located at the Busch Group offices, the diocesan-approved oratory holds weekday Masses and is open for prayer during business hours.

Plan your visit: queenoflifechapel.org. 2532 Dupont Drive, Irvine, CA 92612. (949) 474-7368.

Life begets life, and how apropos that Mother Mary stands larger than life at the **Mariam Mother of Life Shrine** at St. Ephrem Maronite Catholic Church in El

Cajon! Rising above the manmade mountain with a winding staircase to the top, a statuesque stone Mary holds a toddler Jesus with curly hair, his arms open to the world. Completed in 2003, the cone-shaped monument, with an altar built into its base, recalls another Marian appellation: Our Lady of the Bees.

Plan your visit: stephremchurch.com. 750 Medford Street, El Cajon, CA 92020. (619) 337-1350.

✠ FINDING FAITH
in California

He stood only five feet two inches tall, but Saint Junípero Serra (1713-1784) left a big footprint. The Franciscan padre founded nine of California's twenty-one Spanish missions. Soak up history and the saint's spirit on this mission trip through Father Serra country. Beginning with his first mission in San Diego in southernmost California, the missions are listed geographically from south to north, rather than by the chronological order in which they were founded. (Other missions are listed separately. See also 404.)

Founded in 1769, **Mission Basilica San Diego de Alcalá** in San Diego, Father Serra's first mission, is where the California mission chain began. Highlights include the stark-white adobe church with its signature five-bell campanario and the Casa del Padre Serra, part of the original friary where Father Serra stayed during his mission visits.

Plan your visit: missionsandiego.org. 10818 San Diego Mission Road, San Diego, CA 92108. (619) 283-7319.

Famous for its annual spring return of the swallows, **Mission San Juan Capistrano** (1776) in San Juan Capistrano — the seventh of Saint Junípero's missions — includes the Serra Chapel (1782), California's oldest standing building and the only extant California church where Padre Serra offered Mass.

Plan your visit: missionsjc.com. 26801 Ortega Highway, San Juan Capistrano, CA 92675. (949) 234-1300.

Grace was surely at work at **Mission San Gabriel Arcángel** (1771) in San Gabriel. More than 25,000 Indians were baptized here. The fourth of Padre Serra's missions, the church holds the original copper baptismal font, a gift of King Carlos III of Spain, and a sterling silver baptismal shell. On July 11, 2020, a fire ravaged much of the church's roof and interior. Grace still abounds, and the church is being restored.

Plan your visit: sangabrielmissionchurch.org. 428 S. Mission Drive, San Gabriel, CA 91776. (626) 457-3035.

The last of Padre Serra's missions, **Mission San Buenaventura** in Ventura, founded in 1782, is known for a pair of "mystery bells." Some speculate the wooden bells, carved from two-foot blocks of wood, were used during Holy Week when the metal bells were silenced.

Plan your visit: sanbuenaventuramission.org. 211 E. Main Street, San Buenaventura, CA 93001. (805) 643-4318.

It's hard to forget Father Serra's fifth mission: The walls of **Mission San Luis Obispo de Tolosa** (1772) in San Luis Obispo feel enormously tall. As the story goes, mission walls were erected as tall as the trees — in this area, pine trees!

Plan your visit: missionsanluisobispo.org. 751 Palm Street, San Luis Obispo, CA 93401. (805) 781-8220.

Saint Serra's third mission, **Mission San Antonio de Padua** (1771) at Jolon was a trendsetter: It was reportedly the first mission to use red roof tiles, now a common feature in California architecture. A hand painted on a museum wall shows how musical scales and notes were taught to Indian neophytes.

Plan your visit: missionsanantonio.net. End of Mission Road, Jolon, CA 93928. (831) 385-4478.

Mission San Carlos Borromeo de Carmelo (1770) in Carmel, the second of Padre Serra's missions, was his favorite. The saint died here and was laid to rest here. Also called Carmel Mission Basilica, the church holds Father Serra's revered statue of Our Lady of Bethlehem.

Plan your visit: carmelmission.org. 3080 Rio Road, Carmel-By-The-Sea, CA 93923. (831) 624-1271.

The heart of Santa Clara University, **Mission Santa Clara de Asís** (1777) in Santa Clara was

Padre Serra's eighth mission and the first to bear the name of a woman. The Mission Cross in front of the church contains fragments of Father Serra's original founding cross.

Plan your visit: scu.edu/missionchurch. 500 El Camino Real, Santa Clara, CA 95053. (408) 554-4023.

Dwarfed by Mission Dolores Basilica next door (see 404), **Mission San Franciso de Asís** (1776) in San Francisco was the sixth of Father Serra's nine missions. Ohlone Indians painted the eye-catching ceiling in native design. The two swinging, saloon-like doors at the rear open up into a confessional.

Plan your visit: missiondolores.org. 3321 Sixteenth Street, San Francisco, CA 94114. (415) 621-8203.

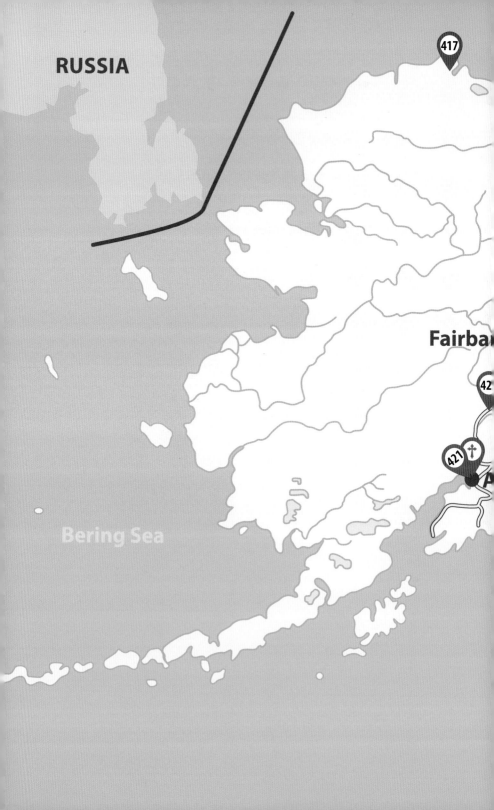

RUSSIA

Fairba

Bering Sea

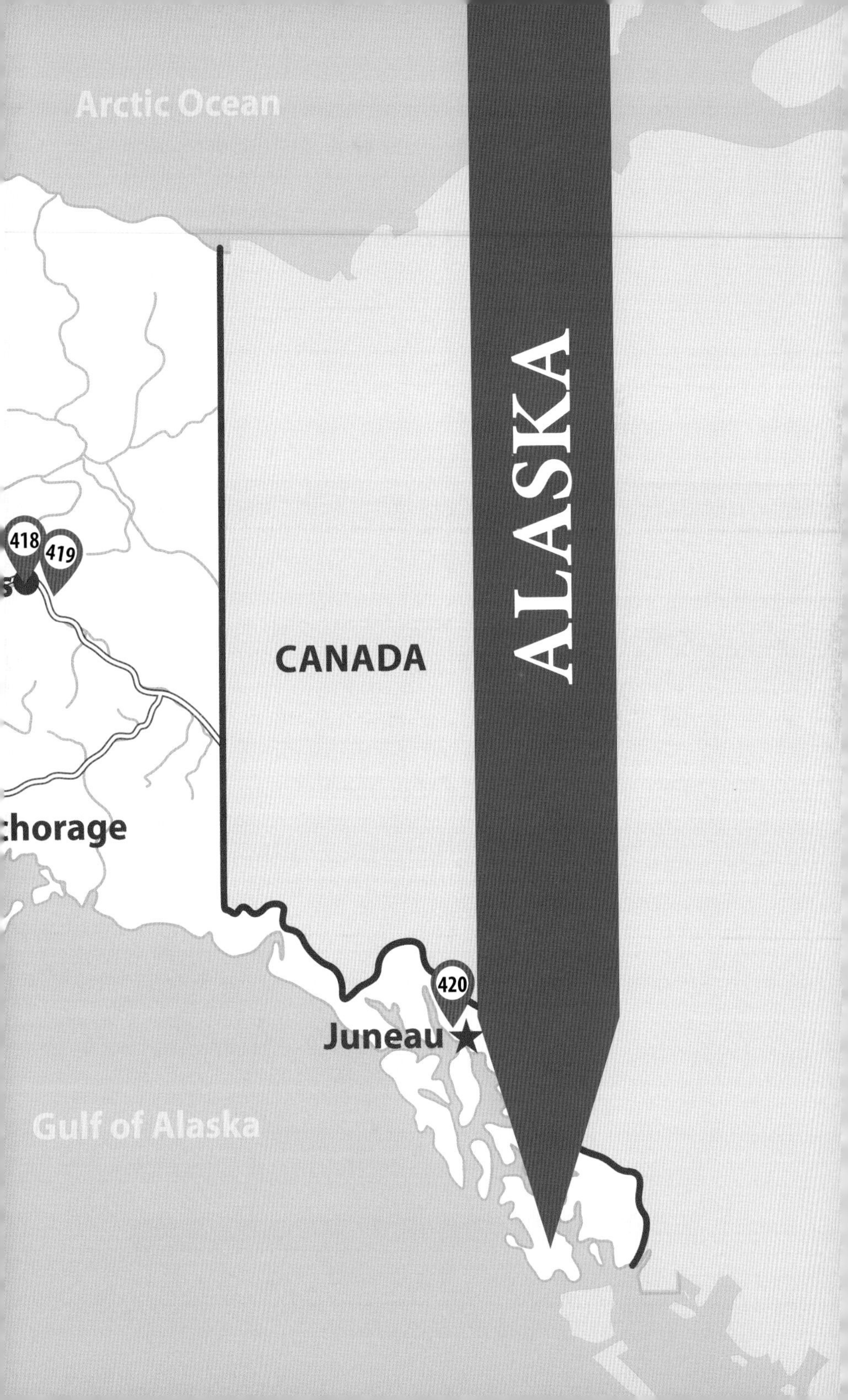

Arctic Ocean

ALASKA

CANADA

418 419

horage

420

Juneau ★

Gulf of Alaska

417 You're on top of the world at **Saint Patrick Catholic Church** in Barrow. Located 330 miles above the Arctic Circle, Saint Patrick's is the northernmost church on planet Earth. Like the darkness that fell over Calvary on Good Friday, Barrow descends into total darkness (the sun doesn't rise) from November 18 to January 24, and then emerges into twenty-four-hour sunshine (the sun doesn't set), from May 10 to August 2.

Plan your visit: facebook.com /barrowstpatrickscatholic. 618 Cunningham Street, Barrow, AK 99723. (907) 852-3515.

418 **Immaculate Conception Catholic Church** in Fairbanks is "the little church that could." In 1911, Father Francis Monroe, SJ, decided to roll the white frame church across the frozen Chena River to the other side. Folks gathered to watch and bets were placed (odds were the church wouldn't make it). As the church was being placed on its new foundation, a cable snapped. But Mary and a second cable held tight. A smiling Mary statue stands beneath the quaint steeple, while pressed tin and stained glass (note the window devoted to Catholic frontier mothers) decorate the inside.

Plan your visit: iccfairbanks.org. 2 Doyon Place, Fairbanks, AK 99701. (907) 452-3533.

419 Where does jolly old Saint Nick live? At **Saint Nich-**

St. Nicholas of Myra Byzantine Catholic Church [421]

olas **Catholic Church** in North Pole, of course! A carved wooden statue of the wonder-working saint greets visitors in a covered shrine outside the church. Dedicated in 1978, the Alaskan-themed church includes a diamond willow cross, log altar and lectern, and tabernacle styled as an Alaskan cache.

Plan your visit: stnicholasnp.org. 707 St. Nicholas Drive, North Pole, AK 99705. (907) 488-2595.

Saint Thérèse of Lisieux is famous for her "little way" (doing little things with great love), so how apropos that little donations — quarters and dollar bills — helped fund the **National Shrine of St. Thérèse** on Shrine Island near Juneau. Surrounded by rugged wilderness, the Shrine Chapel, constructed of beach stone collected by ordinary people, went up in 1938. Outdoor devotional areas include the Good Shepherd Rosary Trail, Biblical and Marian Gardens, and way of the cross.

Plan your visit: shrineofsainttherese.org. 21425 Glacier Highway, Juneau, AK 99801. (907) 586-2227, ext. 24.

421 It's not Rudolph's red nose shining so bright at **St. Nicholas of Myra Byzantine Catholic Church** in Anchorage, but the world's only internally illuminated copper dome. Called the Jewel of the North, the twenty-four-foot-tall perforated dome weighs 1,500 pounds and is crowned with a ten-foot Russian cross. Dozens of Byzantine icons decorate the church interior, including a large icon of the real Santa Claus — Saint Nicholas of Myra.

Plan your visit: ak-byz-cath.org. 2200 Arctic Boulevard, Anchorage, AK 99503. (907) 277-6731.

422 Between November 1932 and January 1933, Our Lady appeared thirty-three times in a hawthorn tree to five children at Beauraing, Belgium. While stationed in Belgium during World War II, Minnesota soldier George Herter obtained a piece of the hallowed tree. When his son fell deathly ill with typhus, he put the piece under the boy's pillow. The boy rallied! In thanksgiving, Herter cast fifty statues of Our Lady of Beauraing, put a tree splinter in each, and placed them around the country. One statue found its way to **St. Bernard's Catholic Church** in Talkeetna and greets pilgrims in an outdoor shrine.

Plan your visit: archdioceseofanchorage.org/parishes/st-bernard. 22136 South F Street, Talkeetna, AK 99676. (907) 733-2424.

✙ FINDING FAITH
in Alaska

Want to visit a "Sistine Chapel" on the ground? You can at the Cloister at **St. Patrick's Church** in Anchorage, one of the country's most unique pilgrimage destinations. The Cloister, a walled-in courtyard with translucent glass, portrays ten "courts," or scenes in salvation history. The architectural and artistic detail ingeniously engages the spirit and the senses. In the Court of Moses, you can see, hear, and feel the parting of the Red Sea: two waterfalls facing each other.

The statuary — adaptations of Old World masterpieces by world-renowned sculptor Roberto Santo — compels contemplation. In *The Court of Sorrows*, Santo's depiction of Michelangelo's *Pietà* imparts a mother's questioning: Rather than looking down at her crucified Son, Mary's face is turned toward heaven. In Santo's homage to Bernini's *David*, the steely-eyed shepherd, slightly crouched with his slingshot in hand, prepares to topple the Philistine giant.

Plan your visit: st.patsak.org. 2111 Muldoon Road, Anchorage, AK 99504. (907) 337-1538.

Hilo

HAWAII

ISLAND OF OAHU

Saint Father Damien de Veuster (see Finding Faith in Vermont, 99, and Finding Faith in Hawaii) was ordained here, and the remains of Saint Marianne Cope (see Finding Faith in Hawaii) are enshrined here. Built of coral block in 1840–1843, it's reportedly the country's oldest cathedral in continuous use. Where are you? Aloha! At the beautiful **Cathedral Basilica of Our Lady of Peace** in Honolulu. For a bit of lore, look up to the twin galleries. In the 1870s, when local Catholics were accused of worshipping idols, the bishop responded in kind: He ordered thirty-six gilded wooden statuettes!

Plan your visit: cathedralofourladyofpeace.com. 1184 Bishop Street, Honolulu, HI 96813. (808) 536-7036.

ISLAND OF MAUI

Ask and you might receive coral from the sea! That's the legacy of the **Coral Miracle Church** at St. Gabriel Mission, in Keanae. In 1860, native Hawaiians decided to build a new church. While rocks abounded, there was no sandy beach. The sand and the coral — needed to make the mortar — would have to come from the sea. Diving for coral was dangerous, and prayers went up. On the appointed day of the dive, a "miracle storm" washed heaps of coral ashore! When the church was finished, another storm swept the surplus coral back to sea.

Plan your visit: stritahaiku.com/15. 115 Wailua Road, Haiku, HI 96708. (808) 575-2601.

Holy Ghost Mission in Kula is steeped in tradition. Built by Portuguese immigrants in the mid-1890s, the quaint eight-sided church is said to imitate the eight-sided crown of Saint Elizabeth, Queen of Portugal (1271–1336). According to one account, when a terrible famine hit Portugal's Azores Islands, Queen Elizabeth and her subjects prayed to the Holy Ghost. On Pentecost Sunday, a ship laden with food sailed into port. In thanksgiving, the queen processed to Lisbon's cathedral and laid her crown on the altar. A replica of Queen Elizabeth's crown is found inside the church.

Plan your visit: kulacatholiccommunity.org. 4300 Lower Kula Road, Kula, HI 96790. (808) 878-1091.

ISLAND OF HAWAII

Discover a painted paradise at **St. Benedict Roman Catholic Church** in Captain Cook. After building the 1899 church, Belgian Picpus priest Father John Velghe picked up his paintbrush. Using house paint, he decorated the wooden walls with murals (the hell scene is dramatic); turned the vaulted ceiling into a Hawaiian postcard with palm fronds and stars; and in the sanctuary, created the illusion of being in Spain's Cathedral of Burgos. If that don't beat the devil, he also painted on wooden pillars, in Hawaiian, the Saint Benedict medal's prayer of exorcism.

Plan your visit: thepaintedchurchhawaii.org. 84-5140 Painted Church Road, Captain Cook, HI 96704. (808) 328-2227.

427 Great is thy peace at **Saint Peter by the Sea Church** in Kailua Kona. Dubbed the Little Blue Church, the charming historic white structure, with blue trim and a blue roof, is topped by a tall steeple and cross. Overlooking the beautiful blue sea, an etched glass window depicts Jesus walking on water to rescue a sinking Saint Peter (see Mt 14:22–33).

Plan your visit: konacatholicchurch.net. 78-6684 Ali'i Drive, Kailua-Kona, HI 96740. (808) 326-7771.

✤ FINDING FAITH
✝ in Hawaii

Where saints lived, pilgrims follow — to the Island of Molokai where Saints Father Damien de
Veuster (1840–1889) (see Finding Faith in Vermont, 99, and 423) and Mother Marianne Cope
(1838–1918) (see 423) cared for exiled lepers. A
Belgian Picpus priest, Father Damien also built
churches.

Greeting you in Kamalo at **Saint Joseph's
Church** — a white frame structure built in 1876
— are statues of the bespectacled priest and
Brother Joseph Dutton. Called "the third leper
saint," Brother Joseph, a Catholic convert, spent
forty-five years tending to the outcasts (see Finding Faith in Vermont).

Plan your visit: damienchurchmolokai.org.
5900 Kamehameha V Highway, Kamalo, HI
96748. (808) 553-5220.

In 1874, Father Damien erected **Our Lady of
Seven Sorrows Church** at Kaunakakai. Pretty
as a postcard, the pristine white church — with
ten Gothic windows and fifty-foot bell tower —
was rebuilt in the 1960s. Today's church retains
the same character, dimensions, and styling of
Father Damien's original church.

Plan your visit: damienchurchmolokai.org.
8011 Kamehameha V Highway, Molokai, HI
96748. (808) 553-5220.

A pilgrimage to the former leper settlement in **Kalaupapa National Historical Park**, at Kalaupapa, is like no other: The remote peninsula is accessed only by plane, mule train, or foot. Lepers built St. Philomena Church in 1872, a year before Father Damien arrived. He expanded the church and, because many lepers had mouth deformities and drooled, it's said that he cut holes in floor boards where they could spit during Mass.

A lei-draped cross marks Father Damien's original grave (in 1936 his remains were reinterred in Belgium), while a statue of Saint Francis of Assisi embracing the Crucified Lord stands at the former tomb of Franciscan Mother Marianne Cope. Her remains are now enshrined at **Honolulu's Cathedral Basilica** of Our Lady of Peace (see 423).

Plan your visit: nps.gov/kala/learn /historyculture/damien.htm, damienchurchmolokai.org/wp/saint -philomenia-church. Kalaupapa Peninsula, Kalawao, Molokai, HI 96742. (808) 567-6802. Advance park permit required.

ACKNOWLEDGMENTS

No man is an island and neither is an author. My deepest gratitude to the hundreds of people who helped with this book: pastors and deacons, parish personnel, editorial staffs of diocesan newspapers, diocesan officials, guardians of convents and monasteries, state and national parks personnel, docents of museums and churches, state tourism departments, and directors and keepers of shrines and monuments. May Heaven bless you with joy unspeakable, and may this book lead many souls to the Throne of Grace.

INDEX

For easy reference, the index uses
site numbers, not page numbers.

ARCHITECTS

ARTISANS

HOLY PEOPLE OF AMERICA

PHOTO CREDITS

NORTHEAST

Maine
p. 22 – Courtesy of Michael Corbin, Mizpah

New Hampshire
p. 27 – Courtesy of Thomas Bebbington, Diocese of Manchester
p. 29 – Courtesy of Thomas Bebbington, Diocese of Manchester

Vermont
p. 33 – Courtesy of Lynn P. Altadonna, Blessed Sacrament Church, Stowe

New York
p. 38 – Courtesy of John Pitts, OLV Homes of Charity, Lackawanna
p. 45 – Steve Cukrov / Shutterstock.com
p. 49 – Courtesy of John Pitts, OLV Homes of Charity, Lackawanna

Massachusetts
p. 55 – Courtesy of Rev. Octavio Cortez, St. Anthony of Padua Church, New Bedford

Rhode Island
p. 65 – Courtesy of Mark Garrepy, Shrine of the Little Flower, Harrisville

Connecticut
p. 70 – Dan Hanscom / Shutterstock.com
p. 73 – James Kirkikis / Shutterstock.com

MID-ATLANTIC

Pennsylvania
p. 79 – Courtesy of Mary Peterson, Central Association of the Miraculous Medal, Philadelphia
p. 85 – Courtesy of Mary Peterson, Central Association of the Miraculous Medal, Philadelphia

New Jersey
p. 93 – VintageJim / Shutterstock.com

Maryland
p. 101 – Don Winter, courtesy of Historic St. Marys City

Missouri

p. 297 – Courtesy of Susan Schneider, National Shrine of Mary, Mother of the Church, Laurie

p. 299 – Courtesy of Howard Matthews, Shrine of St. Joseph, St. Louis

North Dakota

p. 307 – Courtesy of Joni Obrigewitch, Cathedral of the Holy Spirit, Bismarck

South Dakota

p. 315 – Courtesy of Rev. James Kubicki, SJ

Nebraska

p. 323 – Courtesy of Schoenstatt Sisters, Cor Mariae Shrine, Crete

Kansas

p. 332 – Courtesy of Connie Windholz, Basilica of St. Fidelis, Victoria

MOUNTAIN WEST
Montana

p. 343 – Courtesy of Patricia Lawrence, St. Francis Xavier Church, Missoula

Idaho

p. 350 – Idaho Department of Parks & Recreation

Wyoming

p. 355 – Nagel Photography / Shutterstock.com

p. 356 – Matthew Potter

Colorado

p. 363 – Courtesy of JoAnn Seaman, Mother Cabrini Shrine, Golden

Utah

p. 370 – Courtesy of Juliana Boerio-Goates, St. Francis of Assisi Catholic Church, Orem

Nevada

p. 378 – Liz Huntington

SOUTHWEST
Oklahoma

p. 386 – Chris Hohne / Shutterstock.com

Texas

p. 393 – Courtesy of Allie Dieter, St. Peter's Church, Lindsay

p. 396 – JustPixs / Shutterstock.com

p. 399 – William Silver / Shutterstock.com

New Mexico

p. 407 – Courtesy of Monastery of Christ in the Desert, Abiquiu

p. 410 – Robert Cicchetti / Shutterstock.com

Arizona

p. 417 – Marion Amberg

p. 420 – Courtesy of Mission San Xavier del Bac, Tucson

PACIFIC WEST
Washington

p. 426 – Nagel Photography / Shutterstock.com

p. 429 – St. James Cathedral, Seattle

Oregon

p. 435 – ARTYOORAN / Shutterstock.com

p. 436 - Victoria Ditkovsky / Shutterstock.com

California

p. 443 – Kit Leong / Shutterstock.com

p. 446 – Genaker / Shutterstock.com

p. 451 - Tracey B. Kincaid, ABC, Diocese of Orange

Alaska

p. 460 – Courtesy of Rev. Father Joseph Wargacki, St. Nicholas of Myra Byzantine Catholic Church, Anchorage

Hawaii

p. 466 – Courtesy of Patrick Downes, Hawaii Catholic Herald

ABOUT THE AUTHOR

Marion Amberg is an award-winning book author and freelance journalist. Her articles — mainly religion travel pieces and human-interest features — have appeared in more than 100 markets. She is known for her "nose for the unique and unusual" and for her engaging writing style.